NEW MEXICO

For my mom and dad, who first
taught me to love this country.

*Blessing
to the
Season
Frank*

Shane Rowland
Reba K. Rowland

Soon after Mexico declared her independence from Spain in 1821, adventurous Missouri frontiersmen opened trade relations with New Mexico over the famous Santa Fe Trail. View of The Santa Fe Plaza in the 1850s (End of the Santa Fe Trail), *a painting by Gerald P. Cassidy in ca. 1930s oil on canvas, captures the spirit of the day by illustrating the meeting of diverse cultures that took place when huge wagons rumbled into Santa Fe's plaza.* Courtesy, Museum of Fine Arts, Museum of New Mexico, gift of the Historical Society, 1977 (#6977)

American Historical Press
Sun Valley, California

NEW MEXICO

The Distant Land

An Illustrated History

By Dan Murphy
Photo Research by John O. Baxter

© American Historical Press
All Rights Reserved
Published 2000
Printed in the United States of America

Library of Congress Catalogue Card Number: 00-107748
ISBN: 1-892724-09-X

Selected Readings: p. 235
Includes Index

CONTENTS

A Timeline of New Mexico's History   6

CHAPTER I
The Virgin Land   9

CHAPTER II
The First People   19

CHAPTER III
Spanish Explorers   29

CHAPTER IV
Colonization and Conquest   39

CHAPTER V
Spanish Colony, Mexican Territory   53

CHAPTER VI
New Mexico and the United States   71

CHAPTER VII
One of the Fifty   97

CHAPTER VIII
Into the Millennium   145

CHAPTER IX
Chronicles of Leadership   160

Acknowledgment   234

Suggestion for Further Reading   235

Index   236

A TIMELINE OF NEW MEXICO'S HISTORY

c. 25,000 B.C. Sandia people leave earliest evidence of human existence in what is now New Mexico.

c. 10,000–500 B.C. Cochise people are first inhabitants to cultivate corn, squash and beans, the earliest evidence of agriculture in the Southwest.

A.D. 300–1,400 Mogollon culture introduces highly artistic pottery and early architecture in the form of pit houses.

A.D. 1–700 Anasazi Basketmakers elevate weaving to a high art, creating baskets, clothing, sandals, and utensils.

A.D. 700–1,300 Anasazi Pueblo cul-ture culminates in the highly developed Chaco Civilization.

A.D. 1,200 – 1,500 Pueblo Indians establish villages along the Rio Grande and its tributaries.

1536 Cabeza de Baca, Estevan the Moor and two others reach Culiacan, Mexico, after possibly crossing what is now southern New Mexico, and begin rumors of the Seven Cities of Cíbola.

1539 Fray Marcos de Niza and Estevan lead expedition to find Cibola and reach the Zuni village of Haw-

The Ninth Cavalry Band, a group of black soldier-musicians (Buffalo Soldiers) under the direction of Professor Charles Spiegel, entertained Santa Feans on the Plaza in the last quarter of the nineteenth century. In this photo by Ben Wittick, the band posed in front of the plaza's gazebo in 1880. Courtesy, City of Santa Fe.

Europeans first visited Taos in 1540, during an exploration of the northern pueblos made by coronado's Captain Hernando de Alvarado. The party's scribe reported multistoried apartment houses made of adobe, a description that still fits today. State Historic Preservation Bureau

ikuh where Estevan is killed.

1540-42 Francisco Vásquez de Coronado explores area from Gulf of California to present day Kansas, discovers the Grand Canyon.

1580–81 Fray Agustin Rodriguez leads expedition to New Mexico; four members of the party killed by Indians.

1598 Juan de Oñate establishes the first Spanish capital of San Juan de Los Caballeros at the Tewa village of Ohke north of present day Espanola.

1599 Battle at Acoma between natives and Spaniards; seeds of Pueblo Revolt sown.

1600 San Gabriel, second capital of New Mexico, is founded at the confluence of the Rio Grande and the Chama River.

1605 Oñate expedition to the Colorado River; visits El Morro, leaves message on Inscription Rock.

1608 Oñate removed as governor and sent to Mexico City to be tried for mistreatment of the Indians and abuse of power. Decision made by Spanish Crown to continue settlement of New Mexico as a royal province.

1609–10 Governor Pedro de Peralta establishes a new capital at Santa Fe. Construction begins on the Palace of the Governors. Gaspar de Villagra publishes epic history on the founding of New Mexico, the first book printed about any area in the United States.

1626 Spanish Inquisition established in New Mexico.

1641 Governor Luis de Rosas

assassinated by colonists during conflict between the church and state.

1680 Pueblo Indian Revolt; Spanish survivors flee to El Paso del Norte.

Late 1600s Navajos, Apaches, and later Comanches begin raids against Pueblo Indians.

1692–93 Don Diego de Vargas recolonizes Santa Fe. Spanish culture returns to New Mexico.

1695 Santa Cruz de la Cañada founded.

1696 Second Pueblo Revolt; efforts thwarted by Governor De Vargas.

1706 Villa de Albuquerque founded.

1743 French trappers reach Santa Fe and begin limited trade with the Spanish.

1776 Franciscan friars Dominguez and Escalante explore route from New Mexico to California.

1786 Governor Juan Bautista de Anza makes peace with the Comanches.

1807 Zebulon Pike leads first Anglo American expedition into New Mexico. Publishes account of way of life in New Mexico upon return to U.S.

1821 Mexico declares independence from Spain. Santa Fe Trail opened to international trade.

1828 First major gold discovery in western U.S. made in Ortiz Mountains south of Santa Fe.

1836 First school text printed in

New Mexico by Padre Antonio Jose Martinez of Taos.

1837 Chimayo Revolt against Mexican taxation leads to the assassination of Governor Albino Perez and top officials.

1841 Texans invade New Mexico and claim all land east of the Rio Grande. Efforts thwarted by Governor Manuel Armijo.

1846 Mexican-American War begins. Stephen Watts Kearny annexes New Mexico to the United States.

1847 Taos Rebellion against the U.S. military. Governor Charles Bent killed.

1848 Treaty of Guadalupe Hidalgo ends Mexican-American War.

1850 New Mexico (which included present day Arizona, southern Colorado, southern Utah, and southern Nevada) is designated a territory, but denied statehood.

1851 Bishop Jean Baptiste Lamy arrives in New Mexico and establishes schools, hospitals and orphanages throughout the territory.

1854 The Gadsden Purchase from Mexico adds 45,000 square mile to the territory.

1861 Confederates invade New Mexico from Texas. The Confederate Territory of Arizona is declared with the capital at La Mesilla. Territory of Colorado is created. New Mexico loses extreme northernmost section to the new territory.

1862 Battles of Velvarde and Glorieta Pass fought, ends Confederate occupation of New Mexico.

1863–68 Known as the "Long Walk," Navajos and Apaches are relocated to Bosque Redondo; finally allowed to return to their homelands after hundreds die of disease and starvation.

1863 New Mexico is partitioned in half; territory of Arizona is created.

1878 The railroad arrives in New Mexico opening full-scale trade and migration from the east and Midwest. Lincoln County War erupts in southeast New Mexico.

1881 Billy the Kid shot by Sheriff Pat Garrett in Ft. Sumner, N.M.

Although service was frequently uncomfortable and unreliable, stagecoaches provided an important means of transportation in nineteenth-century New Mexico. Standing before the Meredith and Ailman Bank in Silver City, driver and passengers posed for this photo prior to their departure for Georgetown, New Mexico, circa 1885. MNM (#11933)

1886 Geronimo surrenders; Indian hostilities cease in the Southwest.

1898 First movie filmed in New Mexico, *Indian Day School*, by Thomas A. Edison.

1906 People of New Mexico and Arizona vote on issue of Joint Statehood, New Mexico voting in favor and Arizona against.

1910 New Mexico Constitution drafted in preparation for statehood.

1912 New Mexico admitted to the Union as the 47th state.

1916 Pancho Villa raids Columbus, New Mexico.

1920 Adoption of the 19th Amendment gives women the right to vote.

1922 Secretary of State Soledad Chacon and Superintendent of Public Instruction Isabel Eckles elected first women to hold statewide office.

1923–24 Oil is discovered on the Navajo Reservation.

1930–43 As a result of the Great Depression federal New Deal funds provide employment for many and causes numerous public buildings to be constructed.

1942–45 New Mexico soldiers serving in the 200th Coast Artillery during World War II are captured by the Japanese and forced to endure the Bataan Death March. Navajo "Code-talkers" are influential in helping end the war. Secret atomic laboratories established at Los Alamos.

1945 World's first atomic bomb detonated at Trinity Site in southern

New Mexico after its development at Los Alamos.

1947 UFO allegedly crashes between Roswell and Corona, believers claim U.S. government institutes massive cover-up of the incident.

1948 Native Americans win the right to vote in state elections.

1950 Uranium discovered near Grants.

1957 Buddy Holly records "Peggy Sue" at Norman Petty Studio in Clovis.

1966 New state capitol, the "Roundhouse," is dedicated.

1969 Proposed new state constitution is rejected by voters.

1982 Space shuttle Columbia lands at White Sands Space Harbor on Hollomon Air Force Base near Alamogordo.

1992 New Mexico observes Columbus Quicentenary, welcomes Cristobal Colon XX, direct descendent of Christopher Columbus.

1998 New Mexico celebrates its Cuarto Centennial, commemoration its 1598 founding by Don Juan de Oñate.

2000 State population estimated to reach 1,700,000.

Beneath a stormy sky, sheep graze in the shadow of Enchanted Mesa, near Acoma. Found throughout the state, the flat-topped hills known as mesas are New Mexico's most distinctive geographic feature. From the Department of Development Collection, New Mexico State Records Center & Archives (NMSRCA)

The Virgin Land

New Mexico is made out of rocks. Most states, of course, have a basement of rocks, but they are camouflaged, and the state calendars have scenes of rolling green. But in New Mexico the rocks are out in the open, great shelves and cliffs that stand baking in the sun.

New Mexico is a high land. Perhaps fifty million years ago those rocks, some of them formed beneath great seas, were slowly lifted high into the air, some warped and twisted in the process, forming spectacular mountain ranges. But the plains were lifted, too. If the governor of New Mexico, sitting in his office at Santa Fe, decided that he should sit at the same altitude as the governor of Missouri, he would have to dig a well straight down about 6,000 feet. It is the altitude that accounts for New Mexico's cold winters, unexpected in a state so far south, and the cool evenings year-round.

If the governor did decide to dig that hole beneath his office, his constituents would find it a perfectly reasonable act, providing he told them he was looking for water. New Mexico is dry. Westerly winds bring moisture from the Pacific, and the high north-central mountains often receive heavy snowfall, much to the relief of farmers and ranchers in the flatlands below who depend on snowmelt to water their crops. But in coming from the Pacific, those winds have crossed hundreds of miles and several mountain ranges, and the lion's share of water has been wrung out of them. More important to New Mexico are the springtime south and southeasterly winds that come from the Gulf of Mexico, watering the low-lying plains in the southeastern part of the state. The central spine of mountains confines most of the springtime moisture to the eastern plains, but by July moisture from the west begins to reach the Rio Grande Valley. ("It always rains on the Fourth of July picnic," say the old bean farmers in the central part of the state.) Then mornings in Santa Fe, Albuquerque, and Socorro are clear and blue, but by afternoon thunderclouds begin to form over the mountain ranges. They can be huge; the mass of a mountain range, such as the Sangre de Cristos, is enormous, yet the clouds that form on most afternoons in August are higher and wider than the range itself. The clouds promise rain and sometimes they deliver, but these are not the county-wide rains of the Midwest. Individual thunderheads move across the countryside, sometimes four or five in view at once. Some have curtains of rain hanging down that seem to disappear before reaching the ground. The appearance is correct. That is "virga," the condition when rain falls but actually evaporates before it can touch the earth. Other clouds may be dragging an actual rainstorm that will water the earth beneath it, but between such storms there may well be large areas of sunshine. One ranch can be watered while its neighbor stays dry. The state as a whole runs a moisture deficit, the amount of water evaporated in a year being greater than the amount that actually falls. In some parts of the state, particularly in the south, it would take five times as much water as is available in a normal year just to break even with what evaporates.

New Mexico is a huge state, fifth largest in the union. It is far removed from major population centers—an important factor in its history—and distances within

Located west of the Rio Grande, between Albuquerque and Socorro, the Ladrón Mountains are a small, compact range that rise to an elevation of more than 9,000 feet. Spaniards named them "ladrón" (thief) because of the marauding bands of Navajos and Apaches that sought refuge there. NMSRCA

Beginning in Colorado as a mountain stream, the Rio Grande flows south through New Mexico's midsection and crosses the Texas border at Anthony. For centuries its turbulent waters have irrigated the crops of Indians, Hispanos, and Anglos. Early colonists called it the Rio del Norte. Courtesy, National Park Service (NPS)

the state are vast. Ranchers go a long way to town to shop, and children have long rides in school buses. With so much road per person, no state could afford a comprehensive paved highway system, and New Mexico has thousands of miles of dirt roads, much of it state highway. In Santa Fe, the capital, many of the finest homes are on dirt roads, and at the opera one may see elegantly dressed people climbing out of four-wheel-drive vehicles.

The highest part of the state is the north-central mountain core, where the Rockies come down from Colorado and extend for a hundred miles into New Mexico, finally petering out in small rounded hills and the sharp cut of Glorieta Pass. Entrepreneurs have built ski lodges up there, and there is an elk hunting season. The high country could easily be mistaken for land far to the north, with huge forests of ponderosa pine, and even Douglas fir. Hiking to the high country from one of the National Forest Service trailheads, the hiker passes through climates as though he were traveling north; every

1,000 feet upward represents perhaps 200 miles north. The hike may start in piñon-juniper scrublands, but these give way to the ponderosa, and then aspens, breathtaking in autumn. And often at their highest point the mountains seem like arctic tundra, where no trees grow but there is just rock, and miniature plants in a fierce struggle with the cold and wind, and views that go forever.

But New Mexico has another kind of mountain: the small, clearly defined range. Small is a relative term; a rancher who lives near one of these ranges may spend a lifetime learning it well. But a visitor traveling by car can see a range in its entirety, approach it, and drive past it in a few hours. Each of these ranges represents a distinct geologic event, and, especially from an airplane, they are textbook examples of the various ways mountains come to be. Mount Taylor and the Jemez range are both volcanoes. The Sandias are the product of a fault-block thrust: the west side, the side pushed up along the fault, is so steep that it supports a two-

Made of weathered sandstone, Camel Rock is a good example of what erosion has done to New Mexico's terrain. Situated north of Santa Fe near the pueblo of Tesuque, the formation has become a popular stopping place for travelers. NMSRCA

Above
During the centuries since the Jemez eruptions, the soft volcanic ash spewed forth has eroded into a series of fascinating formations. Known as "tent rocks," they continue to intrigue geologists and tourists alike. From the Woodward Collection, NMSRCA

Right
The cholla cactus, a hardy desert plant, is found in many parts of the state. When moisture is adequate, it produces a brilliant magenta blossom. NPS

mile cable tramway with a rise of almost 4,000 feet, while skiers glide down the gently sloped eastern side. These and perhaps three dozen other ranges are oases in the desert, "islands in the sky." Other geologic showplaces are the mountain canyons. Canyons are watercourses, success stories in the ages-long effort of water to claw the mountains down. Distinctive of desert mountains are the outwash plains, broad slopes that come from the canyon mouths, the temporary resting place of all the debris that came out of those canyons: the very stuff of the mountains, spread out on the desert around the base of the mountain like the skirt of a lady sitting on the grass. Early travelers knew that the mountains were sources of water. In danger of death on the desert, they headed for the outwash plains to find a major arroyo, then followed it up to where the water had not yet sunk into the debris.

Much of New Mexico is desert. Scientists define "desert" in various ways, as an area where evaporation exceeds precipitation, or where the annual rainfall is less than twenty inches. To plants and animals that live on the desert it means simply this: to survive, you must adapt to the amount of water available. The very symbol of the desert, the cactus, is a bundle of marvelous adaptations. Leaves have been reduced to spines, exposing less surface to sunlight. The skin is leathery, thereby letting little water evaporate. The root system can be a broad, shallow net, set near the surface to catch all the water possible and store it (hence "barrel cactus"); or roots can go deep, searching for water below. Desert trees, too, tend to have small leaves with leathery surfaces. Some desert plants are even self-pruning. The body of the cholla (pronounced "choy-ya") cactus is segmented, like a string of sausages. In times of drought the plant cuts circulation to the outer segments, which dry or even drop off. This reduces the plant's size (and therefore its need for water) and surface area. (It is also why the cholla is one of the least pleasant cacti to bump into, and why one species is called "jumping cholla." The outer segments, loosely connected, cling easily to anything that brushes against the plant.)

New Mexico desert animals, too, are precisely suited to this dry climate. The mammals are largely nocturnal, avoiding the daytime sun. Some desert rodents never drink water at all; they metabolize it from seeds that seem perfectly dry to humans. Snakes function well in the desert; they are largely nocturnal, and being cold-blooded (not spending energy to keep the body at any particular temperature) they can eat well in the desert, which at best is a sparsely set table. Lizards are a delight to all youngsters visiting the desert for the first time, as they move from sun to shade, adjusting their body temperature, then sit motionless for long periods of time, waiting for some unwary insect to venture in reach of that lightning tongue. New Mexico does not have too little water; it has

Above
Because of its wide distribution and hardy characteristics, the piñon, a variety of pine, has been selected as New Mexico's state tree. A favorite source of firewood, the piñon grows slowly in a region with meager rainfall. Courtesy, Department of Development Collection, NMSRCA

Left
Equally at home in the mountains or on the desert, the omniverous coyote is one of New Mexico's most common mammals. NPS

Bottom
For the sightseer, New Mexico provides some of the Southwest's most spectacular scenery. This photograph taken near Los Alamos looks over the mesas west of the Rio Grande toward the high peaks of the Sangre de Cristo range. Courtesy, Los Alamos National Laboratory

Right
Despite its hostile appearance, the diamondback rattlesnake will usually avoid a confrontation if possible. The rattlesnake is an important figure in the myths and rituals of Southwestern Indians. NPS

precisely the right amount of water for what it is—an arid land, where life must adjust to that aridity.

The rivers of New Mexico are relatively few, but it was along those rivers that history came. The major waterway is the Rio Grande. It rises in the Colorado Rockies and flows down through New Mexico, north to south, dividing the state in half, then forming the Texas-Mexico boundary, and ultimately reaching the Gulf of Mexico. In the northern part of the state, the

river rushes at the bottom of a tremendous gorge, the scene of yearly whitewater races in modern times. Sometimes it emerges onto the flats and moves lazily for a while, a braided stream scattered across a wide, sandy riverbed, shallow enough to walk across. Then it passes in rough cuts through the mountains, carving its canyon through the debris of the Jemez volcano west of Santa Fe and, further south, along the Fray Cristóbal Mountains (where the river has been dammed to form Elephant Butte Reservoir) and finally crossing into Texas at El Paso. It was this "Great River" that drew Indians to the region and served as the lifeline for the Spaniards. It is a large river in New Mexico terms but often surprises first-time visitors, who usually exclaim, "why, you can walk across it!" Sometimes you can. Its normal pattern used to be one of flood during snowmelt, then a trickle the rest of the year. (Today dams largely control this, but there is still seasonal variation.)

Another good-sized river, the Pecos, rises in the Sangre de Cristos and flows south, roughly parallel to the Rio Grande, across the eastern plains of the state, eventually joining the Rio Grande in Texas. The continental divide comes down the western side of New Mexico, and a few streams—including the Gila in the southwest and the San Juan in the northwest—flow to the Colorado River and ultimately the Gulf of California. Aficionados know some of the other rivers in the state—the Chama has its fans, especially among trout fishermen—but the statistics speak for themselves. New Mexico has 121,666 square miles of surface area, of which a mere 155 square miles is water, nearly all of that artificial reservoirs. Still, a watercourse need not be one of the famous rivers to be of importance to the people along it. Some canyons, particularly those near significant mountain ranges, have small perennial streams. Plants thrive along them; so do animals and, in many cases,

that includes humans. Even dry arroyos sometimes run full. (This can be a tragedy for tourists who camp in the broad, sandy bottom of what they take to be a dry canyon.)

Besides mountains, deserts, and rivers, there has been one final craftsman forming the stage for New Mexico's story. The state is a hotbed of volcanism. No mind that there has been no eruption here in recorded history: geologists and historians use different time-scales. For ages the heat and magma of the earth have broken through to the surface in New Mexico. Capulín Mountain, a national park in the state's northeast corner, preserves an enormous, classic cinder cone, and from the top of it the visitor sees that the surrounding terrain is a family of such cones. The whole southwest part of the state is also volcanic, and it was the escaping heat, with its associated steam and gasses, that helped to form minerals that are mined there today. Throughout the state there

One of a cluster of volcanic cinder cones, Capulín Mountain is a familiar landmark for tourists crossing Northeastern New Mexico on U.S. highways 64 and 87. "Capulín" is the Spanish word for chokecherry, a bush that grows abundantly on the slopes of the mountain. NPS

15

are visible reminders of its violent geologic past. A million years ago the Jemez volcano exploded with a force many times that of Mt. St. Helens, leaving behind the Valle Grande, one of the great calderas of the world. Today it is a cattle ranch, and scientists poke their drill bits down through the earth toward the magma mass that still lies just a few miles down. They hope to heat water and create electricity with the barest fraction of the sleeping giant's power. At Shiprock and Cabezon Peak, lava froze in the throat of dying volcanoes, forming hard rock towers that outlasted the surrounding mountains.

Nor is it over; about the time of Christ, lava squeezed from the earth near modern Grants. That flow, miles wide and thirty miles long, is so fresh it is worth a pair of shoes to hike across it, and it deserves the local nickname "malpaís," or "bad land." A similar flow near Carrizozo is possibly even more recent.

Lava extrusions have discernibly af-

Above
Located west of Santa Fe in the Jemez Mountains, the Valle Grande is one of the world's largest calderas, with an area of 176 square miles. Courtesy, Los Alamos Historical Museum

Right
A favorite subject for artists and photographers, Shiprock is Northwestern New Mexico's most famous natural attraction. Regina Tatum Cooke created this painting as part of the Federal Arts Project. From the R. Vernon Hunter Collection, NMSRCA

Each year thousands of visitors come to Southern New Mexico to experience the beautiful and awe-inspiring limestone formations in Carlsbad Caverns. On the surface temperatures are extreme and rainfall sparse, but below ground the caverns are always cool and moist. The area became a national park in 1930. Courtesy, Carlsbad Caverns National Park

fected New Mexico's scenery. Lava is extremely resistant to wind and water, and it protects from erosion the softer material over which it has flowed. At the edge of a flow, however, the softer material beneath, exposed to the elements, erodes rapidly, forming a sharp cliff. The resulting mesas, or perfectly flat-topped hills, are a dramatic feature of the state.

The land of New Mexico is a grand stage. The eastern plains are a mature, timeless landscape, an appropriate transition for approaching motorists who may not realize they are following an ancient trail. The green ribbons of the rivers provide relief. The mesas raise their distinctive outlines, while such oddities as the recent lava flows, the Carlsbad Caverns, and the white sands serve as punctuation. The vastness and the scenic drama are well suited to the story that would unfold: the encounter of people with this beautiful but stern land, and with one another.

Known to generations of New Mexicans as "malpaís" (bad land), the state's rugged lava beds have always been hard on footgear and horses' hoofs. Part of the forty-mile-long flow east of Carrizozo is pictured. From the Department of Development Collection, NMSRCA

Folsom Man depended on great herds of prehistoric buffalo (bison antiquus) for his existence. To secure a supply of meat, hunting parties drove the huge beasts over steep banks or cornered them in arroyos where they could not escape. From the Marjorie F. Lambert Collection, NMSRCA

The First People

It is certain that there were human beings in New Mexico by 10,000 B.C. The mesas and canyons those first people saw would be familiar to New Mexicans today, even down to individual rocks and caves, but the color was different—it was green. The great ice sheets that covered much of North America at that time never came this far south, but their effect came this far. The eastern plains, treeless today, then had shallow lakes surrounded by pine and even spruce trees. Today's Estancia Basin was a lake, as were the Plains of San Augustin.

If someone from today would be surprised at the lush vegetation of the otherwise familiar landscape, he would be astounded at the animals that roamed across it. There were ancient horses (long extinct by the time the Spaniards arrived) and camels, tapirs and sloths, and even great mammoths. With such game it is not surprising that the first human arrivals were big game hunters.

By chance New Mexico has "type sites" (sites where excavation and reports have established the definition of a culture) for several of North America's early Paleo-indian population groups. One of the earliest is Sandia Cave, where meager artifacts of "Sandia Man" have been found in a cave high in the Sandia Mountains above modern Albuquerque. Little is known of these people and how they lived.

Clovis Man's type site, a spot near the modern town of Clovis on the eastern plains, contains numerous heavy projectile points made for hunting. These stone points were attached to a spear that was thrown with an "atl-atl," a tool that in effect lengthened the hunter's forearm, enabling him to throw with tremendous

force. Clovis Man was here when the mammoths were, and occasionally even managed to kill one of the great animals for food. These early hunters seem to have built rude, temporary brush shelters, often near water where they watched for game coming down to drink, as on the shores of ancient Lake Estancia. These ancient beaches show up on aerial photos as benches around dry basins, and archeologists have learned that that is where to look for remains of Clovis Man.

As the climate changed, then came the dying. Many of the largest animals disappeared. But as great grasslands developed on the prairies, the herd animals thrived, especially the magnificent *Bison antiquus,* a long-horned species which became the larder for Clovis Man's successor, Folsom Man. Near the little town of Folsom is the type site that produced the most famous spearhead of all, the Folsom point. (There Folsom points were found in direct association with the animals they had killed and provided the first proof, since amply confirmed, that man had coexisted with the great Pleistocene animals.) Exquisitely flaked and balanced, the Folsom point has a characteristically concave cross-section created by chipping off a long flake longitudinally on either side. Removing that long flake took considerable skill and is difficult to perform even today. (One wonders what a Folsom craftsman's professional opinion was of his predecessors, as he looked at the more crudely chipped Clovis points he must have occasionally picked up.)

Unlike Clovis Man, who specialized in individual kills, Folsom Man drove whole herds of bison over steep banks, or up narrowing arroyos, or into loose sand, then

C H A P T E R   I I

moved in with lances to finish the job. Butchering was done on the site; by careful examination of the order of bone piles, seeing which bones were thrown on first and which later, archeologist Joe Ben Wheat has been able to determine the actual butchering method.

There were other early hunting groups, many of which have been identified by archeologists who specialize in the period of the Paleoindians. The Paleoindians inhabited the land for at least twenty times longer than the United States has existed. We have never found their physical remains. We do not know what they wore, or what they lived in, and we have absolutely no idea what their language sounded like. But it is clear that situations of frantic activity and danger, each enough to provide a lifetime of stories for a modern adventurer, were a familiar part of their lives. They knew the terror of facing an enormous, wounded animal with just a stone-tipped spear; and some even knew the taste of mammoth meat, an animal we shall never even see.

By about 6000 B.C. New Mexico was beginning to display the characteristic browns and reds that attract visitors today (actually a sign of aridity). The great variety of New Mexico's landforms created a range of environments, from moist canyon heads to high timber, from sandy desert and stands of seemingly inhospitable cactus to large areas of pinon trees. To live in this new situation, people learned to use all of these environments. They spread into the canyon heads and the valleys, learning when and where to look for food, when to return to areas with ripening grass seed, and where to find a spring that might still drip a little water.

Life in the Archaic period (approximately 6000 to 1000 B.C.) was quite different from that which had been enjoyed by Paleoindians (10,000 to 6000 B.C.). The herds were gone, now moving east across the great plains. The remaining humans found it necessary to know one area very well and to glean from a variety of its sources. New Mexicans of the Archaic period were hunters and gatherers, moving season by season to where the resources were ripening. The tools Paleoindians left behind are for hunting and butchering big game; Archaic "tool kits" have stone tools for grinding seeds, and projectile points, knives, and scrapers suitable for hunting and preparing a variety of small game.

The achievements that would make it possible for people to master this arid environment probably were not recognized as remarkable at the time. Corn, which would revolutionize their lives one day, probably came in as a handful of seed traded from people who might have migrated slowly, generation by generation, northward from Mexico. You could plant it in some likely spot on your travels and harvest it next time around, if the birds had not found it first. Or you could leave someone there to scare the birds away, so that. . . . There was the revolution: a nomadic people of hunters and gatherers were going to become farmers, accomplishing the unprecedented feat of living in one place. It would take millenia to put the inventions, techniques, and combinations into place to make it work.

With the development of agriculture came the period of what archeologists refer to as the Basketmaker (roughly 1000 B.C. to A.D. 800). At some point people invented nets for catching rabbits and improved tumplines for carrying loads. They modified and improved stone tools that had originally been used for grinding wild seed. Beans and squash became part of the diet. Gradually these New Mexicans began to acquire new skills, again probably from Mexico. They made pottery and cooked in it, grew and used cotton, mastered the bow and arrow, and began building storage cists.

The idea of storing one crop, rather than searching for another, was an important step. Pottery served the purpose, but storage cists, specially designed holes in the floor, had greater size and permanence. Finally, the tendency to stay in one place made it sensible to spend more time building a house for year-round living, rather than the seasonal brush shelters of the nomad. Thus was invented the pithouse, which in one form or another would house perhaps half of all the people who lived in New Mexico before the coming of the Spaniards. It was usually but not always round, was built partially underground, and usually had a ramp entranceway or a hatch and ladder. The roof was made of poles, brush, and dirt. Outside a home like this would be a work area for scraping skins, sewing, chipping spearheads, and grinding grain. Here, too, a Basketmaker could sit in the evening, talk with his neighbors, and chew the native tobacco. Archeologists have found the quids.

The Basketmaker period had much of the Archaic in it, but it was Archaic-plus-corn, and that made a profound difference. Small groups of semi-nomads became farmers living in pithouse villages, with food stored from good years to even out the bad ones.

Having moved from brush shelters on the surface to pithouses underground, the people of New Mexico now came back to the surface again. The first above-ground

Above
Modern-day craftsmen would likely envy the skill of the Anasazi masons who built the Chaco villages. The same people also constructed a remarkable road system at Chaco, but its purpose is not clear. NPS

Left
Because of its astonishing size, pueblo Bonito is the best known of several Anasazi villages in Chaco Canyon. Its residents were traders who also practiced irrigated farming. To insure its preservation, Chaco Canyon is now a national historic park. Courtesy, State Historic Preservation Bureau (SHPB)

Arroyo Hondo, located five miles south of Santa Fe, was a large multi-storied pueblo occupied during the thirteenth and early fourteenth centuries. Archeologists from the School of American Research in Santa Fe first investigated the site in 1971. Because of long habitation by prehistoric peoples, New Mexico is rich in archeological resources. From the School of American Research Collection, NMSRCA

structures of rock and mud began to appear in the seventh and eighth centuries and were evidently used for storage. Eventually, the above-ground houses came to predominate. The ancient pithouse did not disappear entirely, but was transformed into the kiva, a ceremonial structure. Centuries later the Spaniards would find New Mexico's Indians living in rock and mud houses with adjacent kivas. Creating a term that exists yet today, they called the natives "Pueblos." Today the term is applied to the building itself, the village, the individual, and the culture. The term is also used for the period of development that began around A.D. 800.

The most elaborate and intriguing of New Mexico's early pueblos are found at Chaco Canyon. At the middle of the tenth century Chaco contained a typical mix of pithouses and masonry houses, and a relatively large population, but was not vastly different from other centers of the pueblo group we now call Anasazi. But sometime around A.D. 950, building construction be-

gan at an accelerated rate. At first the buildings had essentially the same floor plan as was already common, but writ large: the rooms were twice as big, there were more of them, and a second story might be added. The surge did not stop but carried over generations, culminating in the marvel of Pueblo Bonito, a five-story, 800-room building designed as a harmonious D-shaped whole, containing its own plaza and more than thirty kivas. The masonry technique changed from generation to generation, but some of it is the finest anywhere, with banded effects deliberately created by skillful placement of rock. Eleven of these extraordinarily large, well-built towns are found in the immediate vicinity of Chaco Canyon.

More astonishing still are the enigmatic lines across the countryside that show up clearly on aerial photographs, radiating from Chaco Canyon. Studies have confirmed that these are indeed a network of roadways, built by people who had neither the wheel nor beasts of burden. More than 460 miles of road have been traced so far. They lead to other outlying towns that have Chaco-type architecture. These towns, more than seventy-five identified so far, had some tie back to Chaco Canyon, either political, economic, religious, or cultural.

Chaco Canyon does not fit the mold of Pueblo societies, at least as they are understood now. Such societies usually are egalitarian; at Chaco there are hints of rich folks and poor folks, as finer artifacts are found in the large structures than in the small ones. The architecture is unique, the roads are unique, and the size of the "system," whatever it was, linking towns spread over the San Juan drainage, was unprecedented. There are theories, of course. One is based on the extreme variability of growing conditions in the Chaco area. It is difficult to predict whether a given year will produce a crop or not, and even if one place does, an area a few miles away may be parched. The way to cope with shortages over time is by storage, and the way to cope with shortages in different places is by transfer. The huge rooms at

Chaco could be storage, and the roads could be transfer. Could Chaco have been administering a food redistribution system, to smooth out the unpredictabilities of farming a marginal area?

The reasons for Chaco's decline are not clear, although probably they involved multiple blows of drought and failures of the "system," whatever it was. Quite rapidly, between 1150 and 1200, construction ceased and the population declined radically. It was just about then that the cliff towns at Mesa Verde, 100 miles to the north, were approaching their zenith in population and activity, and it is attractive (and easy) to think of skilled Chacoans moving up there to touch off a great advance. Furthermore, when Mesa Verde declined around 1300, there was a blossoming of the pueblos in the Rio Grande Valley. Did the same crew move over there? Some have guessed so, but probably the truth is more complex. In fact, cultures rarely move in jumps. The better metaphor might be the braided stream,

like the Rio Grande. Look over the bridge in Albuquerque. Water moves within the broad sand bed from one side to the other—a trickle here and a solid stream over there which then changes and moves to a new arrangement of deep and shallow places. Some pools even become isolated to one side, possibly to disappear. It seems even so in the family of cultures.

Meanwhile, in the southern part of the state, a sister culture to the Anasazi was the Mogollón. It may have been the Mogollón who had introduced pottery and even the idea of pithouses to the Anasazi, and in at least one way they exceeded even Chaco: the Mimbres offshoot of the Mogollón produced the finest potters of prehistoric times. By the late 1200s the northern Mogollón had become the innovative ceramic center of the Southwest, but by the mid-1400s the Mogollón had abandoned most of their homes in southwestern New Mexico.

Even as the Anasazi and the Mogollón, the people of the northern Rio Grande

One of the most intriguing archeological sites in New Mexico, the Gila Cliff Dwellings are located forty-four miles north of Silver City. The cliff houses were built in a series of natural caves and occupied by farming people in the thirteenth and fourteenth centuries. The monument also contains pit houses made by an earlier Mogollón culture about A.D. 100 to 400. From the Marjorie F. Lambert Collection, NMSRCA

These artifacts include examples of the geometric designs and living creatures that characterize Mimbres pottery. The exhibit is part of the Eisele Collection at the University of New Mexico's Maxwell Museum. From the Calvin Collection. Courtesy, University of New Mexico General Libary, Special Collections

Right
Hollowed-out caves sheltered some Frijoles residents. They were a farming people who raised corn, beans, and squash, and also made pottery. NPS

Below
Some of the most significant archeological sites in the Northern Rio Grande Valley are situated in Bandelier National Monument, west of Santa Fe. Photo by Fred Mang, Jr., NPS

passed through the pithouse and small pueblo stages. Evidently they were influenced by the Anasazi in the Chaco area, and later by ideas from the Mesa Verde area. By the late 1200s and early 1300s these people lived in adobe or masonry pueblos, usually located on tributaries to the Rio Grande or sometimes near the great river itself. Some of these towns grew to great size, but there was much moving around and, oddly, even large towns were often abandoned, sometimes for reasons that today's archeologists cannot figure out. This common abandoning of villages may be more understandable if we realize that we are sedentary and accept living in one place as the "right" way of things. Recently nomadic people may need as much reason to stay as we do to move.

Some of these pueblo towns, including Taos, Picurís, and Pecos, engaged in extensive trade, especially with the non-pueblo Indians to the east. There nomads, who would come to be known as Apaches and Navajos, lived by hunting the bison on the grasslands. The nomads had meat but no corn, hides but no cotton clothing. The farmer-Pueblos living in the Rio Grande Valley and near it were quick to meet the needs of the Plains Indians on the other side of the mountains just to the east; so

just beyond Glorieta Pass and further south—near Abo Pass—towns developed on the east side of the mountains that specialized in trade with the plains.

The scene in New Mexico was vastly different from the distant, hazy days when big game learned to fear men with spears; there was even a pueblo that traded salt from the desiccated bed of what had been Lake Estancia. Towns had been built, usually square, often one large building surrounding three sides of a plaza. There were shifting political and economic alliances. Art forms were recognizable as being from one region or another. Jewelry was being manufactured and traded. Life was well-ordered, and from what we know of Pueblo culture later, customs were entrenched. Profoundly complicated and meaningful ceremonies happened at predictable times, necessary to keep the universe functioning properly and—specifically—to make the corn grow. Old people told children the stories of the tribe (although this probably happened in Pleistocene times as well). One wonders what this culture might have done, what direction its development might have taken, if history had taken a different turn. But it was 1492, and a tidal wave was gathering in a distant sea. Soon it would engulf New Mexico.

Estancia Valley's salt lakes are vestiges of a much larger body of water, which covered the area during prehistoric times. Salt gathered at the lakes was an important trade item for nearby Pueblo Indians. After the Spanish conquest, large quantities of the salt were sent to New Spain for use in a silver extraction process. NPS

27

During the reign of Philip II, a contract for the colonization of New Mexico was granted to Juan de Oñate, scion of a Zacatecas mining family. Philip died two months after Oñate established his headquarters at the Indian village of Ohke on the Rio Grande. From the Long Collection, NMSRCA

Spanish Explorers

It was a long international history that finally brought a handful of Spaniards trudging into New Mexico. In the hindsight of history books, their coming has a sense almost of inevitability, but from the view of the Indians already living among the canyons and mesas, it was the unexpected bordering on the unbelievable. One suspects that the first word came as rumors from the far south, of men known to us as Columbus and Cortez. After the conquest of Central America, it was an ill-fated expedition led by Pánfilo de Narváez that first brought New Mexico to the attention of Spain. The expedition was a disaster, and only four of its members survived, turning up eight years and thousands of miles later on the northwest coast of Mexico to report a series of remarkable adventures. It is unlikely that these men had actually entered New Mexico. They had struck west from the Rio Grande, some distance below present-day El Paso, toward Sonora. Nevertheless they had heard of Indian towns north of their route, with multi-storied buildings and great riches. These vague rumors of lands-almost-seen had a dramatic effect on the restless and ambitious Spaniards who inhabited the New World outposts of the empire.

To check out the stories, Viceroy Antonio de Mendoza sent a small scouting expedition, in the charge of Fray Marcos de Niza but actually led by one of the survivors, a Moorish slave named Estevan. Desert-hardened Estevan pushed on ahead of the friar until he reached the pueblo of Hawikuh, one of a cluster of small Zuni Indian villages south of present-day Gallup. There Estevan was killed. Exactly how close Fray Marcos came to Hawikuh, or what he saw, is not clear. In any case the Spaniards in Mexico were convinced that there were riches to be had in the tantalizing lands beyond the wild desert which up to now had blocked them from the north. After all, had they not found unexpected riches in Mexico and Peru?

Competition began immediately among the leading men of Mexico, each clamoring to be allowed to gamble his own fortune to lead a northward expedition. The man finally chosen was Francisco Vásquez de Coronado—young, wealthy, well-connected, and governor of the province of Nueva Galicia. The expedition assembled at Compostela, capital of Nueva Galicia, some 800 miles north of Mexico City, and on February 22, 1540, it started north.

There were perhaps 1,200 people, all but 336 of them natives, with more than 1,000 mounts and pack animals and a herd of food animals—cattle, goats, and sheep.

From a centuries-later viewpoint, an expedition seems to be all newness and adventure; it is easy to overlook the sheer physical labor of it. Everything needed by a large group of people had to be carried, every day. Even if carried by a horse, it was pulled down and lifted up as many times a day as necessary. Shovels, clothes, axes, armor, weapons, ammunition, medicines, food, records, spare parts, cooking gear—all of it was hauled north. Just the process of living during the trek took labor. Firewood had to be cut and gathered, water carried. A shelter did not just "appear": it had to be put up and taken down. Animals had to be saddled and un-saddled, packed and unpacked, and tended to. Bedding was not just slept in: it was carried, laid out, and packed up again.

C H A P T E R   I I I

In August of 1540 the forces of conquistador Francisco Vásquez de Coronado first encountered New Mexico's Zuni Indians before the pueblo of Hawikuh. Coronado's army, composed of 300 soldiers and 800 friendly Indians, had marched north from New Spain to explore the fabled "Seven Cities of Cíbola." This colorful representation of Coronado's encounter was painted by Gerald P. Cassidy. NMSRCA

Rivers were swollen, and not one of them was easy to cross. But the army we would call a mob trudged north. The history books say the medieval age was over, but it seemed that here was a piece of it: Coronado in his gilded armor (which must have been an oven on the desert, one presumes used for reviews and combat but not for marching), leading men with arms that any farmer in Europe would have recognized—lances, swords, bows and arrows, and just a few potent, expensive crossbows and arquebusses. As the purpose was exploration and possibly conquest, but not colonization, there were but a dozen or fewer women. And because this was a Spanish expedition of the sixteenth century, there were friars, four identified in the records and several others unnamed, to succor the souls of their countrymen and identify mission fields in the area they would explore. One of them was Marcos de Niza, who had led the first tentative foray with the unfortunate Estevan.

After a trek of nearly six months, the expedition reached Hawikuh—Fray Marcos' gilded city—and found it a miserable collection of stone-and-mud houses. Its people neither came out to trade nor in-vited the explorers into busy marketplaces; instead they resisted. The Spaniards attacked. Neither side had weapons we would consider formidable today. Coronado himself was downed temporarily by a well-aimed stone, his plumed helmet perhaps offering an easy target for Indian marksmen. The fight was short, and the Spaniards prevailed. Europeans had arrived in New Mexico.

Hope dies hard. When pressed, the Indians of Hawikuh told of other cities and, yes, those cities were rich. Coronado split his forces. He sent one detachment west to search for rumored towns in that direction. It found the Hopi villages, sitting in the sun on their timeless mesas. Another detachment, under Captain Hernando de Alvarado, was sent east with an Indian guide known as Bigotes, so called because of his mustache, unusual for an Indian. (Bigotes had arrived at Hawikuh as the leader of a delegation from Pecos, on the eastern fringe of the Pueblo country, sent to investigate the incredible report of the Spaniards' arrival.) In early September 1540 Bigotes led a group of perhaps two dozen Spaniards back toward his homeland. They were the first Europeans to enter

the Rio Grande Valley, the heart of the Pueblo region then, and the heart of New Mexico now.

They reached Acoma, the "Sky City," then swung north and east. The trudging soldiers welcomed the long downslope that brought them to a great river. It was the Rio Grande, which they reached at approximately the site of Albuquerque today. The area was heavily settled even then, for Bigotes had brought them to the heart of the Pueblo country. From there north were numerous Indian towns set amongst fields along the river. Alvarado records that representatives from twelve such towns came to meet him, bringing gifts. He called the "kingdom" (for he could think only as a European) Tiguex.

From there the Spaniards ranged northward to the Jemez, San Juan, and Taos pueblos. Time has been relatively kind to Taos, and today's visitor can, with a little effort, blank out the modern additions and see approximately what Alvarado's little band saw. Of course the two great buildings were eyeless then, for windows came later; but still they sit solidly on opposite sides of the stream that comes down from the massive sacred mountain that protects

the village. By then winter was coming on, and the Spaniards retreated to near present-day Bernalillo. From there Alvarado sent riders to Coronado, still at Hawikuh, with this message: bring the army here for the winter; there are warm rooms and corn.

After dispatching the report to Coronado, Alvarado's band pushed eastward toward Pecos and the plains beyond, hoping to find the great herds of buffalo of which Bigotes and his men had told Coronado. They entered the narrow western opening of Glorieta Pass and descended on the other side to the pueblo of Pecos. There they rested and enjoyed the hospitality of Bigotes' home village, but Alvarado was anxious to find the bison herds and decided to push on. Bigotes remained at Pecos, and the Spaniards took as guides two Plains Indians—captives being held as slaves at Pecos—known as "the Turk" and Sopete.

The group found the great animals in only four days. Now that bison have been reduced to such miserably few numbers, and virtually everyone knows what they look like, it may be hard to recreate the effect of that first encounter. "The most

The Zuni Indians were astonished by the Spaniards' horses and armor. In 1921 Santa Fe artist Gerald P. Cassidy painted this triptych, which depicts the first meeting between Francisco Vásquez de Coronado and New Mexico's indigenous people. The painting now hangs in Santa Fe's Federal Building. NMSRCA

monstrous beasts we have ever seen or heard about," wrote Alvarado, and so multitudinous that he "did not know to what to compare them unless it be to the fish of the sea." But soon the wonder of the bison was replaced by erroneous reports of an even greater wonder, the one the Spaniards had come so far to find: gold.

More than four centuries later it is impossible to know just what the Turk had in mind. The captive may simply have wanted the Spaniards to take him to Quivira, his homeland in what we now call Kansas, or he may have intended to lure them to their deaths on the plains. Perhaps he just enjoyed making a sensation. At any rate the Turk soon discovered the Spaniards' preoccupation with gold and told them that the metal abounded in his homeland. As evidence he claimed that he had had a gold bracelet when captured,

that it had been taken from him, and that even now it was in the possession of none other than Bigotes.

If the Turk wanted to create a sensation, he certainly succeeded. The tiny army, having seen the buffalo, turned around and returned to Pecos. There they questioned Bigotes, who denied the story. The cacique, or religious leader of the Pecos, backed Bigotes' denial. But belief is born of desire, and the Spaniards wanted very much to believe. Bigotes, the cacique, the Turk, and Sopete were all taken in chains back to Tiguex, where Alvarado expected to meet Coronado and the main army. Here indeed was news for the general.

Alvarado and his prisoners arrived at Tiguex to find that Coronado had not yet arrived but had sent Captain García López de Cárdenas with an advance detachment to prepare the way. To be fair to

For centuries, Pueblo women have baked in beehive-shaped ovens called "hornos." Their tasty bread has always been a popular item wherever Indian arts and crafts are displayed. From the Woodward Collection, NMSRCA

Above
Europeans first visited Taos in 1540, during an exploration of the northern pueblos made by Coronado's Captain Hernando de Alvarado. The party's scribe reported multistoried apartment houses made of adobe, a description that still fits today. SHPS

Left
Coronado's men first saw buffalo when they ventured onto the plains east of the Pecos River. There they also met the Querechos, an Apache group who followed the great herds, carrying their hide tepees on dog travois. From the WPA Collection, NMSRCA

Cárdenas, there is evidence that the Spaniards began to prepare their own quarters for winter, but soon the cold set in, and time was short. Cárdenas then "asked" the Indians—the verb is in the records but not enlarged upon—simply to move out of one of their villages and let the Spaniards move in. The Indians left, and the Spaniards moved into the pueblo called Alcanfor to wait for Coronado and the rest of the army.

On the very night Coronado arrived—after a hard march from Hawikuh, by way of El Morro, and up the Rio Grande—the Turk confirmed everything, adding more and more embellishments. Coronado checked with Bigotes and the cacique from Pecos, who continued to deny the existence of the golden bracelet. To make them tell the "truth," apparently the Spaniards' fierce war dogs were used to harass or at least frighten the Pecos witnesses. They stuck to their story, but they would not forget the dog baiting.

The winter was cold and hard. Relations between Spaniards and Indians in the Rio Grande Valley, which had begun hospitably, disintegrated in the hard winter. Coronado sent parties to ask the Indians for food and supplies. Apparently Coronado sincerely wanted to obtain the supplies without bloodshed, but the wish was fantastic. Somebody had to be hungry, and it was not clear to those who had farmed just why it should be they.

The climax came with the horses. Fascinating to the Indians, the huge animals gave the Spaniards almost miraculous mobility. Whether out of curiosity about the animals or in retaliation for the levies, the Indians staged a raid on the herd. Tracing their tracks to a pueblo called Arenal, the Spaniards saw the Indians driving the horses around the plaza, shooting them with arrows. An attempt at diplomacy failed, and the inevitable battle was fierce. The Indians barricaded themselves in their pueblo, which was a formidable defense against the arms of the Spaniards. The Spaniards broke through the mud walls and built smudge fires to force the Indians out. There was terrifying hand-to-hand combat in the dark, smoky rooms, but in the end the struggle became a rout. Possibly because of a mix-up in orders, Indians who thought they had been promised amnesty for surrendering were tied to stakes and burned. The witnesses from Pecos observed it all.

The Battle of Arenal took place at the end of December 1540, and despite the harshness of winter, nearby Indians abandoned their towns and fled into the Sandia Mountains. The Spaniards—learning that the Indians were reassembling in a village called Moho, somewhere above present-day Bernalillo—laid siege to the pueblo. The siege lasted six weeks. The Indians tried to dig a well, but it caved in, killing thirty. With sorrow as old as warfare, they turned over their women and children to the besiegers, hoping for safety for them, and attempted a last, desperate breakout. It was futile. The mounted Spaniards rode them down, lancing them from horseback, and many died trying to swim the frigid waters of the Rio Grande. A tragic pattern had been set and confirmed.

Finally it was spring, and on April 23, 1541, Coronado set out to pursue the golden dreams fostered and fed by the Turk. They crossed the frozen Rio Grande, passed through Glorieta Pass, and reached Pecos. Somehow, now or earlier, the tales of the Turk meshed with a plot by the leaders at Pecos to destroy the Spaniards or at least get rid of them by leading them far out onto the plains. Unaware, Coronado and his men pushed on across the plains, land as flat and featureless as the sea.

Like Alvarado's reconnaissance before them, they found the great larder of the plains, the buffalo. The huge animals were in herds of numbers that staggered the imagination. The expedition encountered bands of Plains Indians who followed the herds, killing and butchering the animals very much as their Paleoindian ancestors had done 100 centuries earlier. The Spaniards had found one of the wonders and treasures of the (future) American West—one that would soon be squandered—but it was not the treasure they sought.

At last it became apparent that the Turk's story was not holding up. Alvarado noted that the Turk's directions were not the same as they had been the previous autumn, and there were discrepancies, too, with what the nomadic buffalo hunters told them. The continued protests of Sopete and Bigotes, who claimed all along that the Turk was lying, may have begun to sink in. In any case there was a confrontation—one wishes the record offered more detail, for it must have been dramatic—and the Turk confessed. He had lied. The houses of his people were only of grass. He had wanted not only to return to his own people but also to get the Spaniards lost on the empty plains.

Coronado decided to send the main part of his army back to Tiguex, while proceeding himself with thirty selected men to investigate this rapidly diminishing Quivira. There was a parting on the plains. The main body returning enlisted some of the Plains Indians as guides to shorten the return trip. The Spaniards were fascinated by the method their guides used. Each morning, taking bearings by the sunrise, the Indians shot an arrow as far as possible in the appropriate direction. They then traveled toward the arrow, but, before

At Petroglyph National Monument, more than 15,000 ancient Indian rock drawings, or petroglyphs, are inscribed on the 17 mile volcanic escarpment west of Albuquerque. Ordinarily, one would have to trek miles into a wilderness area to see as many petroglyphs as Albuquerque has on its doorstep. The meaning of many of these images has been lost to time, but some seem to have deep religious significance. Albuquerque CVB

35

For the Pueblo Indians, the kiva was an important center of their religious life. Conversely, Spaniards hated and feared these underground chambers as the sources of pagan practices. During times of repression, civil and religious authorities frequently ordered their destruction. NPS

they reached it, shot another arrow past it and walked toward that one, thereby achieving a straight line of travel.

Meanwhile Coronado and his detachment pushed on, the vindicated Sopete now in the lead and the Turk in chains. In a month of travel, any day of which would be in today's terms a tremendous adventure—or an hour in a car—they reached Quivira. Where they had hoped for golden chandeliers, they found straw huts. Secretly (for they were in the Turk's land) they strangled and buried the Turk. Then they began the long journey back to Tiguex to rejoin the rest of the army.

By this time the main unit—which had reached Tiguex—had realized Pecos' involvement in the plot to lose the Spaniards on the plains and went to Pecos to wait for Coronado, figuring that their force could

prevent the powerful Pecos pueblo from attempting to wipe his unit out. They were right, and Coronado successfully rejoined his main army. But the success was a hollow one. Winter was at hand, and the expedition could not return to Mexico. They would have to spend another winter at Tiguex, with nothing but the empty-handed return to look forward to in the spring.

At least two and possibly three of the friars elected to stay in the mission field they had discovered. Fray Juan de Padilla returned to Quivira; Luis de Escalona stayed at Pecos; and it seems that a third stayed in Tiguex. The latter two soon found the martyrdom they evidently sought. Though it took a little longer, so did Padilla, who met his death, kneeling, in a shower of arrows. This is known from the eyewitness account of his Portuguese servant, Andrés de Campo, who was taken prisoner but escaped and ultimately made his way back to Mexico five years later.

By then Coronado's expedition was long gone from New Mexico. The army that had descended dramatically on the land gathered its wondrous horses, its metal, its gunpowder, and, leaving behind a small taste of its religion and a branded memory of its power and will, walked back past Acoma, past Hawikuh, and disappeared to the south.

It was two generations before another band of explorers probed north from New Spain into the Pueblo country. The delay was significant, for during it the Council of the Indies in Spain, acting in the name of the Crown, instituted the Ordinances of 1573. The New World experience was presenting new problems for Europe—problems of administration, finance, logistics, even of morality. A vocal faction led by the church had raised serious questions about the treatment of the native peoples. The Ordinances of 1573 reflected a new view. There was to be no "conquest"—the very word was forbidden. A permit from the king was necessary to undertake "pacification," and the rights of Indians were enumerated. Still, the northern frontier of New Spain (what are today the Mexican states just below the Texas-Mexico border) was far from the heartland of the rapidly growing colony that centered on the capital in Mexico City. It was a tough mining frontier, and distant rules bent easily.

In one "boom" town called Santa Bárbara, a particularly devout Franciscan lay brother named Agustín Rodríguez yearned for the mission field rumored to exist to the north. There is no evidence that he knew anything about Coronado's journey two generations before, but he worked with local Indians, and some of them had told him about other Indians to the north. He applied for permission to go north. His band was to receive a military escort of nine soldiers, led by Captain Francisco Sánchez Chamuscado and including one Hernan Gallegos, who would keep a journal (and thus earn the gratitude of historians).

The party left Santa Bárbara on June 5, 1581. Chamuscado may have escorted the friars, but he did not seem overly concerned with their mission. As they entered New Mexico coming up the Rio Grande, he began "taking possession" for the king. The little band ranged the pueblos between present-day Albuquerque and Galisteo Creek, going west to Zuni and east to Pecos and into the plains, but the soldiers were more interested in mineral deposits than Indian souls. One of the friars, Fray Juan de Santa María, was determined to report the subversion of the expedition and left to walk back to Mexico. When the soldiers finally decided to return, the two other friars elected to stay at a pueblo somewhere near present-day Bernalillo.

Captain Chamuscado died of natural causes before the soldiers got back to Santa Bárbara, but the survivors brought back stories of towns to the north worthy of colonization. The buzz that followed was like the one that had followed Fray Marcos' return forty years before, this time with the added touch of concern for the friars who had stayed behind.

In the midst of the buzz was Antonio de Espejo, who with his brother owned successful ranching and mining enterprises in northern New Spain. Temporarily out of favor with the authorities, Espejo was in the north to escape legal difficulties in Mexico City. Here was a chance for a daring man to recoup all in one triumph: he would use his wealth to sponsor a rescue attempt of the friars left behind in the north. In deliberate confusion as to whether he had permission or not, he set out on March 10, 1582, with a small expedition, and once again Spaniards were traveling up the Rio Grande.

The fate of one of the friars had been learned already. Fray Santa María, the one who had set out to walk to Mexico, had never finished his lonely journey. Trudging south through the Estancia Valley, he had stopped and stretched out to rest; Indians killed him where he lay. As for the other two who had stayed behind, Espejo learned that they also had been killed. Having discovered their fate, the soldiers wanted nevertheless to go on. They visited the pueblos, confirming once again that these were not opulent, European-style towns.

Nonetheless, on their return to Mexico there was the predictable uproar of speculation. This time the buzz was loud enough to reach the Crown, and the search began for an official colonizer. In the meantime, however, there would be at least one more ragtag unofficial probe.

This most unlikely expedition of all was that of Gaspar Castaño de Sosa, lieutenant governor of the province of New León and part-time slaver. In a moment of vaunting imagination, he persuaded the whole population of his tiny colonial settlement, some 200 strong, to remove with him to the outback in direct contravention of a viceregal order. They brought wheeled carts, the first ever seen in New Mexico. Their decision to travel up the Pecos was a mistake, for the terrain was broken and rough. There were armed encounters—precisely what the Crown had wished to avoid—and a pursuing expedition caught up with de Sosa at the pueblo of Santa Domingo. De Sosa was returned to Mexico in irons (although he was later pardoned). The Crown was now ready for an official attempt.

El Señor D. Diego de Bargas Zapata Lujan, Pon ze de Leon, Marques de la Na ba de Barcinas, del Orden de S.tiago. Governador, Conquis tador, Pacificador, y Capitan General del Nuebo Mejico, perdió la Vida en Campaña Rasa por libertar los Va sos Sagrados en el Sitio de Bernalillo, año de MDCCIV.

Este cuadro, que el Instituto de Cultura Hispánica ofrece al Museo de Nuebo Mejico, es co pia del verdadero retrato de D. Diego Barzas Zapata, "de la Casa de los Vargas", cuyo original se conserva en la capilla de San Isidro sita en el Pretil de Santisteban de Madrid.

A swaggering nobleman, Diego José de Vargas Zapata y Luján Ponce de León y Contreras—known as Diego de Vargas—is the hero of the reconquest of New Mexico. During a 1692 reconnaissance he personally persuaded Pueblo leaders to accept a Spanish return. When he came back in 1693 with colonists and Franciscans, he was compelled to quell Indian resistance by force. This portrait of Diego de Vargas hangs in the Museum of New Mexico. Courtesy, Museum of New Mexico (MNM) (#11409)

Colonization and Conquest

The man chosen to lead an expedition to colonize, not merely explore, the distant north was Juan de Oñate, son of a wealthy mine operator in Zacatecas. Oñate offered to finance the expedition himself. In return he was to receive a hereditary governorship, along with various other titles and an immense land grant on the new frontier.

On January 7, 1598, the caravan of 130 men, their wives and children, ten Franciscan friars, and an immense herd of bawling animals started north. They traveled on foot, on horseback, and in ox-drawn carts. Instead of following the rivers as others had done, Oñate decided to strike north, straight across the desert, to intercept the Rio Grande where it swung to the east. Unknowingly he finished blazing the Camino Real into New Mexico, a road that one day would carry the commerce of the United States and Mexico—two countries that did not yet exist.

The Pass—"Paso del Norte"—where the river shouldered its way between mountains and where one also had to ford the river, was generally accepted as the entrance to New Mexico, and somewhere on the Rio Grande near there Oñate and the friars performed an elaborate civil and religious ceremony of claiming the region, a ceremony which included the medieval custom of tossing grass and stones into the air. From a nearby hillside a curious Indian pausing to watch would have found it comic: tiny, ant-like figures in the immensity of New Mexico, claiming in a puny voice, lost in the wind, land, riches, and souls for God and king. The souls and riches would prove elusive, and in just twelve years Oñate himself would return the same way, a broken man. But do not disdain that impertinence along the Rio Grande. In some ways the Spaniards made their claim stick. Some four centuries later this land still bears the rich stamp of Spain in customs, food, architecture, and language.

The Spaniards crossed the river and followed it north, seeing with immeasurably more time and curiosity the scenery a motorist sees today hurrying north on I-25 from El Paso. Indians were few, and the land a desert. Near the present-day improbably named town of Truth or Consequences they were forced by rough terrain to the east side of the Caballo and Fray Cristóbal mountain ranges, across a ninety-mile stretch without water or shade. A man named Robledo died at the beginning of the crossing—a small settlement still bears his name. This area is still known as the Jornada del Muerto (Dead Man's Journey).

The caravan reached the Piro Indian villages, causing most of the natives to flee. There the Spaniards paused and rested, eating corn given them by the few Indians who stayed behind. Further north were more villages, and the expedition found welcome relief around present-day Socorro.

At the pueblo called Santa Domingo, north of Bernalillo, there was a happy discovery. Two of the Mexican Indians left behind by Castaño de Sosa's expedition were still there. For seven years they had lived among these river farmers, and they spoke the local tongue. Here the Spaniards were met by seven "chiefs" (a strictly European concept) whom Oñate somehow understood to represent thirty-four villages. This was impossible, but the Spaniards didn't know it and were gratified as

C H A P T E R   I V

For centuries New Mexicans depended on ox carts called "carretas" to bring supplies of all kinds north from New Spain. In the seventeenth century the Franciscans organized and directed supply caravans. This example of a carreta of more recent vintage is on display at the Museum of New Mexico. From the School of American Research Collection, NMSRCA

the representatives swore allegiance to the God and king of Spain. The capabilities of the translators must have been sorely strained.

On July 11, 1598, the expedition reached the end of its journey, near present-day Espanola. There, where the Chama empties into the Rio Grande, near the pueblo today called San Juan, Oñate and his advance party established the first Spanish headquarters in New Mexico. A month later the main caravan, which the group had left behind, arrived at the fledgling colony.

The story of the Oñate colony is usually told in the actions of its leader, especially the extraordinary trips he took. With a retinue of soldiers and friars, he traveled on horseback through Glorieta Pass to Pecos and out onto the plains. He went to the area around present-day Mountainair and, as usual, conducted elaborate ceremonies to accept the allegiance of the pueblos. In one astonishing journey he crossed Arizona to the mouth of the Colorado. On the way back he paused at the ancient watering hole at the foot of the great rock

of El Morro and carved into the rock his name and the date: April 16, 1606.

But just as important as the peripatetic travels of their leader were the experiences and gradual disillusionment of the colonists. Ordinarily a frontier settlement is at the edge of the unknown; just behind it is the known, providing support. But this fledgling colony had leap-frogged 1,500 miles from the colonial heartland. It was a "bubble" frontier, with little or no support. And now winter hit hard, longer and colder than these people from the south had expected. Their crops did badly. The cold dry hills turned out to be just dry hills, with no gold or silver hidden in them.

As for the Indians, some Spaniards saw them as souls to be won, and others disdained them, but probably all underestimated them. Juan de Zaldívar, Oñate's nephew, paid for just this mistake with his life. Sent to Acoma to procure food, he and most of his men were wiped out in an ambush. The Spanish reacted ferociously. Vicente de Zaldívar, younger brother of the slain officer, was sent with seventy soldiers to avenge the deaths. They were brutally successful and brought back more than 500 prisoners—men, women, and children—nearly all sentenced to slavery.

Other conflicts followed, and discontent grew. The missionary effort was drawn back from outlying pueblos and concentrated along the Rio Grande; even there it was often frustrated. Reading the record today it appears that the Spaniards failed to understand the Indians' polytheism, which made them quite willing to adopt the new religion while steadfastly keeping the old. Religious and economic frustrations mounted. The colony dwindled under mass desertions, and in the end Oñate himself began the long trek back to Mexico. His fortune was lost to the defeated enterprise, and all hope of glory was gone.

This turning point in New Mexico history brought a remarkable decision by the Spanish Crown. The New Mexico colony had proved unprofitable, but a missionary effort had begun and could not be aban-

Left
Oñate established his first headquarters on the east bank of the Rio Grande at the Indian village of Ohke. Within a few months the settlers moved across the river to Yuqueyunque (pictured). MNM (#16739)

Below
Oñate left an inscription chiseled in the soft rock at El Morro. Translated into English the inscription reads: "Adelantado don Juan de Oñate passed this way from the discovery of the South Sea, April 16, 1606" (actually 1605). Courtesy, State Parks and Recreation, NMSRCA

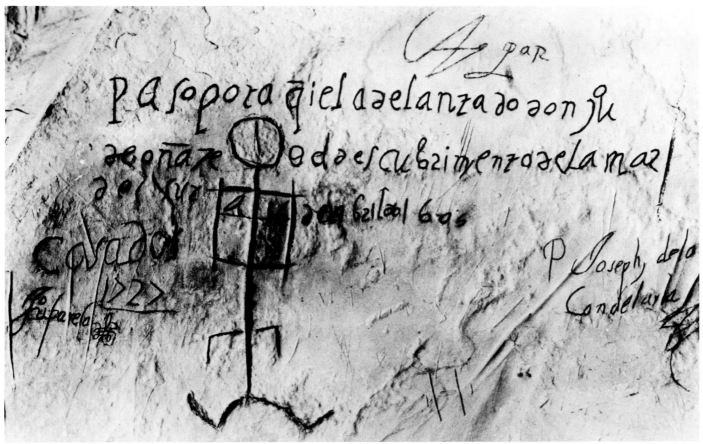

The first serious confrontation between Oñate's men and the Pueblo Indians took place December 4, 1598, on Acoma Mesa. After feigning friendship the natives attacked a Spanish foraging party that had climbed up to the village to secure supplies. Eleven soldiers were killed. Others survived by leaping off the mesa to the plain 400 feet below. Six weeks later the Spaniards retaliated, capturing and burning the pueblo and taking over 500 captives. MNM (#68736)

doned. Thus a new governor was appointed, although to a colony that had changed its nature. Instead of the once-anticipated loads of silver being carried to the homeland, now supply trains to the colony would carry cloth, holy images, nails, and axes for the construction of new missions, largely paid for by the Crown.

In a missionary colony—or at least such was the idea—blue-robed Franciscans would labor patiently at missions in the various pueblos while the civil authorities would govern the Christian population. As soon as the Indians learned Christian and Spanish ways—the two were taken to be synonymous—the region would become a solid member of the Spanish Empire. It did not turn out this way. Instead, the 1600s became what one historian has called "troublous times."

The basic problem was the split between the religious and the governmental sides of Spain's effort. The pile of grey limestone ruins on its lonely hill at almost exactly the center of the state, now the Gran Quivira unit of Salinas National Monument,

may be taken as a case study.

The Indian town had been there for centuries before Oñate came riding up the hill. It was one of the fringe pueblos, a go-between for trade between the Rio Grande pueblos and the Plains Indians, as well as the Apaches. Trade items included pottery, corn, and piñon nuts. The nearby salt beds provided a special trade item and also gave the area its common name, the Salinas Province. As in all other pueblos, there was a rich ceremonial year. There was no difference between civil and religious government; all life was bound up in activities that were at once religious and practical. Planting corn was a religious act, and praying a practical one.

And then Oñate and more than 100 men came up the hill. It was an October day in 1598. The colony at San Juan was just two months old, and already Oñate was on the road, visiting the pueblos he anticipated administering. The record says merely that the villages "rendered obedience to His Majesty," but from other instances we know something of the pomp of

Left
For many years Apaches from the East came to Gran Quivira for trade, but the relationship withered. During the 1670s all the Saline pueblos were abandoned because of drought and Apache hostility. Gran Quivira is now part of Salinas National Monument, administered by the National Park Service. NPS

Below
Erected circa 1630 under the direction of Franciscan friars, the Quarai Mission Church served Pueblo Indians living near the salt lakes east of the Manzano Mountains. NMSRCA

the ceremony. The Indians were instructed that these officers and priests now had authority over them. The lesson was driven home in the next year or so as there were two, possibly three, armed conflicts with the newcomers. It is not clear from the record exactly where the fights were, but if not at this town they were nearby and with friends and relatives of these people. The Spanish were bloodily victorious each time, and the new regime settled in.

In 1626 a priest visited the town. Fray Alonso Benavides was a remarkable man, and his report on the missionary potential in New Mexico would do much to bring the colony to the attention of the church. He recorded that he preached a sermon in the plaza and was well received. In 1629 several new priests came northward with the biannual packtrain, and one of them, Fray Francisco Letrado, was assigned to this town. For the first time there was a full-time Spanish presence. Of course Letrado built a church, its ruins a rectangle of fallen walls today. It must have been a lonely and frustrating job. Today one can

stand in the remains of his living quarters (his rooms are larger than the Indian rooms) and look out and imagine this devoted man, impossibly distant from home and relatives, laboring against the blank wall of a totally different conception of religion, God, and man. There only a short time, Letrado was transferred to Acoma, where on February 22, 1632 (a century to the day before an English child was born in another colony on the other side of the continent and christened George Washington), he was killed by the Indians.

Priests were few and far between in New Mexico, and it was a generation before Fray Letrado was replaced. The church he built fell into ruin; archeologists find that beams from it were used to repair Indian rooms. There were active churches at the pueblos just a day's walk away, though, and in many ways life was affected by Spaniards, even if they were not always present. Indians had to walk to Santa Fe to work in the governor's sweatshops, their fields suffering in their absence. They had to gather salt and lug it in leather sacks over to the Rio Grande, to meet the mule trains that took it south to the mining towns in Parral. There were also demands from the Spaniards for piñon nuts, for cotton mantas. The Indians, whom the priests saw as a mission field, were actually turning out to be the economic base for the colony.

Eventually, in 1660, another priest came. His name was Fray Diego de Santander, and, inevitably, he wanted to build another church. This one would be huge, its fort-like stone walls up to six feet thick, with attached workshops, classrooms, priest's quarters, storerooms, and a corral. The labor, of course, was immense.

Records do not give us the day-to-day details, but there must have been good times, years when the crops were adequate. There were classes for the children, and there was fascination in the mysteries of the candle-light church. But overall, the story was one of disintegration. Throughout the colony the schism between church and state burst wide open, much of it over control of the Indians. There were a few governors who supported the church, but in the main the governors were out to make what they could during their limited term of office, and that meant using Indian labor. But the church, too, made de-

The Palace of the Governors, constructed soon after the founding of Santa Fe in 1610, is the oldest public building in the United States. The adobe structure served as both residence and executive offices for New Mexico's governors under Spanish, Mexican, and United States administrations. Today it contains exhibits of the Museum of New Mexico. NMSRCA

Because of its strategic location in a natural pass between the Rio Grande and the eastern plains, the pueblo of Abó was an important trade center in prehistoric times. Like their neighbors at Gran Quivira, Abó's people belonged to the Tompiro linguistic group. Franciscan missionaries built San Gregorio church beside the pueblo early in the seventeenth century. NPS

mands on the Indians, to tend fields and herds, to gather firewood, to cook.

As for things of the spirit, there was absolute turmoil. Priests demanded that the kiva ceremonies stop and occasionally went so far as to destroy kivas and their paraphenalia; at the same time there were government officials who at least condoned and sometimes even encouraged the dancers. Whom were the Indians to believe? Word spread like wildfire of the time in the church at Quarai that the *alcalde mayor* stood up during the sermon and disputed the priest, who had just said the Indians owed their allegiance to God. The alcalde said no, they owed their allegience to the governor. After several such incidents, the church brought in the Inquisition, a formidable weapon against its enemies. (A friend to historians, though: Inquisition charges brought against anyone, especially a governor, led to testimony, of which Inquisition officials kept meticulous records. Those fragile pages are the source of much of this story.)

Worse still, relations with the Indians' old trading partners, the Apaches, began to break down, at least in part because the Spaniards occasionally captured Apaches and sold them south into man-killing slavery in the silver mines. The Apaches saw that the Spaniards were living with the Pueblos, and, on the theory that "the friend of my enemy is my enemy," began attacking the pueblos. The situation was exacerbated by a drought in the 1660s that would not let up. There had been droughts before, of course, but never under these circumstances. The age-old pueblo ceremonies to make nature do as it ought had been disrupted, so there was no particular reason for the Indians to think it would get better. The Apaches, suffering themselves from the drought, burned fields and stole stored grain. Drought brought starvation; the *alcalde mayor* of the Salinas Province wrote that when his men went to collect corn from the Indians, "they weep and cry out as if they and all their descendants were being killed." (They were.) And disease came riding on the back of starvation.

The source of their troubles was not lost on the Indians. In the late 1660s Indian leader Esteban Clemente rose in the Salinas Province and attempted to organize a

Acoma's original village was situated high atop a steep-sided mesa for defensive purposes. The location made water a precious commodity. Today the old pueblo is still occupied, but most tribal members live in new communities on the flatlands below. From the D. Woodward Collection, NMSRCA

revolt. He was found out and hanged. But the troubles proved too much; by 1676 the hill at Gran Quivira was abandoned by Pueblo and Spaniard alike.

This was Gran Quivira but it could have been Pecos, or Acoma, or the Galisteo pueblos, or any of a dozen others. In this case the pueblo simply fell apart, never to be reoccupied. But others with similar experiences were still occupied, seething with trouble and resentment and about to boil over into the bloody days of August 1680.

There was long preparation for the revolt. Stimulated by hardship and encouraged by signs of Spanish disunity, Pueblo leaders met to discuss what to do, and the idea evolved of throwing the Spaniards out, lock, stock, and barrel. It is incredible that this joint planning took place at all, for traditionally the various Indian pueblos were fiercely independent. Even more remarkable, the planning took place without

the Spaniards' knowledge. It seems that only days before the revolt, the government—headquartered at Santa Fe since 1610—thought everything was as usual.

One of the organizers of the Pueblo Revolt was a San Juan religious leader known as Popé. In a routine exercise at rooting out the Indians' religion in 1675, Spaniards had flogged a number of Indians at Santa Fe, probably including Popé. His revenge would be terrible.

Popé moved to the remote pueblo of Taos in the final months of preparation. From there the word went out to pueblos as distant as Zuni and Hopi, brought by runners who carried a knotted rope. Each knot represented a day left before the uprising; when the last knot was undone, the revolt would begin.

The Spaniards did receive some warning, but it did them little good. On August 8, 1680, Fray Fernando de

Velasco at Pecos learned from Indians there that an uprising was scheduled for the thirteenth. He wrote to Governor Otermín at the Palace of the Governors in Santa Fe, who received the note the next day, along with similar warnings from Taos and elsewhere, and even from captured messengers at Tesuque. For some reason Otermín did not respond quickly, but in any case he probably would not have been quick enough. Either the Indians changed the day once their plan was discovered, or the thirteenth had been a ruse all along. On Saturday the tenth the revolt came.

Death, revenge, and a terrible form of a people's renewal burst upon the Spaniards from a reservoir that had been filling for eighty years. Priests of the new religion were killed in or near their churches. The churches themselves—all of them—were desecrated. Whole Spanish families were wiped out, save those who could flee to the temporary safety of Santa Fe. There the Palace of the Governors became an armed, wailing camp as the refugees straggled in. All in all, more than 400 Spaniards would be killed in the uprising, including twenty-one friars.

By August 12, Indians surrounded the Palace of the Governors. Word reached Governor Otermín that the Rio Abajo (Lower River) ranches near present-day Albuquerque had been totally wiped out. This story later proved to be false and may even have been told deliberately by the Indians, but it brought home to the besieged Spaniards their isolation. In a dramatic gesture one Indian leader, wearing the sash of a slain priest, offered a red cross or a white one—"peace or war." But there was no possibility of reconciliation, and the battle raged.

There is a church in Santa Fe today called "the oldest church." An image of the Blessed Virgin was kept there, and some brave soul rescued it and brought it through the turmoil to the Palace. Soon the besieged could see the smoke of that building mixing with that of burning houses and shops. The little statue would appear again in the story of New Mexico.

It is remarkable that the Spaniards were able to break out of this seemingly impossible situation. Actually there are indications that once the Spaniards chose to leave, the Indians were willing to let them go. On August 21, about 1,000 survivors,

During the 1680 Pueblo revolt, Spaniards from the Rio Abajo (down-river region) assembled at the pueblo of Isleta before retreating down the Rio Grande. That pueblo's church may be the oldest in New Mexico. Although the church has been remodeled frequently, parts of its current foundation and walls were put up about 1613. From the Cobb Collection. Courtesy, University of New Mexico General Library, Special Collections

During the 1680 revolt, Pecos Indians destroyed the massive mission church that the Franciscans had erected south of their pueblo. After the Vargas reconquest, a smaller church was superimposed on the old foundations. This aerial view shows the remains of that church and adjoining convento, following National Park Service stabilization. NPS

many of them now widowed or orphaned, made their way out of Santa Fe and started downriver.

Santo Domingo . . . San Felipe . . . at one settlement after another their worst fears were realized. Bodies lay motionless in the sun, the charred remains of buildings behind them. Somewhere along the way Otermín learned that, although the revolt had indeed included the Rio Abajo, there had been survivors who even now were fleeing southward, in the belief that all those at Santa Fe had perished. He sent word for them to wait and caught up at the campsite of Fray Cristóbal. Together the ragged, grieving crowd of 2,500 trudged south to El Paso, where at last they felt out of reach of the terror. The first attempt at European colonization of New Mexico had been extinguished.

Far to the north, there was rejoicing. The images in the churches were destroyed, as were many of the buildings themselves. The great church at Pecos, largest in New Mexico until the modern age, went up in a huge blaze, and its burned adobe blocks reappeared in brand-new kivas. The Palace of the Governors was divided into the small Indian rooms that characterized a traditional pueblo. The old kachina dances were performed again and again, celebrating freedom and the chance to renew old ways. It was an orgy of purification.

It was twelve years before the Spaniards came back, but the celebrating did not last that long. With Spanish repression removed, the alliance quickly collapsed, and age-old rivalries reasserted themselves. Soon there was warfare between the recent allies, and the Apaches and Utes began raiding again.

Of course the Spaniards were not completely forgotten. From year to year there were probes from the south, as Otermín and others made various attempts to reconquer the lost territory. In some ways it is curious that the authorities in Mexico City kept trying, for the colony never had returned much. But the world scene was changing, and Spain was losing its monopoly in the New World. France especially was a threat, with its growing presence in the eastern part of North America. Even if New Mexico could never deliver the riches once imagined, it could serve as a buffer to keep France from approaching the heartland of New Spain.

RECONQUEST

It was dark inside the wrappings. La Conquistadora, the small statue of the Virgin that had been rescued and taken south during the Pueblo Revolt, was now carefully wrapped and being carried in a jolting, screeching oxcart, approaching Santa Fe once again. The Spaniards were back.

Bringing La Conquistadora was the reconquerer who would eventually succeed at the job, with the formidable name Diego José de Vargas Zapata y Lujan Ponce de León y Contreras, commonly referred to as Diego de Vargas. Vargas had gathered 300 men at El Paso, and in August of 1692—twelve years and one week after the first terrible day of the revolt—set out to see if reconquest was possible. The way was hard, and caution was the watchword, for the few previous tentative probes had found the Indians still implacable. Still, 300 men is a significant force. They reached the north country to find pueblos recently abandoned, with crops near harvest. Santo Domingo was empty, as was Cochití. It was obvious that the Indians had fled to the hills and were watching the invaders from there.

Vargas' force approached Santa Fe. Of course the Indians knew they were coming, but what would the reception be? Before dawn on September 13, the tense army gathered silently in a broken-down rancho a few miles from Santa Fe. (It had once belonged to Roque Madrid, Vargas' *maestre de campo,* who must have had memories that night.) The attempt to retake Santa Fe was to be peaceful if possible, but swords were sharpened and ready.

The next day the Indians were defiant. They gathered on the walls of the palace and shouted at the Spaniards assembled

Standing high on a hill overlooking Santa Fe, the Cross of the Martyrs was erected in 1920 by the Knights of Columbus and the Historical Society of New Mexico as a memorial to the Franciscan friars killed during the Pueblo Revolt of 1680. After the neighborhood around the cross became heavily populated, civic groups put up a second cross on a nearby hill for use during ceremonial processions. MNM (#52461)

before them. But Vargas quickly demonstrated the remarkable courage and restraint that were to serve him so well. Seeing the acequia, the irrigation ditch that supplied water to the city, he cut it off—as the Indians had done in 1680—and boldly walked into Santa Fe with an assumption of victory. The defiance withered, and Vargas won without a fight.

At Pecos the Indians abandoned the pueblo and fled to the hills; Vargas captured several and, after five days, released them with messages of peace. Vargas then left without damaging the pueblo or stealing its stores. It was a critical decision, for the Pecos would become the Spaniards' most important allies in the difficult decade to come.

The pattern would repeat itself throughout New Mexico. Tesuque . . . San Ildefonso . . . Picurís . . . at pueblo after pueblo Vargas arrived with restrained but obvious force, and with nervous relief the Indians capitulated. Undoubtedly there was something of a domino effect at work, for each pueblo had heard that the pueblo

After the successful recapture of Santa Fe from Pueblo Indian rebels late in 1693, victorious Spanish soldiers attributed their success to a small statue of Our Lady of the Rosary, which they had brought back after a long exile near present El Paso. The image soon became known as "La Conquistadora." Photo by Robert Martin, MNM (#41984)

before had accepted this Spaniard, which made it easier for them also to do so. Time and time again the soldiers heard "the speech," reclaiming the land and all its people in the name of King Carlos II. Priests were kept busy baptizing children born since the revolt and blessing marriages which had taken place. The army marched through the snow to Taos, and even that powerful pueblo, once headquarters for the revolt, came to cheer the speech and accept the baptism. They promised to keep peace with their neighbors, and warned Vargas of opposition in some of the western pueblos.

Vargas then headed south. He revisited Pecos; this time the Indians welcomed him with boughs and crosses and pledges of allegiance. He visited Santo Domingo and Cochití and was warned of trouble to come at Jemez. It was true, but there, too, his courage and will prevailed without bloodshed.

Now Vargas determined to push on to the western pueblos. He sent part of the army and much of the baggage to wait for him at El Paso, and headed west with a select force. They approached the virtually impregnable mesa at Acoma. Again the general bargained, waited, and chose the precise moment to seize a bloodless victory. The record was unbroken, and when the army stopped at El Morro for water a few days later, Vargas added another message, still visible today, to New Mexico's rock of history: "Here was General Don Diego de Vargas, who conquered all New Mexico for our holy faith and the royal crown at his own expense, the year 1692."

The Hopi mesas brought the greatest danger and the highest drama of the 1692 expedition. Yet even there, facing a seemingly implacable foe, Vargas somehow prevailed by sheer force of personality. Natives who had him vastly outpowered ultimately submitted without a fight and, on bended knee, received "the Reconqueror."

Vargas wasted no time preparing to build on the foundation he had won. Returning to El Paso amid great rejoicing, he once again spent day after day on horseback, this time going from village to village persuading ranchers and miners to join him in settling the land he had reconquered. Although he had hoped for 500 families, he succeeded in enlisting only seventy. Still, by October 1693 he was ready to head north again, this time leading settlers, Indians, herds of cattle and horses, and 100 soldiers to man the presidio in Santa Fe. From now on the seemingly easy glory of reconquest was going to become the hard work of settlement.

His second trek north was cold and difficult. There were rumors that the Pueblo Indians were reverting to their old animosity. When the settlers finally arrived at Santa Fe, they were locked out; the stymied colony camped in the snow outside.

Vargas wished to avoid armed conflict, but this time he could not. Twenty-two Spaniards died of exposure during the snowy wait, while negotiations and mutual insults dragged on. On December 29, 1693, the Spaniards attacked. After a two-day-long battle, the victorious Spaniards executed seventy Indians and enslaved about 400 more for a time. Those who escaped fled through the snow to the outlying pueblos and spread the word: the Spaniards were back.

Four pueblos, most importantly Pecos, cast their lot with the Spaniards, but the rest remained in rebellion. Their stronghold was Black Mesa, behind San Ildefonso. Vargas spent much of 1694 trying to subdue the Indians who held out there, and eventually, by destroying their fields, he succeeded. (Ironically he organized his Pueblo allies with a knotted rope—the same means the Indians had used in the Pueblo Revolt of 1680.) Even then the Spanish hold on New Mexico was tenuous, and in 1696 the northern pueblos revolted again. The outburst was sudden, bloody, and frightening—but Vargas was no Otermín. He and his troops were constantly in the saddle reasserting Spanish dominion. It proved to be the last organized, massive Indian resistance and the beginning of a new era, when the sons and daughters of Spain would sink permanent roots into New Mexico's parched, rocky soil.

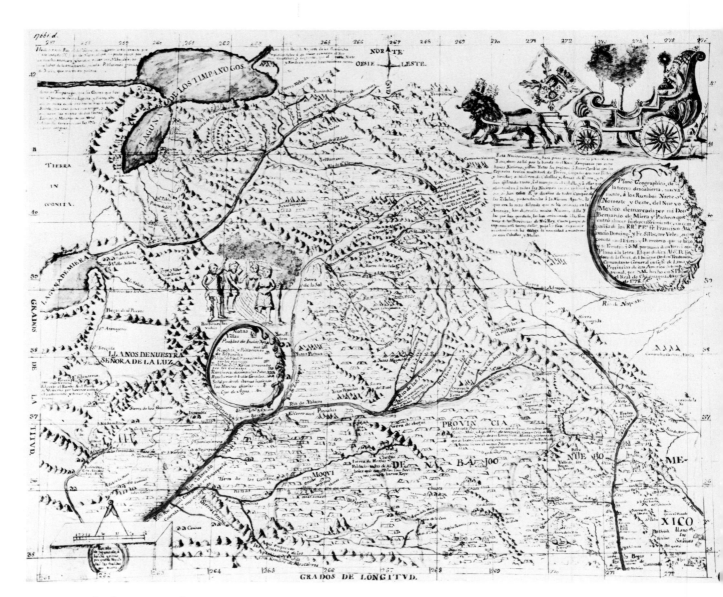

In the summer of 1776, two Franciscan friars, Fray Francisco Atanasio Domínguez and Fray Sylvestre Vélez de Escalante, set out on a six-month expedition to locate a route from New Mexico to California. Accompanied by a small military force, they explored much of southwestern Colorado, Utah, and northern Arizona, but failed to reach California. This map was drawn in 1778 by Bernardo Miera y Pacheco, an expedition member. MNM (#92063)

Spanish Colony, Mexican Territory

History spends much of its time looking at great events, at pivotal points where one force takes over from another. In this light the 1700s were calm, almost static in New Mexico. The century began with the reconquest, and at the end of the century Spain was still in control. Changes were slow and incremental; the 1700s do not get much space in New Mexico history books. In some ways, the history of the state was being written far away on the east coast, where some rambunctious colonies of England revolted and formed a new nation ... but those were just distant rumors in New Mexico.

Of course, to the people living in this "quiet" century—one where not one nation managed to seize power from another—the century did not seem quiet at all. It was a difficult time, filled with hard work and considerable danger. In the previous century the Spanish economy had been built on the backs of the Pueblo Indians by demands for tribute and labor—and that had led to the Pueblo Revolt of 1680. Now Spain was to build a colony that lived on its own labor from the land. That it succeeded at all is a measure of the will of the people who did it, for New Mexico has never been an easy place to make a living.

They began along the river, of course, where there was water and soil for farming. Some of the best land was along the middle Rio Grande, and in 1706 Governor Francisco Cuervo y Valdes formally established a new villa there. Possibly seeking royal favor—his appointment replacing the great Vargas was provisional, pending con-

firmation—he named it for the viceroy in Mexico, the Duke of Alburquerque (the extra "r" has since been dropped). There were broad, well-watered lands along the river, and Tijeras Pass offered a route through the mountains to the plains. One day the tiny farming village would become a great center of the Southwest.

Naturally, these parcels so desirable to the Spanish colonial farmers had not gone unnoticed by Pueblo Indian farmers, and competition was inevitable. In theory, the king owned all the land and could grant it to whomever he chose. This radical position was tempered, though, by a quite genuine belief in the rights of Indians, and various Pueblos retained the areas they had long inhabited. There were numerous court cases involving Spaniards accused of trespassing on Indian lands, and often enough the Indians won. Mutual infringements took many forms. Some irrigation systems were operated jointly by Indians and Spaniards, with resulting conflicts over who was to make repairs and who got first crack at the water. Cattle wandering onto fields were a continuing sore point, as were "unused" grounds owned by one party but desired by another.

As Spanish children reached maturity, the limited farmlands became inadequate. The normal solution was to petition the governor for new land grants. One such case can stand for many. In 1751 twelve families petitioned the governor for land where they would found a new settlement, in a small, well-watered valley in the Sangre de Cristos high above Santa Fe. The petition was researched: did anyone

On July 15, 1751, Don Tomás Vélez Cachupín, governor of New Mexico and commander of the Santa Fe presidio, approved a request made by twelve families for a land grant at Las Trampas. The settlers were given the tract in an ancient ritual conducted by the alcalde mayor, a leading local official. From the Spanish Archives of New Mexico, NMSRCA

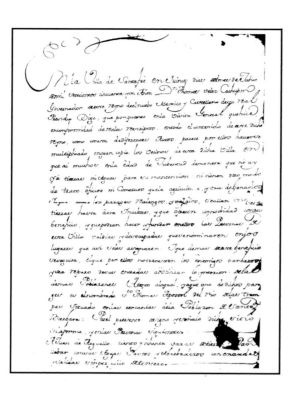

else want the land? Was there a prior grant? (The Spanish bureaucracy was meticulously legal.) In this case the petition was granted. The alcalde accompanied the settlers to the valley that would be their new home. He showed them the boundaries which had been set out by the governor, after which they repeated the medieval ritual of pulling up grass and throwing rocks within the boundaries they had been granted. The tiny village of San José de Gracias de Las Trampas came into being.

In accordance with frontier policy, the village was laid out for defense, with the houses and church fronting on an enclosed square, presenting blank, defensible walls to the outside. An acequia from a point on the stream somewhat higher in the valley was brought down the side of the valley. From it water could be channeled into fields, which were long and narrow so that each field could touch the acequia. They built their church with adobe from a nearby hillside, cleared fields, raised children. In 1776, as an unheard war raged on the other side of a continent, there were 278 people in Las Trampas. There were good years, when the rains came and the frosts stayed away, when children were raised in

health; but there were disastrous years too, of crop failure, of Indian raids, and the terrible time in the 1780s when smallpox swept the valley. All this and more came to be part of the village memory.

In 1982 this writer spent some time helping plaster the church in Las Trampas. It was worth four or five history courses to hear the worn, strong-spirited people who live there talk of the village. A dog's bark across the valley is easily heard, and a pickup truck intrudes only rarely. When we went to a hillside to get dirt for adobe, they explained that this was where their fathers had dug it the first time—in 1760—and they still got it there "so the color would be the same." But perhaps it was too easy to be carried away with the peace of those autumn days. The people also talked of the disaster of unemployment, of men injured in the mines a few miles away, and of the difficulties of hauling timber in winter.

In spite of competition in the fields and in the courts, Pueblo and Spaniard drew together to ward off danger from new directions. The Apaches, who had begun their rise the previous century, continued it with a vengeance; and the Navajos to the west and northwest saw rich pickings in the isolated Spanish and Pueblo settlements, especially as they gained arms and horses from the Spaniards. Utes appeared in the north, and Comanches began riding in from the plains to the east. Isolated villages were in almost constant danger, and Pueblos just a generation after the revolt found themselves garnering praise as effective military auxiliaries during Spanish counterraids. Scattered ranches and settlements, like Las Trampas, often suffered small, sudden, violent raids. Sometimes they were conducted on a large scale. In 1760 Comanches attacked a hacienda near Taos and killed at least fourteen, taking many others prisoner. In 1775 it was Comanches again who attacked the Pueblo of Sandia and drove off the horses, then trapped and killed the thirty-two Pueblo men who pursued them. Two years later Apaches attacked Valencia and killed twenty-three settlers. Albuquerque itself

lost citizens to occasional raids and, once, its whole *remuda* (string of horses). The ordinary response was for community leaders to pursue the raiders, almost always without result. Against such hit-and-run tactics the soldiers of the presidio and their Pueblo auxiliaries could hardly be effective.

The constant exchange between Spaniard and Indian, sometimes military and sometimes trading, gave rise to a class of people unique to New Mexico. *Genízaros*, they were and are called, Indians by race but Spanish by culture. Many Indian children were captured or bartered for, and ended up in the Spanish settlements. Others simply wandered in. Never quite accepted as Spaniards, they became neither Indian nor fully Spanish. They secured land grants, settled in villages of their own—Abiquiu north of Santa Fe is one—and played a major role in the colony. One historian has estimated that by the late 1700s they were one-third of the population.

In 1779 Don Juan Bautista de Anza, one of New Mexico's greatest governors, took the war to the Comanches' doorstep

*Far Left
Far from urban centers where it could be bought, New Mexicans began to make their own religious art. Part of the Museum of New Mexico collection, this representation of San Rafael is the work of Don Bernardo Miera y Pacheco, an important eighteenth-century cartographer who accompanied the Domínguez-Escalante expedition in 1776. SHPB*

*Below
Las Trampas still retains the feeling of an eighteenth-century village. At that time Spanish governmental regulations required that frontier settlements be laid out around a central plaza for defense. MNM (#11561)*

in eastern Colorado. The Comanches were utterly surprised and defeated, and Anza forced a treaty that was respected by both sides for generations. But attacks continued from other quarters. In fact, the problem would last another century, through another government entirely, and on into a third.

Remarkably, hostilities were generally suspended for the annual Indian trade fairs, a tradition of long standing, as Indians from the plains met at Pecos, Taos, or Abiquiu to trade for the goods of the Rio Grande pueblos. The Spaniards participated in these but had their own trading adventure as well: the caravan to Mexico City or, by the mid-1700s, Chihuahua. A half-dozen or so New Mexico merchants assembled at the point and time announced by the governor to form the annual caravan. Then settlers from villages and ranches joined with items to take south, to be traded for products not available on the remote frontier. They brought a few crops but also tanned hides, wool, piñon nuts, and salt from the salt lakes near present-day Estancia. Pretty soon the long, dusty caravan moved, often escorted by some ragged soldiers from the presidio in Santa Fe. It is the regret of every New Mexico historian that no diaries of members of the annual caravans have surfaced. We know the caravans made their way downriver past present-day Socorro, struggled across the Jornada del Muerto, and rested briefly at El Paso. There they picked up a few more merchants with barrels of "Pass wine" and continued on across the terrible sand dunes of the Medanos and down the long, hard trail to Chihuahua. The dust of the approaching caravan sent prices skyrocketing, and a complex system of coinage and exchange rates guaranteed that no northerner was going to come out ahead of the game.

Of course the New Mexico traders knew what was happening—their empty purses told them—but they were between the rock of necessity and the hard place of Spanish policy. The policy ruled that Spanish colonies must trade only with Spanish colonies or the motherland. There were two very different views of the northern colony. For those living in it, it was home, where one worked to stay warm, to have food, to raise a family, and to live the good life. For those of this view, the merchant who appeared unexpectedly from the east, speaking perhaps French but selling his wares at a good price, was a godsend. (In 1739 just this happened, when the Mallet brothers appeared with trade goods. It was not the last time.) But in the view from Mexico City, New Mexico was the first line of defense in a game of global politics. Spain had been first into the New World, and her glorious empire was not without competitors. England and France had established themselves on the eastern half of the northern landmass and were obviously not content to stay there. Struggles in the Old World were reflected in the new, and the prairies were proving too porous a barrier. Like those houses in remote, threatened villages, New Mexico could present her doors to the motherland, her blank walls to everyone else. Travel was strictly regulated in New Mexico. When a caravan or group of traders came through town, the *alcalde mayor* was re-

quired to notify the governor of all who were in it. A permit was required to travel almost anywhere. By wading through the mountain of paperwork that continually came into his office, the governor was immediately aware of any newcomers in the territory and anyone heading toward the border. Much of this red tape that so overburdened the governor was so that the authorities down in Mexico could keep track of events in New Mexico. Spain was just as worried about French and English traders—and after the revolution, the vigorous entrepreneurs from the fledgling United States—as she was about their soldiers.

Spain had reason to be worried.

In 1806 a small, ragged United States Army exploring party, led by Lieutenant Zebulon Pike, was struggling across the plains. As they approached the Rocky Mountains they either became or pretended to become lost. Historians still debate just what their orders were; lost or not, the group was inevitably following the restless westering of the young United States. The Spaniards sent a force onto the plains to intercept the weathered band. There is something symbolic about those two forces: on one side was the United States, represented by Pike and his eighteen trail-

Left
During the eighteenth century most New Mexicans were subsistence farmers whose patron saint was San Isidro Labrador. Carved by José Benito Ortega, a santero *from Mora, this image is displayed at the Museum of New Mexico. According to tradition, the angel assures that San Isidro receives divine assistance. SHPB*

Opposite, top
Described by one authority as "the most perfectly-preserved Spanish Colonial church in the United States," the Church of San José de Gracia was built in the 1760s at Las Trampas, a mountain village thirty-five miles south of Taos. SHPB

Opposite, bottom
Although Spanish settlers and their northern Ute neighbors fought, they traded actively between skirmishes. The deerskins that the settlers obtained from the Utes and other tribes were among the few items for which there was a demand in Chihuahua and other commercial centers to the south. From the McNitt Collection, NMSRCA

In late February 1807, a Spanish patrol captured Zebulon M. Pike and his men on Conejos Creek in present southern Colorado. After preliminary questioning in Santa Fe the prisoners were marched to Chihuahua for further interrogation before being allowed to return to the United States. Pike was killed April 27, 1813, during the Battle of York, a significant engagement of the War of 1812 fought near present Toronto. MNM (#7757)

weary men; while on the other was the Spanish Lieutenant don Facundo Melgares and his 600 men, their remuda of over 2,000 horses, according to some sources, carefully selected even for color. How could one know that this powerful force was almost the last gasp of an empire that was losing its three centuries' hold on New Mexico, the small ragged force the first intimation of an empire that was coming? The clue came a little later. The two detachments failed to encounter each other on the plains, but a few months later Pike was desperately bivouacked in the Colorado mountains, caught by winter. Melgares captured—perhaps rescued is a better word—the pitiful force and brought it into Santa Fe. They were trespassers, the old regulations were still in effect, and Melgares was told to take Pike to Chihuahua for the authorities to decide what to do with this international intruder. After a dinner (with plenty of wine, Pike noted) in

the venerable mud Palace of the Governors, they left into the snowy night, first in the governor's carriage and then on horseback. They made their way down La Bajada—the steep, rugged hill that for centuries had been a bane to oxcart drivers on the Camino Real—and stopped for the night in the little village at its foot. Melgares went to sleep, while Pike stayed up to talk with the local priest. If ever there was a representative of Old Spain, it is the local frontier priest, but this one's conversation surprised Pike. The priest wanted to know what the United States was like and when they were coming, giving Pike the impression that he, the priest, would be glad when that happened.

The "quiet" century, the 1700s, in which no empire replaced another, was over. People had lived and died, families and villages had been established, and rival empires had learned a little more of the distant land. Perhaps unintentionally, preparations had been made for tremendous change in New Mexico.

Two influences from the United States arrived in New Mexico early in the 1800s. One went around the world and came by way of Spain; the other came straight across the plains in canvas-covered wagons. They met in Santa Fe.

It is too simple to credit the U.S. example alone with igniting the democratic revolutionary fires that burned in so many places in the late 1700s, but the Revolutionary War in the English colonies had been the most successful, and the most obvious, challenge to the old order. Europeans had watched it with fear or envy, depending on their social perspective. After Napoleon's occupation of Spain, in 1810 a government-in-exile instituted changes that were almost democratic. For the first time in memory they called a *"cortes,"* a type of parliament used long before. Orders to elect representatives went across the ocean to New Spain and in a saddlebag up the long, lonely Camino Real to distant New Mexico. A New Mexico representative, Don Pedro Bautista Pino, actually made the trip to Spain to give New Mexico a voice in deliberations

that were called to give Spain a constitution. As it turned out, when circumstances in Europe changed and the monarch was restored, he declared the whole thing had been a mistake. Nevertheless, fires once started are not so easily put out. Revolution—bloody, confused, and stumbling, but still revolution—broke out in New Spain. In September 1821 New Mexico was no longer the most distant outpost of a European-based Spanish Empire; instead it was the most distant outpost of a new country, Mexico.

Most New Mexicans probably never noticed. The various maneuverings of the revolution itself had been but distant rumors, and when finally the revolution was over, it was weeks before the word arrived in Santa Fe. (The governor reported to Mexico City that there was a glorious celebration at the news.) Still, New Mexico was as distant a place as ever. There were irrigation ditches to clean, sheep to

shear, the sick to tend, Indian attacks to fear, grasshopper hordes to fight. . . . Distant politics were distant indeed.

The other influence from the United States, the one that came in wagons, was far more immediate. The barrier of the plains had proved porous. The Spaniards had worried about this; in fact, their agent Pedro Vial in his several crossings had shown that practical routes existed. Lieutenant Zebulon Pike's widely circulated report, prepared after his arrest and trip to Mexico, had alerted U.S. merchants to the starved markets in Santa Fe. The payoff, which came after the 1821 Mexican Revolution, was precipitated by a small-time Missouri trader named William Becknell.

It happened that his timing was just right. In the autumn of 1821 Becknell was out on the prairie with a few goods, looking for trade with Indians or whomever else he might encounter on the edges of the forbidden Spanish colony, when a de-

Known as La Bajada (the descent) the rocky escarpment south of Santa Fe has defied travelers for centuries. Although cars and trucks have replaced squeaking carretas and a modern highway now approximates the historic Camino Real, the hill still challenges motorists on snowy days. From the Virginia Johnson Collection, NMSRCA

Right
After his ordination as a priest at Durango, Mexico, in 1822 Father Antonio José Martínez became a powerful figure in New Mexico's ecclesiastical and political affairs. He strongly opposed granting large tracts of land to outsiders. In recent years Martínez has evolved into a folk hero for many New Mexicans. MNM (#10308)

tachment of friendly Spanish—no, Mexican—soldiers met him near Raton Pass and invited him in to Santa Fe. There he met the governor, Facundo Melgares, the same man who as a Spanish soldier some fifteen years before had brought Pike in. The message this time was clear and far-reaching: We are now Mexico; we make our own rules; and finally we can trade for your goods. Come on in!

Becknell quickly sold his few goods at a tremendous profit and hurried back to the States. It is said that when he unloaded in Franklin, Missouri, he slashed the leather sack holding his silver profit and let the

Spanish coins tumble onto the street. It was a dramatic announcement and did not go unnoticed.

Becknell returned in 1822, making two changes that set the pattern for the future. First, he used wagons instead of pack animals, proving they could be manhandled across the prairie. Second, remembering the struggle over Raton Pass, he took a shortcut from the Arkansas River to the Cimarron River to avoid the haul over the pass. It saved 100 miles, but the dry crossing would cost lives before the trail days were over.

The trade grew explosively. Hard-

scrabble Missouri farmers and storekeepers heard about the profits and jumped on the bandwagon—or rather the Conestoga, virtual symbol of the Santa Fe Trail, whose distinctive sagging bottom and sloped sides kept the cargo stable. Every spring the meadows around the jump-off towns along the Missouri River saw the wagons gather. Many journals and at least one great book, Josiah Gregg's *Commerce of the Prairies,* describe the scene. Each year many men (and animals) were new, and it was chaos. Luckily, the beginning of the route was relatively easy. First-timers copied old-timers in packing the all-important cargo. Cantankerous mules were broken to harness, and routines worked out. By Council Grove, 150 miles out, men knew their jobs, one another, and their animals a little better. They cut hardwood logs for replacement axles (there would be none out on the prairies, they heard around the campfires) and organized for the true crossing, which at that point began.

It is symbolic of American ways that

Bottom, left Reproduced from an early edition of Gregg's Commerce of the Prairies, *this engraving illustrates a wagon train crossing the plains of the Santa Fe Trail. The expedition is flanked by prairie dogs, buffalo, and watchful Indians. MNM (#87450)*

Bottom, right Josiah Gregg's Commerce of the Prairies, *first published in 1844, is the definitive account of the Santa Fe trade between Missouri and New Mexico. The book describes Gregg's adventures on the trail between 1831 and 1840. Gregg brought the first printing press to New Mexico in 1834. MNM (#9896)*

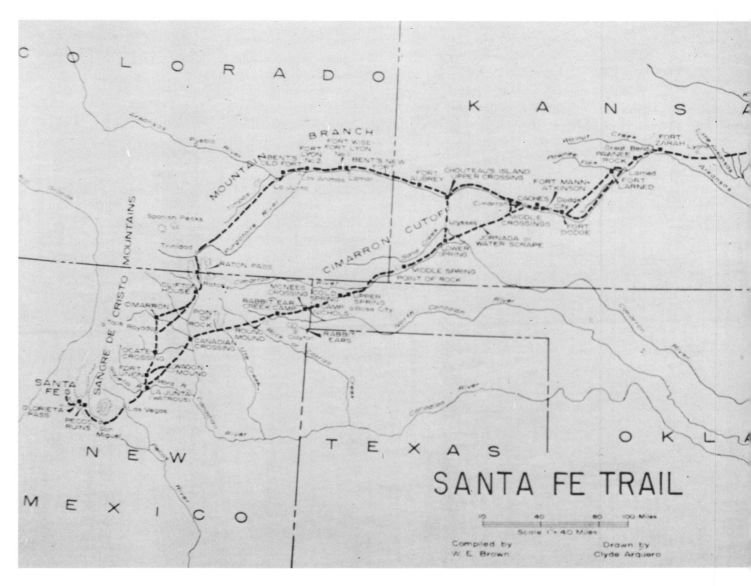

SANTA FE TRAIL

Both the Mountain Branch and the shortcut known as the Cimarron Cut-off are depicted in this map of the Santa Fe Trail. In later years the trail gradually shortened as railroads pushed west and preempted its function. MNM (#45001)

the merchants noisily demanded help from the government, but when the help came it proved unwieldy, so the merchants ignored it anyway. The government decided to map the trail but inexplicably mapped it to Taos; the merchants knew the way and went to Santa Fe. Army escorts for protection from the Indian proved almost useless, so soon the caravans were organized into slowly plodding fortresses.

The Santa Fe Trail was not a single, set trail. If there were no Indians about, the wagons might pull abreast of one another and move across the prairie grass in a broad line, avoiding one another's dust. River crossings, always difficult, might have been best in one place one year, another place the next. Wet weather meant

taking the high ground, dry weather dictated a different route. A caravan might have had to go well out of its way to camp near firewood or pasture.

Many a frontiersman, notably Kit Carson who hired onto a Santa Fe wagon train as a runaway, got his first taste of the American West in the Santa Fe trade. The images worked their way into the national folklore. There would be paintings, songs, and legends about the vast prairie, the night sky, campfire talk, Indians on the horizon, and the exhilarating buffalo chase. It was all true, but it wasn't the reason for the trade. The reason was there in the wagons: the flannels and silks and linens, the percussion caps and cooking pots and traps and mirrors, the combs and

SOURCES:
Joseph C. Brown Map, 1827; Josiah Gregg Map, 1844; Lt. John G. Parke
Kansas State Historical Society Map, 1913; Kenyon Riddle Map, 1949; S

into town now called "Old Santa Fe Trail." They had arrived. The hired hands scattered out to the predictable joys of the strange adobe town, while the wagon owners argued, pleaded with, and bribed customs officials, and rented shop space on the plaza. It was time to turn this adventure into profit.

New Mexico certainly needed goods, but this was a flood; in just a few years the New Mexico market was glutted. Still, there was Mexico, just a little further walk. The Santa Fe Trail connected with the centuries-older Camino Real, and soon the wagons were not even unloading in Santa Fe, but continuing on down to Chihuahua. The Chihuahua merchants found that the game had been turned around.

What went back to the States? Silver, some gold (after it was discovered in the Ortiz Mountains southeast of Santa Fe in 1828, setting off a minor rush), furs, and mules. The wagons were not needed for the return trip, so even they were sold for a profit, converted into more silver and mules. Thus Missouri became a hard silver state and gained the long-eared state symbol that lasts to this day. There were other exchanges, too. Traders learned some Spanish, and New Mexicans learned some English. Spanish surnames began showing up on the rolls of finishing schools in St. Louis. If New Mexico under Spain had

wallpaper and champagne and whiskey. (Traders found they could make a profit even after drinking the latter, so valuable were the bottles to the Indians!)

One day the Sangre de Cristos would be sighted, a thin line on the horizon. The great wagons trudged down the front range, passed the almost-abandoned pueblo of Pecos with its pitiful handful of citizens (soon even they left, and the wagons came past an abandoned ruin, the wagoneers sightseeing, camping in the rooms in bad weather, and stealing souvenirs), and wound through Glorieta Pass. A day out from Santa Fe the traders stopped, shaved, and got out long-saved clean clothes, put new "poppers" on the bullwhips, and came down the long hill

Ceran St. Vrain, a leading trader on the Santa Fe Trail, first came to New Mexico in 1825. Six years later he formed a partnership with Charles Bent, which resulted in the construction of Bent's Fort on the Arkansas River. In 1847 Bent was murdered at Taos while serving as New Mexico's first governor after the United States conquest. To avenge his partner's death, St. Vrain enlisted a company of mountain men in Santa Fe who marched north to chastise the rebels. From the Department of Development Collection, NMSRCA

When trade over the Santa Fe Trail was at its peak, merchants often filled the plaza with heavily-laden Conestoga wagons drawn by teams of mules or oxen. Because Mexican authorities sometimes levied import duties on each wagon, the traders piled their goods into enormous loads before entering the city. MNM (#11254)

been an adobe fortress with its blank wall toward the outside world, that wall now had windows in it, and almost a door.

New Mexico under Mexico was changing, and not just by what the wagons were bringing across the prairie. Mexico never did get a firm grip on the colony. The government in Mexico City changed almost monthly; instructions to the colony were slow and confusing; and actual help almost never came up the long road from Mexico City. Spain, having learned that giving an annual gift to the nomadic Indians was much cheaper than fighting them, had worked out a pretty reliable system to see that the necessary funds reached New Mexico. These funds dried up under Mexico. The raids began again, as bad as they ever had been.

The colony the Indians were attacking

was not quite sure of its own identity. Age-old ties to Spain had been broken, and ties to an independent Mexico were only tissue. More and more Anglos were coming and staying, marrying into New Mexican families and establishing businesses.

In 1837 taxes were instituted to replace the lost financial support from Mexico. This outraged many New Mexicans, especially the poor in the north. The new governor, Albino Pérez, was not born here, they cried (he was from Mexico, not born in New Mexico). Why should he—this outsider—now levy taxes? From the discontent came another revolt. Governor Pérez and several of his officials were killed, and the rebels entered Santa Fe on August 10, 1837—ironically the very day of the Pueblo Revolt of 1680. But this re-

Under Mexican law, traders were required to obtain a guía (commercial passport) at Santa Fe before transporting goods down the trail for sale in the interior states. In this example John Bradley and James G. Sweeney requested a license to carry merchandise valued at 559 pesos and seven reales to Chihuahua and Sonora. Their invoice included ribbon, buttons, thimbles, scissors, knives, razors, and spoons. From the Mexican Archives of New Mexico, NMSRCA

GOVERNOR PEREZ
was assassinated on this
Aug. 9. 1837.
ERECTED BY
SUNSHINE CHAPTER. D. A. R.

Angered by governmental reorganization and a new tax plan, revolutionists from Northern New Mexico assassinated Mexican Governor Albino Pérez on August 9, 1837, during a short-lived rebellion. In 1903 the Daughters of the American Revolution put up this commemorative monument. NMSRCA

volt was neither so organized nor so successful as that long-ago one had been. Manuel Armijo, a merchant with land holdings near Albuquerque and Socorro and one of the remarkable characters of New Mexico history, led an army to Santa Fe to put down the rebellion. The pretender governor was killed, and Armijo assumed the governorship.

Texas, another northern colony which also had the experience of being Spanish one day and vaguely Mexican the next, had a similar revolt, but it was successful. Anglo-Americans had filtered into Texas

in such numbers that the colony was almost a U.S. territory. (The first illegal crossings of the river border between the U.S. and Mexico were not south to north, but in the opposite direction.) When Texas succeeded in pulling away from Mexico in 1836, the rebels confidently expected to become part of the United States. The slavery question interfered, and Texas was left as a republic, looking greedily at the weak New Mexican colony to the west. In 1841 Texans invaded New Mexico with a force of about 270 armed men and about fifty merchants. Historians argue about

Manuel Armijo, one of New Mexico's most controversial figures, served three terms as governor under Mexican administration. During the Mexican War, as U.S. troops approached Santa Fe, Armijo hastily fortified Apache Canyon, east of the city. He later changed his mind however, before any fighting took place and fled south without firing a shot. From the Shishkin Collection, NMSRCA

San Miguel del Vado was the last stop for travelers on the Santa Fe Trail before reaching New Mexico's capital. In 1841 several members of the Texas-Santa Fe expedition were imprisoned there following capture by militia forces. MNM (#13944)

just what the Texas invasion of New Mexico in 1841 was trying to do—or whether it was even an invasion. If Texas was trying to establish trade, why the troops? Or if it was an invasion, why the merchants? A leading theory is that they wanted to take over Santa Fe and thereby capture the lucrative Santa Fe Trail trade. (One historian finally gave up the argument and simply declared it a "hare-brained scheme.")

The much-rumored, much-feared force approached New Mexico in the autumn of 1841. Governor Armijo—harassed by Indian attacks, governing a population that had revolted four years before, aware that Texas had special ties to the United States and therefore possibly to wealthy and influential traders in New Mexico, was ordered by Santa Anna to stop the invaders. He took his hastily assembled army out to meet them. The Texans turned out to be a pitiful lot. The poorly organized march from Texas had been a disaster. Lost, starved, and weak, the Texans were straggling up the Pecos River toward San Mi-

guel, where they could join the Santa Fe Trail and at least find their way to Santa Fe and some desperately needed food. The New Mexicans easily disarmed the force and marched it down to Mexico.

So New Mexico rocked along through the twenty-five years of Mexican rule. Government support and leadership from the south dried up. Indian attacks increased, and New Mexico was too weak and poor to do much about them. Wagons from the east kept coming through Glorieta Pass, bearing goods and ideas in like

measure. Governor Armijo, skilled at fishing in troubled waters, had put down the revolt of New Mexicans, struggled against the Indians, and blunted the "invasion" from Texas, while amassing a fortune for himself from the Santa Fe trade.

But in 1846 there were new rumors of invasion from the east, and this time they were no exaggeration. An army was coming down the Santa Fe Trail, and a turning point was coming that would permanently change the future of New Mexico, Mexico, and the United States.

From this imposing headquarters, L.G. Murphy and his partners sold a wide variety of merchandise to local ranchers and also negotiated lucrative government contracts for army and Indian supplies. The building later served as the Lincoln County Courthouse. NMSRCA

New Mexico and the United States

President Polk had been elected with a mandate for U.S. territorial expansion, and he meant to fulfill it. A skirmish with Mexican troops in Texas was the spark, and on May 13, 1846, the United States declared war on Mexico. The next month tough, experienced Stephen Watts Kearny led a hastily assembled and provisioned "Army of the West" out of Fort Leavenworth, Kansas, and down the same Santa Fe Trail that had seen two decades of traders. In fact, some traders went along with the expedition, confident that whatever the outcome, they might still turn a profit.

Governor Armijo, sitting in the Palace of the Governors in Santa Fe, knew the troops were coming and debated what to do. He made brave noises about defense and issued ringing calls to the citizenry, but he probably knew that the invading army was too strong. Did he really want to resist it? For many staunch Catholic New Mexicans, the invaders were uncivilized Protestants, to be resisted at all costs. But most people were now using U.S. products in one way or another, and many—including Armijo himself—were locked into financial deals with U.S. merchants. Two brothers, long famous in the Santa Fe trade, accompanied the army. James Magoffin was along as an emissary of the U.S. Secretary of State, while his brother James (with his bride Susan, who kept a fascinating diary on the trip) brought along yet another wagon train.

Kearny's army paused at Bent's Old Fort, on the Arkansas River in Colorado, and Kearny sent James Magoffin on to talk with Governor Armijo. We do not know what passed between them, but it seems pretty clear that, one way or another, Magoffin was persuasive. The army continued its approach, pausing in Las Vegas long enough for Colonel Kearny to climb on a roof and announce the conquest of the territory, balancing the threat of force with promises of a new and just government. Still not sure what Armijo would do, Kearny marched his army into Glorieta Pass. Armijo was waiting with cannon and men at the west end of the canyon—a bottleneck the invaders would need to pass through in order to reach Santa Fe. But to the surprise of his own men, some of whom were furious, shortly before Kearny arrived at Armijo's defensive position, Armijo told the local militia to go home, and he himself rode off toward Mexico with the Mexican regulars. It has been an American fashion to disdain Armijo—conquerors have rarely been generous with those who lose. Until unexpected documents surface somewhere, we can only speculate as to why Armijo gave up. Perhaps Armijo was simply interested in delaying the Americans until the wagon train which he and another trader (an Anglo) owned was far enough south to escape the army. Perhaps he saw that the approaching army was too large to hope to defeat. The U.S. army proceeded unopposed and on August 18 raised the Stars and Stripes over Santa Fe. Political form had caught up with commercial reality.

Kearny improvised a government, named Charles Bent governor and installed other officials, and then took part

Right
As a youth of seventeen, fresh from the midwest, Lewis H. Garrard accompanied an avenging party of mountain men from Bent's Fort to Taos. Although they arrived too late to take part in the battle at the pueblo, Garrard later wrote an eyewitness account of the trials and executions of rebel leaders. From the Garrard Collection, NMSRCA

Far right
When the Army of the West reached Bent's Fort on the Arkansas River, General S.W. Kearny sent James Wiley Magoffin (pictured), a trader with many contacts in New Mexico, on to Santa Fe to confer with Governor Armijo. No one knows what took place at their meeting, but soon afterwards Armijo abandoned his defenses and retreated to Mexico. MNM (#10310)

Bottom, far right
On May 13, 1846, President James Polk proclaimed that a state of war existed between the United States and Mexico. In late June Brigadier General Stephen Watts Kearny (pictured) led an expeditionary force known as the Army of the West out of Fort Leavenworth, Missouri, for the conquest of New Mexico and California. From the Shishkin Collection, NMSRCA

of his army and went to California, chasing Manifest Destiny. Actually New Mexico was not as acquiescent as he had expected. Especially in Taos the citizens resented the takeover by the United States. There were rumblings, and finally the outburst came. On January 19, 1847, men still loyal to Mexico, joined by Taos Pueblo Indians, killed Governor Bent in his home. Troops marched north from Santa Fe to put down the rebellion. It was bloody, possibly the more so because Bent had been a prominent and popular man— with the Anglo-Americans. The ruin of the church where the Indians took refuge still stands in the pueblo. The rebellion was over, leaving the United States in unquestioned control of distant New Mexico.

The people of Taos, especially the poor, had long had a champion in Padre Antonio José Martínez. Padre Martínez had the only printing press in New Mexico at the time (General Kearny's pronouncements were printed on it), which the priest had used to print religious material and material that espoused the causes and

rights of the poor. He was accused of having helped forment the rebellion, but it is more likely that his zeal reflected—but did not cause—local feeling.

The United States' control of New Mexico was confirmed after the War with Mexico by the Treaty of Guadalupe Hidalgo, signed on February 2, 1848. Once an outpost of Spain, then of Mexico, New Mexico now became a distant outpost of the United States.

There was still some patching up to do. The Treaty of Guadalupe Hidalgo left some land on the southwestern edge of New Mexico in dispute, area that lay athwart the route of a proposed railroad to California. The United States bought the land, known as the Gadsden Purchase, in 1853 for ten million dollars, and the continental United States (save Alaska) was basically filled out to the form it has today.

Meanwhile gold had been discovered in California, and it seemed the whole nation was heading west. Most of the "Forty-Niners" took the northern route, over the

NOTICE.

BEING duly authorized by the President of the United States of America, I hereby make the following appointments for the Government of New Mexico, a territory of the United States.

The officers thus appointed will be obeyed and respected accordingly.

CHARLES BENT to be Governor.
Donaciano Vigil   "   Sec of Territory.
Richard Dallam   "   Marshall.
Francis P. Blair   "   U. S. D. . A 'y
Charles Blummer   "   Treasurer.
Eugene Leitensdorfer   "   Aud. of Pub. Acc.
Joal Houghton, Antonio Jose Otero, Charles Beaubien to be Judges of "the Superior Court."

Given at Santa Fe, the Capitol of the Territory of New Mexico, this 22d day of September 1846 and in the 71st year of the Independence of the United States.

S. W. KEARNY,
Brig. General
U. S. Army.

*Above
On August 15, 1846, General Kearny and his staff rode into the plaza at Las Vegas where they were met by the local alcalde. From the roof of this building Kearny announced that local officials would be retained in office after swearing allegiance to the U.S. From the Department of Development Collection, NMSRCA*

*Left
On September 22, 1846, General Kearny issued a proclamation announcing his appointments for civil offices in New Mexico. From the Territorial Archives of New Mexico, NMSRCA*

73

Oregon and California Trail, but many came through New Mexico. Regular stagecoach service from Missouri to Santa Fe began in 1849. With U.S. land law, lawyers came pouring in to establish offices and, they hoped, to grow with the territory. Increased protection from hostile Indians was one of the things General Kearny had promised, and in fact much effort and money was expended for that purpose. Indian raids weren't reduced by very much, but the numerous army posts, supply contracts, and surveying and road-building activities were an economic boon.

Along with the economic benefits of belonging to the United States came the political liability of being drawn into an implacable quarrel brewing to the east. Indian and Hispanic New Mexicans had no particular stake in the slavery issue; according to one record there were only twenty-two blacks in the entire territory, most of them servants of army officers. But Anglos (in New Mexico usage, "Anglo" refers to someone non-Hispanic and non-Indian, but not necessarily from the British Isles) were pouring in, bringing with them their affinities from home.

Above
Charles Bent, a former Santa Fe trader, was experienced in the region's business and political matters. This photograph of Charles Bent is a reproduction of a family miniature. From the Jaramillo-Bent Collection, NMSRCA

Right
While visiting his family during the winter of 1847, Governor Charles Bent was murdered by a band of Mexican nationalists and Indians from the pueblo of Taos. The Bent House is now a museum and art gallery. SHPB

Left
The rebellion of 1847 ended at the pueblo of Taos, where the insurgents barricaded themselves behind the thick adobe walls of the San Gerónimo mission. In the ensuing bombardment the church was almost completely destroyed, but the ruins are now preserved as a tribal monument. SHPB

Bottom
Despite Apache hostility, stage service expanded in the Southwest during the 1850s. As part of its long route from St. Louis to San Francisco, the Butterfield Overland Mail Company crossed Southern New Mexico. Today these ruins at Stein's Pass southwest of Lordsburg are all that remain of a once bustling station. SHPB

Above
In a region of great distances, livery stables provided an important service. This stable was built in 1883 and belonged to R.H. Cowan, a former stagecoach driver who settled at Springer. SHPB

Far Right
Henry H. Sibley, a West Point graduate from Louisiana, was commanding officer at Fort Union on the eve of the Civil War. Like many other Southern sympathizers, he resigned his commission and cast his lot with the Confederacy. MNM (#50541)

Many supported the Confederate cause.

General Henry Sibley, for instance, had been born in Louisiana and educated at West Point. In 1860 he was commandant at Fort Union, the important fort on the Santa Fe Trail a few miles north of Las Vegas, the traveler's first relief after the long prairie crossing. Now as the split neared, Sibley faced a hard choice. Would he stay with the Union, or go with the new Confederacy? Sibley chose the Confederacy, as did many other army officers of Southern birth, and approached Jefferson Davis, president of the Confederate States of America, with a proposal. He would raise an army of Texas volunteers and invade New Mexico, coming up the Rio Grande. The plan had some sense to it. There seemed little to stop Sibley from reaching the Colorado gold fields, which would relieve the Confederacy's strapped financial condition. From there he hoped to move west, capturing the California gold fields and establishing ports on the

Colonel Edward R.S. Canby (pictured) commanded Union forces in New Mexico. In the winter of 1862 Confederate troops under the command of Brigadier General H.H. Sibley marched up the Rio Grande from Texas and defeated Canby's men at the Battle of Valverde. From the McNitt Collection, NMSRCA

Pacific Coast to nullify the Union blockade of Southern ports. Plus, with a dramatic taking of half a continent early in the war, he hoped to sway France and England to side with the South. There is a flaw: modern strategists believe that even if Sibley had succeeded in the ambitious plan, he would have had too few men to govern the territory conquered. As it turned out, it never came to the test.

Sibley assembled his invasion force and came up the Rio Grande, entering New Mexico just above El Paso and occupying the Mesilla Valley and Fort Fillmore. At Valverde they met their first resistance from Colonel E.R.S. Canby, in charge of Union military forces defending New Mexico. The Confederates won, bypassing Fort Craig and the Union forces and heading toward Albuquerque. Colonel Canby found himself behind the Confeder-

ate army, pursuing them toward Albuquerque—which he was supposed to be defending. He sent word to have the Union supplies in Albuquerque destroyed before the Confederates could get them. His agents succeeded in destroying some, and some were destroyed by the Confederates themselves, who may have enjoyed too much the "spirits" available to them after a hard march. Leaving Albuquerque, Sibley split his forces and sent part through Tijeras Pass to head up the back side of the Sandia Mountains, while the other part went north and occupied Santa Fe. For the two weeks that the Confederates occupied the capital, New Mexico was, in effect, Confederate territory.

Meanwhile, telegrams had gone to Governor Gilpin of the Colorado territory, pleading with him to rush volunteers down to defend New Mexico. Because he was

Above
The chimneys of Fort Union still guard the plains north of Las Vegas. The fort was first built in 1851 and subsequently relocated twice. It was originally intended to protect the Santa Fe Trail and serve as a regional supply depot. NPS

Right
Troops stationed at Fort Union often retreated to Loma Parda for amusement. Although popular with the rank and file, the large number of dance halls, gambling dens and brothels enraged the fort's top brass. What is now left of Loma Parda is pictured in 1974. SHPB

actually defending Colorado by doing so, Gilpin hastily complied. The Colorado Volunteers were a tough lot, many of them miners from the rapidly developing gold fields. They made an astonishing march, still one of the fastest in the annals of the U.S. Army. Leaving Denver on February 22, 1862, and marching down along the front range in snow and cold, they arrived at Fort Union on March 10. They had covered 400 miles—much of it through deep snow, and crossed Raton Pass—in thirteen days. At Fort Union they had a squabble with the man Canby had left in charge, about staying there to defend the fort, or moving on to seek the enemy. They chose the latter and, joined by forces from the fort, marched south along the Santa Fe Trail. By the night of March 25 they were at the east end of Glorieta Pass; they did not know it yet but Confederates were at the other end. There was a chance encounter of patrols in the pass and the next day a spirited skirmish. Now each army knew that a determined foe waited nearby. On the night of the twenty-sev-

enth, men cleaned their guns and lay in the dark with eyes open; tomorrow would bring a battle.

The Union army moved into Glorieta Pass. About halfway through they stopped for rest and water at Pigeon's Ranch, a well-known way station on the Santa Fe Trail in more peaceful times. They had barely stacked their arms when the scouts sent ahead came running back. The enemy was just around the bend. Moments later the Confederate artillery came crashing in. Men grabbed their arms—or anyone's—and rushed into line.

The battle was bloody. Both sides had cannon, but much of the fighting was skirmishing in the brush. Overall the Confederates prevailed, forcing the Union back a mile or so.

But the seeming Confederate victory was to prove short-lived. At the beginning of the day one of the Colorado officers, Colonel John M. Chivington, had been detached with some 430 men to climb the heights alongside the canyon and circle behind the Confederate forces. Chivington,

Reinforced by Colorado volunteers, Union forces redeemed themselves in March of 1862 when they met the Confederates in a decisive battle near Glorieta Pass. Pigeon's Ranch, situated in Apache Canyon at the west end of the pass, was the site of sharp fighting and was occupied by both sides at various times. This photo of Pigeon's Ranch was taken circa 1900. From the Cultural Properties Review Committee Collection, NMSRCA

In 1939 the Daughters of the Confederacy placed this monument near the village of Glorieta to commemorate the soldiers who fell in the battle fought there. The battle is sometimes called the "Gettysburg of the West." From the Department of Development Collection, NMSRCA

blankets, medicine, harnesses. It took but a few hours to complete the work of destruction. They burned the wagons and bayonetted the mules, and as darkness fell they went up onto the heights again and returned to the Union camp at the east end of the canyon.

The seeming Confederate victory had crumbled. An army could not live off the land in arid New Mexico, and there was nothing for the Confederates to do but straggle south. And straggle they did. Harassed by Canby, who had been joined by the victorious Fort Union forces, the Confederates buried two of their cannon in Albuquerque (they were dug up years later, and one is now in the Museum of Albuquerque), were defeated in a skirmish at Peralta, and eventually made their way back to Texas.

As army troops were pulled back east to fight in the Civil War, Apaches and Navajo, their freedom of movement and life ever more circumscribed by the culture burgeoning around them, reacted to the intolerable pressure by resuming raiding with a vengeance—which of course was intolerable to the surrounding culture. (The mirror image is not funny; it is tragic.) The army, in the person of General James H. Carleton, called in Kit Carson to solve the problem. Historians, novelists, and movie makers never have figured out just how to treat what happened then. It is impossible today to think with the mind of anyone who lived in those times, Indian or Anglo. We have the "facts"—probably more than they did—but we have experienced neither the horror of seeing our children killed and our property lost in a raid, nor the constant pressure of a culture for whom our right is their evil, our taboos their way of life. (The previous sentence can be read from either direction, the Indian and the Anglo-Hispanic looking at each other over a cultural abyss.) There were some on both sides who would have preferred annihilation as the final solution, and some even tried it. Carson, a remarkable man whose biographers are forced into extremes whether they are for him or against him, followed a middle ground. He

who had been a preacher in Colorado when he signed up for the volunteers, had refused a commission as chaplain, insisting that if he was going to be in the army, he would fight. With him were New Mexican volunteers led by Manuel A. Cháves, an experienced frontiersmen and fighter. For some reason Chivington went too far, and came out several miles behind the Confederate rear on the heights above the canyon mouth, looking down on the spot where sixteen years before Governor Armijo had stationed his men and then fled. Looking down now, Chivington's men saw the complete Confederate supply train, some 600 mules and 80 wagons, lightly guarded. There was most of the equipment of the invading army: ammunition, clothes,

pursued first the Apaches and then the Navajos, destroying their crops, cutting their fruit trees, and leaving them almost no alternative but to come into the tight, concentrated camp that the government prepared for them. (The Apaches left in a desperate move.) The camp was named for its lonely grove of trees along the trickling Pecos River in the sun-blasted east New Mexico plains: Bosque Redondo. The name and the "Long Walk" it took to get there live still in Navajo memory, not often spoken but not ever forgotten. Cramped, starving, humiliated, sick, the Navajo scratched the dry dirt in a futile effort at farming, and waited for the dole of food that was always short, either from bureaucratic bungling or outright fraud

among the suppliers. Navajo children listened to yearning stories of the beautiful land of mesas and mountains they had come from. It was a tragedy, and perhaps the only conceivable alleviation in it is that the tribe did survive. In 1868 the government finally admitted that the experiment in forced farming was a failure. A treaty was signed and the Navajo began the trek home. There they rebuilt, accommodating that had to be made to the powerful culture which now shared their homeland. Today the Navajo are the largest Indian nation within the United States, their reservation mostly in Arizona but spilling into northwestern New Mexico. They seem to have the same problems making a bureaucracy work that the rest

To implement his hardline Indian policy, General Carleton relied on New Mexico volunteers commanded by Colonel Christopher "Kit" Carson (pictured). After subduing the Mescalero Apaches in the summer of 1863, Carson began a vigorous campaign against the Navajos. From the Department of Development Collection, NMSRCA

Carleton hoped that the Navajos gathered at Bosque Redondo would learn to become farmers. His experiment failed, however, partly because the number of Indians confined there far exceeded preliminary estimates. From the McNitt Collection, NMSRCA

of the country has, and the desert is still a hard place to make a living. Still, tens of thousands of tourists annually see for themselves that it is indeed a beautiful land that they remembered and today inhabit again.

But in the complex web of the way humans get along—or don't—nothing can be isolated; everything affects everything else. At the army posts, Bosque Redondo, and other reservations there were people to be fed, and that meant a market for beef. Furthermore, the railroad was creeping across the plains from the east, and if you could get cattle to the railhead, your herds could be shipped back to eastern cities to be sold at a fine profit. Cattle raising boomed on the eastern plains. The opportunity was not lost on the ambitious, and not only New Mexicans. Note the players in the famous Lincoln County War: Colonel Emil Fritz, from Germany; James J. Dolan, Major Lawrence G. Murphy, and John G. Riley, all from Ireland; Alexander A. McSween, Canada; John G. Tunstall, England; and various other actors attracted by New Mexico's risky business opportunities. The Lincoln County War was the struggle for economic control of the county that developed into a series of shooting sprees. At least one element in the Lincoln County War was competition, pure and simple, for the contracts to supply beef and flour to various government markets. But also there was competition for political power and land, along with ethnic rivalries thrown in to add venom to ambition. The territorial government, dominated by the "Santa Fe Ring," was incapable of controlling the situation and, indeed, took sides and may have been responsible for some of the violence. The situation degenerated into gunfire and the Saturday-matinee drama of a burning house and a desperate breakout through "a hail of bullets." This time, however, it was not just a matinee, but real sons and husbands kicking and dying in the dirt. There is little noble in it, and it is strange that one of the characters, a possibly psychotic killer named William Bonney but nicknamed "Billy the Kid," has achieved mythological sainthood.

The Santa Fe Ring was unable or unwilling to control the Lincoln County War neutrally because it was not neutral. Historians differ in their interpretation of the ring—some even deny its existence—because no "ring" has a charter, outlining who is in it, who isn't, and what they are

for. Rather, in a troubled simmering pot there are enterprising people who see that, by cooperating, they may be able to grab a delectable morsel that is floating by. New Mexico had more than its share of enterprising people. Two names keep coming up in discussions of the Ring: "Smooth Steve" Stephen B. Elkins and "Tomcat" Thomas Catron. Both were lawyers, intelligent, ambitious, and active in politics. Politics means alliances, and they made them, with leading merchants, with county political leaders, and with corporations eager to do business in New Mexico. The alliances shifted with the project in hand; a foe in the election of a judge now might become an ally in a land deal later. And land deals were about the biggest opportunity going in New Mexico.

The problems of land ownership, which still plague New Mexico, were the direct result of one culture imposing its laws over another, which happened not once but twice, to thoroughly confuse the situation. The Indians had clear ideas, even with property markers, of what belonged to each pueblo. To a surprising degree, when the Spaniards came in they honored these, at least in reduced versions. To its own people Spain made individual and community "grants." These were not surveyed with anything approaching modern means, and trying to figure out where a "large cottonwood tree" used to be, or what "the skirt of the mountain" means, is problem enough. But even more troublesome was the Spanish idea of ownership. Individuals

*Above
Supplies were seldom adequate at Fort Sumner to feed the Indians on the Bosque Redondo reservation. This circa 1866 Signal Corps photograph from the National Archives depicts a group of Navajos assembled for a head count. From the McNitt Collection, NMSRCA*

*Left
Billy the Kid (1859-1881), also known as William H. Bonney, was said to have killed 21 men, one for each year of his life. Three months after his escape from the Lincoln County Courthouse, he was killed in Fort Sumner by Sheriff Pat Garrett. This tintype (circa 1879) is the only authenticated picture of the outlaw. Lincoln Heritage Trust*

*Ellipse
In 1876 Alexander A. McSween gained an important ally when a young Englishman named John H. Tunstall came to Lincoln. Tunstall, pictured in 1875, was searching for ranch investments and had just completed a tour of British Columbia and California. NMSRCA*

*Below
Once established in Lincoln, John G. Tunstall invested in grazing land and livestock. Encouraged by Alexander A. McSween, he erected a new building for his store, depicted in this photograph. NMSRCA*

in a village owned their croplands, but by far the larger amount of the grant was used communally for pasture and wood gathering. Finally over this palimpsest came the United States, with its tidy ideas of clearly surveyed land, clearly conveyed to another person by a bill of sale, with much of it kept by the government as public lands. "Tidy," that is, if ownership was clear and agreed upon to begin with. It never was. How could the U.S. system cope with the concept of communal lands? Furthermore, too many of the persons involved had a personal stake in the outcome.

A case in point is the Maxwell Grant, which led into another "county war," the Colfax County War. Governor Manuel Armijo—who in the last days of the Mexican period had so many dealings with the Americans—had made the grant in the 1840s to a group headed by Charles Beaubien. Eventually ex-mountain man Lucien

Left ellipse
Soon after New Mexico achieved statehood, the legislature elected Thomas B. Catron to be one of its first U.S. senators. Catron, a Santa Fe attorney, is frequently identified as a leader of the Santa Fe Ring. From the Olsen Collection, NMSRCA

Far left ellipse
Stephen B. Elkins, a leader of the so-called Santa Fe Ring, was born in 1841 and graduated from the University of Missouri in 1860. In 1872 he became president of the Maxwell Land Grant and Railway Company and also served two terms as New Mexico's territorial delegate to Congress. Photo by Sarony, MNM (#10202)

Left
Lucien Maxwell's ranch was a popular stopping place on the mountain branch of the Santa Fe Trail in the 1860s. From this base Maxwell consolidated the claims of various heirs to the Beaubien-Miranda land grant, which he sold in 1870 to an investment syndicate for $1,350,000. The ranch is pictured in this circa 1940 painting. From the School of American Research Collection, NMSRCA

Now a ghost town south of Lordsburg, Shakespeare was once Ralston, a lively mining camp. In 1872 the area received a lot of bad publicity because of a diamond salting scheme intended to swindle unwary investors. To improve the town's image, its name was changed from Ralston to Shakespeare in 1879. The town is pictured as it appeared in 1973. SHPB

Maxwell, Beaubien's son-in-law, bought it, but it was not clear exactly what he had bought. Was it two million acres? Or one-twentieth of that? Both figures had their adherents. The grant was roughly Colfax County, up on the northeast border. The visitor driving in today on I-25, after coming over Raton Pass, drives through the Maxwell Grant for the next hour or so. Early on, the United States Secretary of the Interior had ruled that the grant would be limited to 97,000 acres due to an old Mexican law, and settlers promptly claimed the other part. (Many had already moved onto it, believing it to be public land.) Here is where the cooperative effort afforded by the Ring was crucial. A state surveyor—a Ring man—surveyed the grant out at the two-million-acre figure, instantly outraging the settlers then threatened with displacement. The resulting mess was in the courts for years. "Smooth Steve" Elkins became president of a company competing with rival groups to control the land, and ran for Congress (and won) largely to promote its interests. There were killings, and even the prosecutions which followed seem to have been politically controlled. The issue was too big to die quietly, and eventually another survey, by Elkins' brother, reduced the inflammatory two million acres to a "mere" 1.7 million. Eventually this figure held up,

although the bitterness can still occasionally be heard.

In the decades following the Civil War, the United States became aware of the West. By 1878 the Atchison, Topeka & Santa Fe Railroad and its rival, the Denver & Rio Grande Western, had both reached Pueblo, Colorado, and began a race to see who would first claim the best route south, along "Uncle Dick" Wootton's toll road over Raton Pass into New Mexico. AT&SF men had lobbied the legislature in Santa Fe all the previous session to get a charter for their New Mexico subsidiary. During the autumn an AT&SF civil engineer named William R. Morley, pretending to be a sheepherder so as not to rouse the suspicions of D&RG men,

had pretty well figured out the route and grades over the pass. According to one of those dramatic stories of the West that just may be true, both lines sent crews to the little town of El Moro at the foot of the Colorado side of the pass on a cold night in February 1878. While the D&RG crew lodged for the night in the hotel, the AT&SF men went on up the hill to "Uncle Dick" Wootton's and made a deal. They moved a few shovelfuls of dirt and by dawn claimed the pass by right of first construction. The total compensation paid to Wootton was a lifetime pass on the railroad and twenty-five dollars a month for groceries—later increased to seventy-five dollars.

The first locomotive entered the terri-

Formerly a stage station known as Willow Springs, Raton began to grow soon after the Atchison, Topeka, and Santa Fe tracks crossed Raton Pass in 1878. This photograph shows First Street in the 1880s, with railway company buildings in the foreground. From the Raton Museum Photo Collections

In 1877 William R. Morley established the present route of the Santa Fe Railroad. According to tradition he prevented rivals with the Denver & Rio Grande Railroad from learning his plan by disguising himself as a sheepherder while completing his survey. MNM (#77764)

Santa Fe and go directly to Albuquerque where, with the legal and financial co-operation of city fathers, the railroad had decided to build its regional depot and yards. It was obvious now that the railroad's main goal was the Pacific coast, and New Mexico was just a way station. Afraid it might be left to wither on—off—the vine, Santa Fe civic leaders, including the famous Bishop Lamy whose signature was first on the petition circulated to voters, floated a bond issue and succeeded in procuring a branch line. Bishop Lamy also owned the land where the connection was made, and the little town there today is called Lamy.

The line pushed on down the Rio Grande and approached Albuquerque. The railroad had decided to build its regional depot and yards in Albuquerque. Here is one of the fascinating "what-might-have-beens" of history. AT&SF officials had first wanted to build terminal facilities in Bernalillo, but venerable José Leandro Perea, *patron* of that settlement, had demanded too high a price for the land they needed. Why did he do this? For one, a wealthy man, Perea did not need the money. Also, it is entirely possible that the progress promised by the railroad did not strike him as progress at all, and he would as soon have had it built somewhere else. If that was his wish, he succeeded. Triggered by the coming of the railroad, Albuquerque began rushing to become the major city it is today; and Bernalillo continued to be . . . what it is now. An argument as to who won would have passionate supporters on each side.

There was more railroad building to be done, although an astonishing one-third of New Mexico's trackage was built from 1879 to 1881. The Denver & Rio Grande Western did eventually get lines into the state, one coming down from the San Luis Valley and reaching Santa Fe from the north, the other crossing the northern part of the state to its terminus in Durango. (After the freight business fell off, a part of this narrow-gauge northern line was converted to a tourist attraction, now one of the finest ways to see that part of the

tory about December 1, 1878. For a while the engine that pulled loads over the pass was the most powerful in the world, appropriately enough called the "Uncle Dick." The line pushed south past Las Vegas and then turned west into Glorieta Pass following the route of the old Santa Fe Trail, still the most logical way through the mountains. But by now a simple fact of geography and engineering had become obvious: you could not get to Santa Fe without going up a hill. As a result, the Santa Fe Railroad decided to bypass

Left
Accompanied by other French-born ecclesiastics, Archbishop Jean Baptiste Lamy (standing, with cane in hand) enjoys his garden on a summer afternoon. Joseph Priest Machbeuf, his protégé and confidant, is standing to the far right. Jean Baptiste Salpointe, who succeeded Lamy as archbishop, is seated to the left. From the Farrar Collection, NMSRCA

Bottom, left
After emerging from the narrow confines of Apache Canyon, the main line of the Santa Fe Railroad continued southwest through Galisteo Basin toward Albuquerque, instead of climbing the steep grade up to the city of Santa Fe. Despite outraged protests from civic leaders, New Mexico's capital had to content itself with a branch line. Photo by George C. Bennett, MNM (#37441)

Bottom, right
In 1880 the Denver & Rio Grande Railroad constructed one of the most difficult routes into New Mexico, a branch that extended over Cumbres Pass from Antonito, Colorado, to Chama. From Chama, the narrow gauge line continued on to the Colorado mining towns of Durango and Silverton. SHPB

Right
Like Americans everywhere, New Mexico's citizens hungered for culture in the late nineteenth century. Even grand opera found its way to the frontier. Traveling companies such as this one at Socorro brightened the theatrical season with selections from Verdi and Bizet. Courtesy, Socorro Historical Society

Far right
A pioneer archeologist and ethnohistorian, Adolph F. Bandelier was born in Berne, Switzerland, in 1840. He first visited New Mexico in 1880. Subsequently he conducted the first comprehensive survey of the region's prehistoric ruins. During his investigations he traveled thousands of miles on foot or horseback, remaining at various Indian villages for weeks at a time. From the Ramona Indian School Collection. Courtesy, University of New Mexico General Library, Special Collections

state.) Tracks were laid on down the river to El Paso by the AT&SF, and in two main corridors it went west and connected to California. As agriculture and later minerals were developed in the southeastern plains, steel rails were laid there too.

What did the railroad do for New Mexico? It is almost incalculable. Before, New Mexico had been a distant place. All of the ways to get here had been hard: the six- to nine-month ox-cart trek from Mexico City in the seventeenth century, the long plodding of the freight caravans across the plains from Kansas City, and—not much better—the gut-wrenching sway-ride of the stagecoach. Suddenly, getting to New Mexico was a matter of two or

three days. Freight rates dropped dramatically. Goods from the East poured in, and prices dropped. (Historian Marc Simmons has documented what the new rates did just for the sheep industry, with easy transportation of wool.) People, too, could come more easily, their way made almost luxurious by the railroad's genius of profitable hospitality, Fred Harvey. The diary of an anthropologist (another species the railroad began bringing in quantity) is telling. Adolf Bandelier stepped down from the train in Lamy in August 1880, the first year of the train's existence. Two years later he came again and on March 19, 1882, wrote in his diary after walking around Santa Fe, "the city has

grown considerably. New houses have sprung up, some two-story . . . with metallic roofs." (Those tin roofs were one more product brought by the railroad, for it was expensive to haul sheets of tin from Kansas City via freight wagon.) It is not true to say that the railroad was the end of the Santa Fe Trail. Freight, people, and ideas still made their way in both directions across the prairies, tying this distant place to the more populous East. Santa Fe was married to the rest of the United States, as the ceremony says, for better or worse.

With the railroads and modern extraction methods, mining finally came into its own. From the beginning, European explorers had pursued the shining vision of gold and silver, but for the most part New Mexico's ore deposits proved disappointing. One notable exception was (and is) the great Santa Rita copper mine in the southwest corner of the state. In 1800 an Apache Indian guide showed Spanish Lieutenant Colonel José Manuel Carrasco the copper deposits, and the next year Spaniards began working the mine, sending the ore to Chihuahua and Mexico City by burro trains. Apache troubles closed the workings at various times. Eventually the "easy" copper gave out, but when open-pit methods were developed around 1910, the Santa Rita mine became one of the largest open-pit operations in the world.

Despite its luxurious accommodations the Montezuma Hotel was not a financial success. After its sale by the Santa Fe, the Montezuma changed hands several times and was occupied by a wide variety of tenants. Recently remodeled, it now houses a branch of United World College. From the Department of Development Collection, NMSRCA

Right
Determined pros-
pectors panned for
gold along New
Mexico's streams
and canyons in the
last decades of the
nineteenth century.
Water was an in-
dispensable element
in placer mining.
From the McDon-
ald Collection,
NMSRCA

Below
Despite frequent
military campaigns
conducted against
the Apache by
Spanish, Mexican,
and United States
troops, warriors
fought for their
rights in the South-
west for three cen-
turies. From the
McNitt Collection,
NMSRCA

Other dramatic but generally short-lived strikes have punctuated New Mexico's history. Not far from Santa Rita is Silver City, a town much like many other New Mexico towns today, but a legendary place in its heyday. Prospectors finding themselves suddenly rich imported an orchestra from San Francisco to play in a rough, roaring mining town still experiencing Apache raids, and at the mere rumor of a new strike the town would empty of able-bodied men in a few hours. Yet that is not the whole story of this mining town. Wealth dug from the ground built a solid community of more than brick houses. Silver City developed a library and an outstanding early educational system. It was a "boomtown," but its citizens made it last.

In 1828 gold was discovered in the Ortiz Mountains south of Santa Fe, and a minor rush followed. The Ortiz gold fields, too, soon gave out, largely because of the difficulty of obtaining water for the necessary processing. Thomas Edison erected a processing plant there in the late 1800s, trying to use static electricity to extract the gold, but the attempt failed. Technolo-

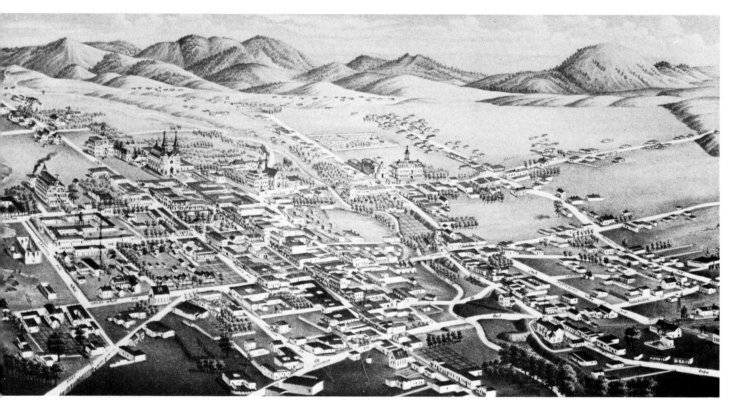

*Above
American artist
Henry Wellge
(1850-1917) drew
Bird's Eye View of
the City of Santa
Fe, N.M. in 1882.
Courtesy, Amon
Carter Museum,
Fort Worth*

*Left
Maintenance of law
and order some-
times required
strong measures by
local officials to re-
strain nineteenth-
century despera-
does. This jail, lo-
cated in Tomé, a
village south of Al-
buquerque, has
walls four feet thick
made of volcanic
rock covered with
adobe. Erected in
1875, Tomé Jail is
all that remains of
a larger building
that served for a
short time as the
Valencia County
Courthouse. SHPB*

Centuries after the Anasazi abandoned it, Navajos occupied Chaco Canyon. These horsemen rode into pueblo Bonito in 1891 for a celebration staged by Richard Wetherill, who operated a trading post there. Wetherill—a famous amateur archeologist—and his brothers discovered the awesome ruins at Mesa Verde, Colorado, in 1888. From the McNitt Collection, NMSRCA

gy has at last caught up, however, and today a modern mining operation uses complex, electrolytic technology to recover gold too fine to be seen by the naked eye.

Gold was discovered at Elizabethtown in the Maxwell Land Grant, but again there was no water to process the ore, despite heroic attempts at building "the Big Ditch," which wound forty-one miles to bring water from eleven miles away. White Oaks in Lincoln County had its heyday, but today it is windblown and almost abandoned. One of the great legends—this one true—is of the "Bridal Chamber." This incredible chamber, discovered in a mine near Hillsboro in the 1880s, yielded more than three million dollars—in 1880 dollars—of horn (free, almost pure) silver. A spur line was run into the chamber and silver was simply loaded directly onto the cars. The area just west of Socorro proved rich in lead, zinc, copper, and silver, and attracted another "run," which proved more permanent. In

1889 the legislature created the School of Mines in Socorro, now the New Mexico Institute of Mining and Technology.

To realize the true value of minerals in New Mexico, however, one must escape the hypnotic effect of the romantic two, gold and silver. Carlsbad has long had an industry in potash; it may be less dramatic, but fortunes have been built upon it. When the nation discovered the secret power of uranium, rich deposits around Grants created a boom that lasted for two decades but which, like so many other mining booms, has declined drastically. New Mexico's greatest long-term mining potential probably lies in her reserves of fossil fuels: coal in the northwest corner of the state, and oil and natural gas both there and in the southeast.

New Mexico's growth, from a distant colony of Mexico to a valued U.S. territory with vast economic opportunities and natural resources, would only continue in the coming years of statehood.

Above
School construction increased rapidly after 1891. Youthful scholars struggled with "the three Rs" in buildings like this one at White Oaks, a gold-mining town northeast of Carrizozo. SHPB

Left
During the 1880s and 1890s many new industries began operations in New Mexico, including Albuquerque's Southwestern Brewery and Ice Company. After its completion in 1899, this handsome, five-story building was the tallest in the territory, according to the local press. SHPB

President William Howard Taft stopped briefly in Albuquerque while enroute to a conference with Mexican President Porfirio Díaz in 1909. On October 15 a large crowd of citizens gathered at the Alvarado Hotel to greet the President. A banquet that evening was marked by a sharp exchange concerning statehood for New Mexico between Taft and politician Albert B. Fall. From the Hubbell Collection, NMSRCA

One of the Fifty

New Mexico was now bound to the United States, for better or worse, by railroad ties and tracks of steel. To risk stretching a metaphor too far, would the union be legitimated with the gold of statehood? Since 1850, or 1846 if you count General Kearny's makeshift government, New Mexico had been a territory, and it was to remain in that status longer than any other part of the nation. In six decades, supporters of statehood managed to get more than fifty statehood bills introduced in Congress; none of them succeeded. There is a story that one bill was defeated because the territorial representative, "Smooth Steve" Elkins, mistakenly shook hands with a Northern reconstructionist congressman, thereby alienating Southern representatives. Of course there is more to it than that. Some local merchants worried that taxes would increase once federal support given to territories ceased. Local officials feared they would lose their political power. Still, by and large the citizens did want statehood, and New Mexico repeatedly called constitutional conventions and drafted constitutions to present to the federal government. Nothing happened.

The federal government found itself with a knotty problem, some aspects of which were not easily discussed. The general pattern of U.S. expansion had been to acquire "blank" (Indian-occupied) territory, settle it, and absorb it as a new state—rather like welcoming back into the firm a son who had gone out and started his own company. Now, for the first time, the United States was being asked to absorb a preexisting, alien culture that was in fact much older than the United States itself. The problem of land law and communal ownership was only one manifesta-

tion of the dilemma. There were also the questions of language and religion, as an essentially Protestant, English-speaking nation looked with suspicion upon a Spanish-speaking, Roman Catholic enclave where in 1890 almost all of the schools were parochial and the church supplied the teachers for the rest. Suspicions were compounded by stories of shootings and hangings and of those "county wars," although other territories—Missouri, for example, which became wealthy on the Santa Fe trade—had been made a state while it was still notoriously lawless.

These problems stymied all attempts at statehood for more than half a century. Still, one by one they were met, battered down, or smoothed over. Finally, on January 6, 1912, New Mexico became the forty-seventh state in the union. William C. McDonald of White Oaks was elected the first state governor of New Mexico.

New Mexico now found itself fully joined to the United States, while heritage and geography still tied it to Mexico. It is not surprising that Mexican troubles spilled across the border. In 1916, during a period of revolution in Mexico, the U.S. government supported one side, thoroughly alienating the famous Pancho Villa, who was attempting to take control. Either from spite over his rejection by the U.S. State Department, or perhaps in a subtle plot to force the United States to invade Mexico and thus oppose his rival Venustiano Carranza, early on the morning of March 9, 1916, Pancho Villa's forces raided the New Mexican border town of Columbus. He got his invasion. Brigadier General John J. "Black Jack" Pershing entered Mexico with 7,000 men to pursue Villa. He never caught up with Villa but

Right
Maintenance and repair of railroad equipment brought heavy industry to New Mexico for the first time. Albuquerque's Atlantic & Pacific shops gave the town a substantial payroll. Eventually the Atlantic & Pacific became part of the Santa Fe system. From the Department of Development Collection, NMSRCA

Below
With the expansion of railroad lines in the 1880s, New Mexico's range cattle industry boomed. This 1914 painting by Taos artist Oscar E. Berninghaus portrays a group of cowboys relaxing at the chuckwagon during a roundup. NMSRCA

Left
When the Spanish-American War broke out in 1898, New Mexico quickly filled its enlistment quota, following President William McKinley's call for volunteers. Commanded by Lieutenant-Colonel Theodore Roosevelt, these troops became known as rough-riders. The contingent pictured traveled to San Antonio, Texas, for training. It is easy to see from this photo that patriotic fever ran high. From the Adelia Collier Collection, NMSRCA

Bottom
Although modest in size, Santa Rosa's first bank was an object of civic pride. When rumors spread that deperadoes intended a holdup, local citizens stood guard around the institution and foiled the scheme. From the Cultural Properties Review Committee Collection, NMSRCA

Above
Ratified by the voters on January 21, 1911, New Mexico's first constitution was extremely conservative. Unlike similar documents approved by other Western states, it had no provisions for such democratic reform measures as initiative, recall, or women's suffrage. Photo by William R. Walton, MNM (#8119)

Opposite, top
In 1907 a group of politicians enroute to the inauguration of Governor Curry posed for a photograph. The tall man in the back row is Pat Garrett, who shot and killed Billy the Kid. To Garrett's right is William C. McDonald. Third from the right in the front row sits Albert B. Fall. NMSRCA

Opposite, bottom
Hoping to limit damage, local citizens organized fire companies such as this one, pictured in 1905. From the Cobb Collection. Courtesy, University of New Mexico General Library, Special Collections

Right
Appointed governor of New Mexico by President William McKinley in 1897, Miguel A. Otero was the only Hispano to hold that position prior to statehood. Otero served until 1906, the longest term of any chief executive. When the Spanish-American War broke out in 1898, Otero's enthusiastic response to the call for volunteers caused New Mexico's quota of roughriders to be raised within a few days. From the Otero Collection. Courtesy, University of New Mexico General Library, Special Collections

*Right
William C.
McDonald, New
Mexico's first gov-
ernor after state-
hood, came to New
Mexico from up-
state New York in
1880. McDonald, a
surveyor and ranch-
er, resided at White
Oaks in Lincoln
County when elect-
ed to the state's
highest executive
office. MNM
(#50589)*

*Top, far right
Before dawn on
March 9, 1916, fol-
lowers of Mexican
caudillo Francisco
"Pancho" Villa
struck the border
town of Columbus.
Despite initial suc-
cess, the raiders en-
countered strong
resistance from the
U.S. Army garrison
and were forced to
withdraw. Eighteen
Americans and ap-
proximately one
hundred Mexicans
were killed in the
attack. NMSRCA*

*Bottom
On January 15,
1912, William C.
McDonald was in-
augurated as gover-
nor before a throng
of enthusiastic citi-
zens. Chief Justice
Clarence J. Roberts
administered the
oath of office.
MNM (#27293)*

did run into Mexican national forces at Parral. Seven U.S. soldiers were killed, and hotheads on both sides called for war. Cooler heads prevailed, partly because war was coming—in Europe. Pershing's forces withdrew from Mexico, and further bloodshed was avoided.

The war in Europe, which overshadowed the fuss with Pancho Villa, reached New Mexico too. A State Council of Defense was created to help with the effort, although the $75,000 they made available seems remarkably small by today's standards. Approximately 17,000 New Mexicans served in the armed forces, perhaps the strongest proof possible, if any were needed, that New Mexico was a full-fledged part of the United States.

The Great Depression of the 1930s hit New Mexico hard, especially in coal production: in four years the tonnage mined dropped by 72 percent. Later, as trains

*Far left
Octoviano A. Larrazolo was elected governor in 1918. At the end of his term, he created a storm of controversy when he pardoned sixteen Villistas. From the State Officials Collection. Courtesy, University of New Mexico General Library, Special Collections*

*Below
Following Pancho Villa's raid on Columbus, President Woodrow Wilson ordered General John Pershing to lead an expeditionary force in pursuit of the famous bandit. MNM (#5816)*

Above
Although Pancho Villa managed to elude Pershing's troops, the "Punitive Expedition" gave the army an opportunity to test new equipment. From the Farrar Collection, NMSRCA

Far right
Albert B. Fall, a veteran legislator and judge, held office under both political parties. Fall's career ended in disgrace, due to his role as President Warren G. Harding's Secretary of Interior in the Teapot Dome oil scandal. From the Olsen Collection, NMSRCA

converted to diesel, coal town after coal town shut down. Nevertheless, coal lies beneath some one-fifth of New Mexico's surface, and such an energy source could not be ignored for very long. Modern technologies for strip mining, as well as demands for the low-sulphur coal available in the state, brought about a resurgence of the San Juan Basin in the 1970s. The coal reserves there lie near the surface, easily strippable; on satellite photographs one can actually see a relatively dark band arcing from Farmington southeastward, formed by the numerous outcroppings of coal on the surface. Now the coal is used not for running trains or heating homes, but for the production of electricity. New Mexico itself consumes only about one-third the electrical power it produces, the rest leaving (as have many of New Mexico's sons and daughters) for the lights of big cities elsewhere.

The petroleum industry is a relatively

Left
From the arrival of the railroads until the end of World War II, coal mining was an important industry in New Mexico. While coal enjoyed a strong demand for industrial and home heating purposes, company towns such as Madrid grew up beside the mines in which the corporation controlled every aspect of life. From the McKittrick Collection, NMSRCA

Bottom, left
Since the 1920s petroleum production has been important in Southeastern New Mexico's economy. The region, known as Little Texas, is heavily dependent on the oil and gas industry. This Continental-Shell refinery near Hobbs extracted highly volatile "casinghead" gasoline from natural gas, which was then blended with lower grades to produce a fuel suitable for automobiles. From the Department of Development Collection, NMSRCA

Bottom, right
During the 1920s the oil and gas business began to boom in New Mexico, particularly in the state's southeast and northwest quadrants. The exploration shown here took place near Shiprock in San Juan County. From the Department of Development Collection, NMSRCA

The huge open-pit copper mine at Santa Rita is one of Southwestern New Mexico's most important industries. Although the mine was worked by Chihuahua entrepreneurs in the early 1800s, it was not until after 1910 that mechanization permitted extensive exploitation of the rich mineral deposits. The unusual geological formation on the horizon is called "The Kneeling Nun." From the Department of Development Collection, NMSRCA

young one, its growth reflecting that of the internal combustion engine. In 1928 New Mexico produced 1.2 million barrels of oil; in 1983 the figure was more than seventy-one million barrels. The state has two main petroleum and natural gas producing areas: the San Juan Basin in the northwest, and the southeastern region centered around Carlsbad, an area known to geologists as the Permian Basin. Both of these corners of the state have experienced the "boom and bust" cycles of the industry, but the trend has been steadily upward, and today New Mexico is one of the leading energy producing states in the union.

New Mexico's natural resources have been an economic boon, not only in providing minerals and fuels but also in attracting people. Early train passengers may have reached the state more quickly than they would have in stagecoaches, but conditions were not that much better. Meal

stops were hurried, the food generally awful. Then a genius named Fred Harvey took over passenger services for the line, and soon Harvey Houses (and their carefully chosen, hardworking attendants, "Harvey Girls") were famous among grateful travelers.

The favorable publicity attracted visitors, many of whom wanted to see more of the fascinating country glimpsed through a train window. Thus there developed a business in short automobile tours to Indian pueblos and other attractions, known as the Indian Detours, with well-trained guides and well-equipped cars. Throughout the 1920s thousands of visitors from the East had the pleasure of an Indian Detour. The Indian Detour finally disappeared, a victim of the Depression and the rise of the private automobile, but by then the nation as a whole was aware of the Southwest. Calendars in every state carried pic-

Completed in 1898, the Castañeda was one of a series of luxury hotels built by the Santa Fe Railroad and operated by the Fred Harvey Company. An English immigrant, Harvey developed a profitable business by providing tourists with pleasing meals and accomodations. To staff his dining rooms Harvey hired attractive, courteous waitresses known as "Harvey girls." He also established Indian Detours, a guide service for travelers desiring side trips to points of interest in New Mexico and Arizona. Photo by Edward Kemp. MNM (#46947)

Cattle ranching has been an important element to New Mexico's economy for more than one hundred years. For all working cowboys branding livestock is part of the regular ranch routine. The Tom Mix hats these San Gabriel Ranch cowpokes are wearing date this photo to around the 1920s. Photo by Edward Kemp, MNM (#53705)

Above
The Villa Real of Albuquerque, founded in 1706 around the customery Spanish style plaza. Named after a Spanish Duke, Albuquerque is still called the "Duke City." Photo by Ron Behrman. ACVB

Right
Since Spanish colonial times Navajo blankets have always been among the most sought after of Southwestern Indian crafts. Today they bring higher prices than ever before because of recent interest in indigenous artifacts. From the Bullock Collection, NMSRCA

tures of a Santa Fe train dwarfed by mesas and desert, or of Indians in colorful dress against breathtaking scenery. New Mexico had created an image in the national consciousness as a place of wonderful light, of colorful, mysterious people, and of a romantic almost-lost way of life.

Artists were attracted to the image—and the reality—of New Mexico. A broken wagon wheel stopped two artists on their way to Mexico in 1898, and they "discovered" Taos. Bert Phillips and Ernest Blumenschein wrote their friends about the wonderful light, the incredible vistas, and the fascinating Indian ceremonials. Some came to see for themselves and stayed, living in adobe houses on dirt lanes. Taos found itself with an artists' colony, of residents who painted when the light was high—and partied when it was not. The intellectual ferment attracted writers as well. Perhaps the most famous was D.H. Lawrence, who came to Taos as the guest of that remarkable heiress, Mabel Dodge Luhan, and, like so many

Above
After an apprenticeship at New York's Art Students League, W. Herbert "Buck" Dunton came to Taos in 1912. His paintings interpreted the American West. From the School of American Research Collection, NMSRCA

Left
Refurbishing a house's walls with a new coat of adobe plaster has traditionally been regarded as women's work. It is often a cooperative enterprise that brings neighbors together. From the E. Boyd Collection, NMSRCA

Above
Arthur Rothstein shot this photo in Taos pueblo in 1936. It is taken from The American West in the Thirties: 122 Photographs by Arthur Rothstein. *Courtesy, Dover Publications*

Right
Also taken from The American West in the Thirties: 122 Photographs by Arthur Rothstein, *this photo depicts Governor Sandoval and a youngster at Taos pueblo in 1936. Courtesy, Dover Publications*

No one knows how long Indian artisans have been selling their pottery and jewelry under the portal at the Palace of the Governors, although it seems as if they have always been around. Each day hundreds of tourists carefully inspect and bargain for a wide assortment of crafts displayed by Pueblo, Navajos, and other tribes, as pictured in this photo from 1962. From the Department of Development Collection, NMSRCA

Renowned nationwide for her beautiful pottery, María Martínez (sitting at right) became one of the state's most famous artisans. The award-winning artist, a resident of the pueblo of San Ildefonso, was photographed circa 1950 with her husband Julian and an admiring tourist. From the Department of Development Collection, NMSRCA

Opposite, bottom right
Taken from The Depression Years: As Photographed by Arthur Rothstein, this picture shows an Indian in New Mexico in 1938. Courtesy, Dover Publications

others, was captivated by the place. New Mexico has returned the feeling, to judge by the numerous books, articles, and meetings celebrating Lawrence's New Mexico connection.

Taos continues as a significant center of American art, but Santa Fe and Albuquerque have thriving colonies as well. Even Roswell, a relatively new town on the eastern plains, has what must be one of the most remarkable museums, with a spectacular art collection, for a town its size anywhere. And the art has passed well beyond the limits of regionalism. The Southwest-based art of Georgia O'Keeffe has influenced many American artists. New Mexico studios routinely show works as exciting, and as confusing, as one could find in New York or Paris. Of course there also remains the great backbone of art more obviously sprung from New Mexico soil.

The clean, clear air of the high desert attracted others besides artists. Some people came for their health. The early de-

cades of this century were darkened by tuberculosis, and a long stay in a sanitorium was considered the most effective cure. Many patients found the climate of New Mexico salubrious. In fact many were cured, although one doubts the 90 percent rate claimed by some at the time. And just as artists came to visit and stayed, these health-seekers stayed to make significant contributions to the state, their descendants becoming native-born New Mexicans.

Along with millions of other Americans, New Mexicans of every background were stunned as they listened to their kitchen radios and hushed the kids on December 7, 1941. The Japanese had attacked Pearl Harbor. War had come to America, and New Mexicans would be in the thick of it. The world now knows of the Navajo "Talkers," who by speaking in their native language provided a radio code that the enemy could not break. Fewer people realize that, by a quirk of fate, it was largely New Mexicans who filled the coastal anti-aircraft regiments in the Philippines that fell to Japan when it captured Bataan. The Bataan Death March is remembered today in the villages and farms of New Mexico almost as a second "Long Walk" for the state. When the grim tally was in, New Mexico had suffered the highest war casualty rate, in proportion to population, of all the states in the union.

The war brought another change to New Mexico, and to the world. In mid-November of 1942 two men in an unmarked car slowly made their way up a dirt road, climbing the shoulder of a volcano. Just a million years ago this mountain had exploded incredibly, belching hundreds of cubic miles of ash and rock which then spread around its base. Eventually erosion cut steep canyons into this conglomerated "tuff," leaving long, narrow, isolated, flat-topped mesas. Atop one mesa was a private boys' school called Los Alamos. The two men—a physicist named Robert Oppenheimer and a general named Leslie Groves—got out of the car and rapidly made their decision. In the interest of the war effort they would condemn this

Top
To promote irrigation and flood control, the Federal Reclamation Service constructed Elephant Butte Dam across the Rio Grande near Hot Springs (now Truth or Consequences). The dam was the first of several major water projects within the state and was completed in 1916. From the Department of Development Collection, NMSRCA

Opposite, bottom
From the late nineteenth century up until the present, the windmill has proved to be a reliable water source for irrigation, stock water, and household use in rural areas. Rising high over the plain east of Sandía pueblo, the windmill pictured helps provide for a herd of thirsty Angus cattle. NMSRCA

Above
This 1940 photo shows the 200th regiment at summer camp near Las Vegas. From the Department of Development Collection, NMSRCA

Right
During World War II New Mexicans did their part. This circa 1942 poster encouraged Indians, Hispanos, and Anglos to buy war bonds and stamps. From the R. Vernon Hunter Collection, NMSRCA

Left
A one-room school at Versylvania is pictured in Taos in 1941. Photo by Irving Rusinow. From the Bureau of Agricultural Economics. Courtesy, National Archives

Opposite, bottom right
Unaware of the terrible struggle that lay ahead, National Guardsmen paraded the colors during 1940 summer maneuvers. From the Department of Development Collection, NMSRCA

Below
To honor the state's soldiers who fought at Bataan, the former state capitol was renamed "The Bataan Memorial Building." From the Department of Development Collection, NMSRCA

Right
On the anniversary of the bombing of Pearl Harbor, President John F. Kennedy stopped briefly in Santa Fe on December 7, 1962, only a few weeks after the Cuban missile crisis. Following a short speech the President boarded a helicopter for Los Alamos, where he was briefed concerning experiments in space rocketry. The official party included Vice-President Lyndon B. Johnson and Senator Clinton P. Anderson. MNM (#9545)

Opposite
Although there are now hundreds of other names chiseled into its soft sandstone face, El Morro has scarcely changed otherwise since 1605 when Oñate carved his inscription there. In 1906 President Theodore Roosevelt gave the area federal protection to assure its preservation. Today El Morro is a national monument. NPS

Right
Each year during the 1930s and 1940s Madrid mounted an elaborate display of Christmas lights. Although sponsored by the coal company, miners performed much of the work on their own time. In this photo an electrical holiday greeting frames the smoking breaker. From the McKittrick Collection, NMSRCA

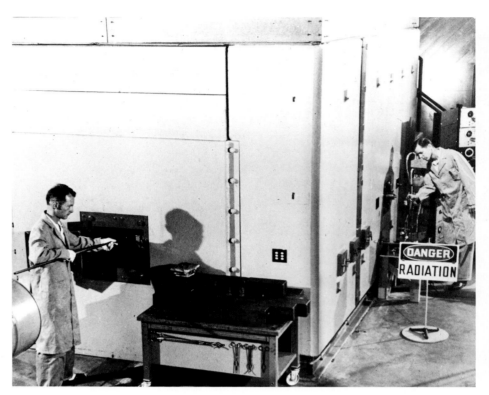

Above
Los Alamos Scientific Laboratory has led the nation in atomic research since its inception. The tools hanging in the foreground might resemble tongs from an old-fashioned blacksmith shop, but the fire in this laboratory is thousands of times hotter than any forge. From the Frank Waters Collection. Courtesy, University of New Mexico General Library, Special Collections

Right
Scientists at the laboratory are conducting experiments in a wide variety of fields. Courtesy, Los Alamos National Laboratory.

Left
In one of the most interesting experiments performed at Holloman Air Force Base, chimpanzees were used to test man's reactions to conditions in space. Space chimps Ham (left) and Enos (right), pictured circa 1961, are preparing for lift-off. On January 31, 1961, Ham became the first chimp to enter space when he rode a Redstone rocket on a transatlantic flight. From the Holloman Air Force Base Collection. Courtesy, University of New Mexico General Library, Special Collections.

Opposite, top right
As a young physics professor from Berkeley in 1922, Dr. J. Robert Oppenheimer took a pack trip over the Pajarito Plateau, the future site of Los Alamos. Twenty years later, during World War II, he was one of the scientists who selected Los Alamos Ranch School as headquarters for the top-secret Manhattan Project, which developed the atomic bomb. Oppenheimer is pictured circa 1945. From the Kittrick Collection, NMSRCA

isolated school and use the buildings for a laboratory. They were working on something of the utmost urgency and secrecy though no one knew for certain if it was even possible. They were going to build an atomic bomb.

Working in isolation on this ridge, the team they gathered built the device in less than three years. In July 1945 they hauled it down the dirt road to an even more isolated spot about 150 miles to the south. There, at 5:30 a.m. on July 16, they tested it. The blast was stunning, of a nature never before seen on earth, and thunder rolled across the valley. New Mexico and the world had entered the atomic age.

In the more than 50 years since the end of World War II, New Mexico has drawn ever closer to the nation of which it is a part. The railroad, which did so much to forge the link, has been overshadowed now by the automobile and the airplane. Above all, the mass media-especially network television-seem to eliminate the very idea of distance. Today, New Mexicans hear their news in the same accent as does everyone else in the country. Modern movies open in Albuquerque the same week they do in Los Angeles and New York. Young people dance to the same music that their peers are listening to across the nation. A few years ago this writer watched the World Series on color television in the pueblo home of an Indian friend. (He was a Cardinals fan.)

The economy of modern New Mexico includes a mixture of farming, ranching, mining, forestry, manufacturing, and tourismas well as high technology at Los Alamos, Sandia Laboratories, and Kirtland Air Force Base in Albuquerque.

Above
As automobiles became more popular in the years between the two world wars, state officials struggled to build a highway system to accomodate them, yet horses and mules still powered some of the road-building equipment. *From the Department of Development Collection, NMSRCA*

Right
In 1941 the Interstate Commerce Commission approved abandonment of the famous Chili Line, *the Denver & Rio Grande branch from Alamosa, Colorado, to Santa Fe.* SHPB

Soon after Mexico declared her independence from Spain in 1821, adventurous Missouri frontiersmen opened trade relations with New Mexico over the famous Santa Fe Trail. View of The Santa Fe Plaza in the 1850s (End of the Santa Fe Trail), *a painting by Gerald P. Cassidy in ca. 1930s oil on canvas, captures the spirit of the day by illustrating the meeting of diverse cultures that took place when huge wagons rumbled into Santa Fe's plaza. Courtesy, Museum of Fine Arts, Museum of New Mexico, gift of the Historical Society, 1977 (#6977)*

Right
American artist
Seth Eastman com-
posed this work, ti-
tled Fort Defiance
at Canoncito Boni-
to, New Mexico, *in*
1860 from a sketch
by Lieutenant Colo-
nel J.H. Eaton.
Courtesy, Amon
Carter Museum,
Fort Worth

Above
German artist
Rudolf D.L.
Cronau titled this
1885 work of his
Eine Strasse in Alt-
Albuquerque./Neu-

Mexiko *(a street in*
old Albuquerque,
New Mexico).
Courtesy, Amon
Carter Museum,
Fort Worth

Left
Design elements from this petroglyph in Galisteo Basin include simple stars, ceremonial masks, birds, and animals. They were most likely made by primitive artists some time after the fourteenth century. From the Marjorie F. Lambert Collection, NMSRCA

Left
Created from A.D. 1000-1200, Mimbres classic pottery is truly a unique art form, unmatched by any other prehistoric Southwestern pottery. The hole in the bowl pictured indicates that the vessel has been "killed," ritually, before being placed in a grave. From the Marjorie F. Lambert Collection, NMSRCA

Above
Decorations painted on the interior walls of San José Church combine Spanish- and Indian-design motifs. Pueblo symbols for sun, rain, thunder, and other elemental forces are integrated with heavy painted scrolls reminiscent of seventeenth-century Mexican church interiors. Photo by Betsy Swanson, SHPB

Left, center
The Mimbres people, a branch of the larger Mogollón prehistoric culture, made many beautiful artifacts. The turquoise frog and necklace pictured were discovered in Luna County and created between A.D. 1000-1200. From the Marjorie F. Lambert Collection, NMSRCA

Above
Bandelier National Monument is administered by the National Park Service. As an interpretative aid, the Park Service has established a self-guided tour through the ruins in Frijoles Canyon. SHPB

Right
Established after the United States conquest in 1846, Mesilla was once the economic and political center of Southern New Mexico and Arizona. The artist of this painting, titled Old Mesilla Plaza, *is unknown. MNM (#37917)*

Tucked into a beautiful mountain valley on the west slope of the Sangre de Cristo range, the pueblo of Picurís is about thirty miles south of Taos. Like Taos, Picurís belongs to the northern Tiwa linguistic group and is famous for its pottery, which is usually undecorated but glitters with bits of mica. From the Marjorie F. Lambert Collection, NMSRCA

In Pueblo Indian villages the kiva is the traditional center for community religious life. Its shape can be rectangular or round like this one at San Ildefonso. The two poles pointing skyward are part of a ladder that provides access into the building. From the Marjorie F. Lambert Collection, NMSRCA

Right
The San Gerónimo Church at the Pueblo of Taos replaced an earlier building destroyed in 1847 during a revolt staged by Taos Indians and Mexican nationalists against the United States conquest during the Mexican War.
© Corrie Photography

Below
Sandhill cranes are among the species stopping over on the Rio Grande River during winter migratory flights at Bosque del Apache Natural Wildlife Refuge, in Socorro.
© Frank Tiller 1999

Pueblo is the Spanish word for a town or village. The Pueblo Indians had already been living in multi-storied apartment-type dwellings for 1,000 years and had a highly developed culture when the Spanish arrived. The Indian and Pueblo Cultural Center in Albuquerque tells the story of the Pueblo people from pre-history to the present and Indian dances are held on the weekends in the Center's open air plaza. Photo by Ron Behrman. ACVB

Approximately 5,000 snow geese taking flight at sunrise. Thirty to forty thousand geese winter in Bosque del Apache National Wildlife Refuge each year. © Frank Tiller 1999

127

During the
reoccupation of
New Mexico by
General Diego de
Vargas in 1693
and 1694, Indians
from San Ildefonso
fled to Black Mesa,
a natural fortress
just north of their
Pueblo. Later,
other Tewas from
nearby villages
joined them. To-
gether they were
besieged by Span-
ish forces until
September 1694
when they finally
agreed to sur-
render. From the
Marjorie F.
Lambert Collec-
tion, NMSRCA.

Left
Flanked by the San Andres Mountains on the west and the Sacramentos to the east, White Sands National Monument lies in South-Central New Mexico's Tulurosa Basin. For centuries snow and rain water from the two high ranges have eroded the gypsum deposits below, creating huge wave-like dunes of dazzling white sand. The area became a national monument in 1933. Photo by Frank Tiller.

Bottom
Although New Mexico is typically an arid land with a scanty amount of rainfall, a few well-timed summer showers can change a barren plain into a desert flower garden almost overnight, as shown in this 1950 photograph. Photo by Nat Dodge, NPS.

Opposite page
El Santuario de Chimayo, erected circa 1816, is one of New Mexico's most famous religous shrines. Earth from the floor of one of the chapels is believed to have miraculous healing powers. During Holy Week, pilgrims from a wide area converge on Chimayo for Good Friday services. © Corrie Photography

Below
The spectacular Cloudcroft trestle, situated on the Alamagordo and Sacramento Mountain Railroad, was erected in 1890 to span Mexican Canyon. Promoters built the A & SM to haul timber out of the mountains and carry tourists to an ornate resort hotel at Cloudcroft. Economic conditions forced abandonment of the line in 1947. The Cloudcroft trestle is pictured in 1981. Photo by Betty Swanson, SHPB

Right
Soon after the first frost touches the state's mountain ranges, the aspen foliage turns from green to a brilliant gold. Every fall scores of motorists head for the hills to experience the dramatic color change. Others ride the Cumbres and Toltec Scenic Railway from Chama to Antonito, Colorado, passing through a particularly spectacular area. Courtesy, Ludwig and Laino

Left
After a short struggle, General Diego de Vargas recaptured Santa Fe from Pueblo Indian rebels in December of 1693. Each year his triumphant reentry into the city is acted out during Santa Fe's fiesta. Courtesy, Ludwig and Laino

Bottom, left
To commemorate the recapture of Santa Fe by General Diego de Vargas in 1693, the small statue of "La Conquistadora" is carried in procession each year from Saint Francis Cathedral to Rosario Chapel. The chapel was erected in 1806 and stands on the site where Vargas camped while besieging the city. Courtesy, Ludwig and Laino

Bottom, right
Chile is an important crop in New Mexico and a vital part of the local cuisine. Aficionados disagree as to whether the most potent chile comes from the northern or southern parts of the state, but both are said to be hot! Photo by Betsy Swanson, SHPB

131

Left
Leon Kroll came to New Mexico for a brief stay in the summer of 1917. While visiting his friends Robert Henri and George Bellows, both well-known Eastern artists, Kroll painted The Hills of Santa Fe, *pictured here. MNM (#45495)*

Opposite
Velino Herrera created this vivid watercolor, Pueblo Mother, *in 1939. Herrera, born in 1902 in Zia pueblo, started painting at the age of fifteen and later adopted the nickname Ma-PeWi. Courtesy, Amon Carter Museum, Fort Worth*

Bottom, left
Gustave Baumann, one of New Mexico's most popular artists, is best known for his woodblock prints depicting trees, flowers, and mountain scenery near Santa Fe and Taos. The view from the road leading into Ranchos de Taos plaza is shown in this print. Courtesy, Fine Arts Museum, MNM

Bottom, right
Fritz Scholder is a New Mexico artist with a national reputation who frequently incorporated contemporary Indian themes into his early work. Because of their social content his paintings and lithographs struck a responsive chord during the Native American protest movement of the 1960s and 1970s. Courtesy, Fine Arts Museum, MNM

The world's finest quarter horses and the Southwest's best thoroughbreds race at Ruidoso Downs Race Track. Horses race to the wire as excited onlookers watch. Photo by Bill Pitt, Jr. Courtesy, Ruidoso Downs Racing, Inc.

Visitors enjoy snowboarding and world class skiing at Ski Apache near Ruidoso, which boasts New Mexico's largest lift capacity and runs the state's only four passenger gondola. Owned and operated by the Mescalero Apache Tribe, it can accommodate over 15,000 skiers per hour. Photo by Mark Doth. Courtesy, Village of Ruidoso

Near-perfect flying conditions make Albuquerque the "Balloon Capital of the World" and the site of the world's largest ballooning event, the Kodak Albuquerque International Balloon Fiesta held in early October. Even during non-fiesta months, the early morning skies are frequently dotted with hot air balloons. Photo by Ron Behrman. ACVB

Below
The world's longest single-span aerial tramway, the Sandia Peak Tram, five miles northeast of Albuquerque, whisks passengers up 2.7 miles of cable to the 10,000 foot Sandia Peak. In biological terms, this is like going from Mexico to Canada in 20 minutes. Wildlife such as mule deer and black bears sometimes appear on the slopes below the noise-less tram car. At the top, visitors enjoy the 11,000 square mile view, explore hiking trails, ride the Sandia Peak ski lift, or exper-ience sunset din-ing at the res-taurant perched on top of the mountain. Photo by Jay Black-wood. ACVB

The Indian Market, with St. Francis Cathedral in the background, is the biggest annual event in Santa Fe and attracts large crowds. © Corrie Photography

In the 1940s skiing became a popular sport in New Mexico. Attracted by the region's bright winter sunshine and lighter-than-air powder snow, skiers came to the Southwest from all over the nation. In an era of laced leather boots and wooden skis, this chairlift was a remarkable innovation. These pioneer skiers posed for a picture at the Santa Fe Ski Basin circa 1947. From the Department of Development Collection, NMSRCA

Situated on the Colorado-New Mexico border, Raton Pass presented a formidable obstacle to nineteenth-century railroad engineers seeking a feasible route into the territory. This view looks over the present city of Raton to the distant mesas and plains beyond. From the Department of Development Collection, NMSRCA

Above
The Santa Fe Opera presented its first performance July 3, 1957, in a brand-new outdoor theater five miles north of the city. Success marked the opera's early years, but the original building was destroyed by fire during July of 1967 in the midst of the summer season. Undismayed, opera founder and general manager John O. Crosby completed the season in a downtown school gymnasium. The opera house was rebuilt and then reconstructed for a third time in 1998. Photo by Robert Reck. Courtesy, Santa Fe Opera

Right
Audiences love the beautiful new theater and especially the electronic libretto system that gives operagoers an English transla-tion on a screen directly in front of them. Pictured are Kim Joseph-son and Elizabeth Futral in Rigo-letto. Photo by Ken Howard. Courtesy, Santa Fe Opera

Albuquerque's ideal climate has long been one of its most notable attractions. The city's 5,000 foot altitude and southern latitude produce a mild, dry climate with definite changes of season. With a population nearing 700,000, the Albuquerque metro area is large enough to offer a varied nightlife, while the nearby Sandia Mountains provide a wealth of recreational opportunities. Photo by Ron Behrman. ACVB

For centuries, Hispanic villages along the Rio Grande have lit luminarias (popularly defined as "little lights") as a sign of rejoicing. Originally, luminarias were small bonfires. With the arrival of plentiful brown wrapping paper over the Santa Fe Trail, people began making paper lanterns to enclose their festival lights. On Christmas Eve, entire neighborhoods light luminarias to guide the faithful to midnight mass and as a symbol of joy. Photo by Ron Behrman. ACVB

Since the early part of the 20th century, New Mexico has attracted a wide variety of writers, artists and movie persons as well as famous business people and important politicians who have enjoyed its welcoming atmosphere and mild climate. Santa Fe has attracted renowned writers such as Richard Bradford (Red Sky at Morning), Willa Cather (Death Comes for the Archbishop) and Wallace Stegner (Angle of Repose). Artist Georgia O'Keeffe first visited New Mexico in 1929, eventually settlling in Abiquiu, north of Santa Fe. Conrad Hilton (1887–1979), famed hotelier, was born in Socorro County and served in the first State Legislature from 1912–1915, prior to opening his first hotel. In more recent times, NMSU playwright-in-residence Mark Medoff won a Tony Award in 1980 for his play Children of a Lesser God, later made into a movie.

Below right
Willa Cather (1876–1947) was a teacher, a journalist and critic as well as what she was best known as—a writer. The Pulitzer Prize winning author of One of Ours *is probably best known for* My Antonia *and* Death Comes For The Archbishop, *portraying New Mexico in the late 1800s. Photo by Nickolas Muray. Courtesy, MNM #111734*

Below left
Fray Angelico Chavez (1911–1996), for whom the library at the Palace of Governors was named, the author of My Penitente Land, *is known primarily for his historical writing and was also a self-taught painter. Pictured here on the left is Chavez, with archeologist Sylvanus G. Morley (center), and artist Ernest L. Blumenschein, one of the founding members of the Taos Society of Artists. Photo by Robert H. Martin. Courtesy, MNM #41361*

Opposite page above Georgia O'Keeffe (1887–1986), near "The Pink House," Taos, New Mexico in 1929. One of New Mexico's most famous artists, she summered in the state for many years, finally taking up permanent residence in 1949 after the death of her husband, famed photographer Alfred Stieglitz. O'Keeffe continued to paint until the late 1970s when failing eyesight forced her to give up her life's work, and she then began producing clay objects until her health failed in 1984. Courtesy, MNM #9763

Left Internationally famous artist, Peter Hurd (1904–1984), born in Roswell was married to Henriette Wyeth, also a painter and the sister of Andrew Wyeth. Hurd, who met Henriette when he went to Pennsylvania to study with her father N.C. Wyeth, painted southwestern landscape themes. Courtesy, MNM #90701

Left below Manuel Lujan, Jr., U.S. Representative first elected to office in 1969 would go on to serve until 1989. He then spent four years as Secretary of the Interior in the George Bush administration, a time fraught with controversy. Courtesy, MNM # 52338

Radio telescopes stand as lonely sentinels in the vast plains of San Agustin. Part of the VLA (very large array), National Radio Astronomy Observatory near Socorro, New Mexico. Total number of dishes in VLA are 27. © 1999 Frank Tiller

Above Dripping Springs historic and recreation area, east of Las Cruces in the Organ Mountains. Courtesy, Las Cruces Convention & Visitors Bureau.

Right World renowned Santa Clara Pueblo potter, Maria Martinez, famous for her "black-on-black" pottery designs. Pictured is a traditional "wedding vase" given to newly weds on their wedding day. Courtesy, City of Santa Fe

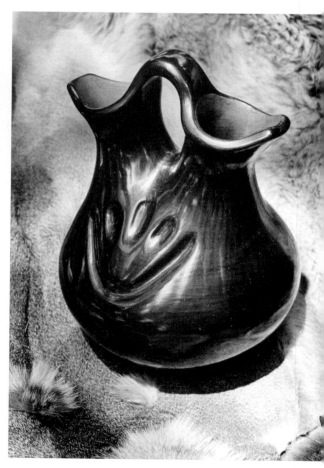

*Tent Rock near
Cochito Pueblo.
© Corrie Photog-
raphy*

During the Christmas Holidays many Santa Feans decorate their businesses and homes with "Farolitos". A Farol is Spanish for lantern, a farolito is a "little lantern." A Farol is a traditional New Mexican ornamentation— typically constructed of a brown paper bag, filled with sand on the bottom, containing a candle. In this photo, the Santa Fe plaza is decorated with Farolitos for the Christmas holiday. Courtesy, City of Santa Fe

INTO THE MILLENNIUM

In 1998, New Mexico celebrated the 400th anniversary of its founding by Don Juan de Oñate and the "Land of Enchantment" continued to flourish. Although this apt phrase has never been officially adopted as the state's nickname, it has been in use since the mid-'30s and celebrates the beauty, multi-culturalism, outdoor recreation, and warm hospitality of the richly diverse landscape from the mountains to the desert.

New Mexico's pride in the distinction of being the 47th state is illustrated by the unique 47-star U.S. flag. Only two are known to exist, one is at the Palace of the Governors in Santa Fe and the other is displayed at the Tularosa Basin Historical Society Museum. The 47-star flag was never an official U.S. flag—since they are only produced in July of the year there is a change in the number of states. The flag was evidently manufactured to represent New Mexico's entrance into the union, early in 1912, during the 39-day period between New Mexico and Arizona's entrance as the 48th state.

New Mexico is one of the fastest growing states in the U.S. approaching 1,740,000 residents by 2000. While mining extractives is the state's number one industry and cattle ranching is still among the state's leading enterprises, the economy has been bolstered as tourism has become one of New Mexico's growth industries and is now second in importance. Visitors enjoy New Mexico's many art galleries, the range of recreation areas, and its varied climate.

Artists in an array of fields—both the home grown and transplanted variety—have been attracted to, and inspired by, the beauty of New Mexico's landscape. The diversity of New Mexico's art reflects its rich cultural heritage.

Art galleries and history abound in Taos and Santa Fe. When Mabel Dodge Luhan and later D.H. Lawrence, first wrote about Taos early in the century, they inspired artists from around the world to similarly travel west. Writers such as Richard Bradford (*Red Sky at Morning*), Willa Cather (*Death Comes for the Archbishop*) and Wallace Stegner (*Angle of Repose*) came to Santa Fe and wrote about the area. One of the region's most famous residents, artist Georgia O'Keeffe first visited New Mexico in 1929, spending many summers in the state before taking up permanent residence. Her work had a tremendous impact on how people perceived this part of the world and a museum dedicated to her art opened in Santa Fe in 1997.

Not to be outdone by their well known neighbors, Ruidoso, just north of Alamogordo, is listed as one of *The 100 Best Small Art Towns in America* in John Villani's book and is home to a variety of artists and craftsmen with a large number of galleries representing their work. The area is the home of the Hubbard Museum of the American West (formerly known as Museum of the Horse), and close by is the courthouse in Lincoln, where the infamous Billy the Kid made his escape.

Also nearby is the Smokey the Bear Museum in Capitan. In 1945, the U.S. Forest Service began using a bear as a symbol for a forest fire prevention campaign. When a two-and-a-half month old, black bear cub was found clinging to the trunk of a burned tree after a fire in the Capitan Mountains in May 1990, the rangers decided to call him "Smokey." The following month he was taken to the National Zoo in Washington, D.C. and New Mexico's bear became the living symbol of the already well-known fire preventing Smokey Bear.

Hollywood has sought out New Mexico's unique and diverse locations and mild climate for shooting a variety of films, dating back to the silent Westerns with Tom Mix. In fact, Thomas Alva Edison came to the state and filmed *Indian Day School* in

Right
One of only two known 47-star flags that were produced has been displayed at the Tularosa Basin Historical Society Museum in Alamogordo since being donated by Wade Topping in 1999. Courtesy, Tularosa Basin Historical Society Museum

Below
Navajo artist, R.C. Gorman is know as much for his flamboyant personality as his colorful paintings of Navajo women. Courtesy, MNM #156932

1898—beginning a long relationship between New Mexico and the film industry. In recent years, movies such as *Butch Cassidy and the Sundance Kid*, *The Milagro Beanfield War*, and *Wyatt Earp* have featured the New Mexico landscape.

Many celebrities have chosen to relocate to New Mexico—some permanently and some seasonally—and a number have generously given back to the state. The

Above
Jackalope pottery, with several locations throughout the state features unique items for residents and tourists. Pictured here is the store in Santa Fe which contains an eclectic mix of items for sale in a sprawling open-air setting. Children enjoy music and puppet shows while their parents shop. © Corrie Photography

Greer Garson Theatre Center on the campus of the College of Santa Fe, is named for the actress, who along with her husband Buddy Fogelson, was a long-time resident and contributed much to the area. They also helped to establish the Pecos National Monument with their donation of land to the National Park Service.

The Pueblos have retained their unique individual cultures and languages, yet share similar religions, lifestyles and philosophies. They have a common economy but have independent governments. Although traditionally Indians have relied on farming, pottery-making, jewelry and various crafts for their livelihoods, more and more they have combined their cultural beliefs with employment in a variety of fields away from the reservations. In recent years, efforts have been underway to develop their economy at home, as well. The most

*Mariachis entertain in Santa Fe.
© Corrie Photography*

*Fresco artist, Frederico Vigil, pictured here with one of his canvases has created many historical paintings.
© Corrie Photography*

147

Right
Gary E. Johnson, Governor since 1994, is the first to be elected to two consecutive four-year terms. Courtesy, the office of Governor Johnson

Below
Local pottery for sale at the Indian Market in Santa Fe. ©1999 Chris Corrie

controversial of these has been the growth of casinos. In fact, the Camel Rock tourist attraction even has a casino just across the road.

The Hispanic culture also has been a great contributor to the heart of New Mexico, combining their traditions and religious influences with contemporary society. The adobe mission church architecture still effects the style of homes found in Santa Fe today.

Gary E. Johnson is the first Governor of New Mexico to be elected to two consecu-

tive four-year terms. His goal has been to improve the quality of life for New Mexico's citizens. To that end, his strongest focus has been improving education by making it more accountable and he is a booster of school vouchers. Sometimes controversial, he is a supporter of legalized drugs and has also worked towards raising the state's economic level by running the state as if it were a business. Johnson, a successful businessman before becoming governor, also holds the distinction of being a triathlete. Among the varied activities he has participated in to promote physical fitness are his five bike treks across the state.

New Mexico is atypical in yet another way—it has a "citizen" Legislature. None of its members is paid a salary. They work on a short schedule and are restricted to fiscal matters, subjects introduced or bills previously passed, and since vetoed, by the Governor.

While Santa Fe is the state capital, today its resident population is third behind Albuquerque and Las Cruces. Most growth in the state has occurred in metropolitan areas. Las Cruces, the second largest city in the state, is one of the fastest growing communities in the United States. Its population increased by nearly 62 percent between 1980 and 1985. With its ideal

Vactioners enjoy rafting on the Rio Grande outside of Santa Fe. © Corrie Photography

Right
A spectacular sculpture, "Free Spirits at Noisy Water" in front of the Hubbard Museum of the American West (formerly the Museum of the Horse) at Ruidoso Downs chronicles the contributions of the horse through a richly diverse collections of fine art, family heirlooms and western memorabilia. Courtesy, The Hubbard Museum of the American West

Near right
The Santa Fe Southern railway is in use for public and private events and day trips to Lamy, as well as transporting freight. © Corrie Photography

Far right
Shoppers carefully select their fruits and vegetables at the Farmers Market in the train station parking lot near downtown Santa Fe. This is very popular on Saturdays and Tuesday mornings offering unique food from the area. © 2000 Chris Corrie

150

Organ Mountains, east of Las Cruces. Courtesy, Las Cruces CVB

Below
The Hubbard Museum of the American West in Ruidoso is one of the most respected museums in the state, housing the Museum of the Horse and the Anne C. Stradling Collection. It features a magnificent collection of carriages, wagons, saddles, fine art and Indian artifacts. The role of the horse is highlighted in great detail. Photo by Mark Doth. Courtesy, Village of Ruidoso

location in south-central New Mexico—225 miles south of Albuquerque and 45 miles north of El Paso, Texas—and 350 days of sunshine per year, it's no wonder why.

Albuquerque's name came from the Duke of Alburquerque (the "r" was later dropped), who was the viceroy of New Spain. Santa Fe means "holy faith" in Spanish. Where the name Las Cruces comes from is the subject of some disagreement. The most popular theory is that sometime during the 1700s a bishop, a priest, a Mexican army colonel, four trappers and four choirboys were attacked near the Rio Grande and only one choirboy survived. He put up crosses at the site and the area became known as El Pueblo del Jardin de Las Cruces, or City of the Garden of the Crosses. Another theory holds that crosses in the area marked the sites of various Apache attacks. This is similar to yet another theory that holds that in 1830, Las Cruces was the site of an attack on 40 or more travelers from Taos during which none of the travelers survived. The most peaceful theory is that the name is simply the Spanish translation for crossing, or crossroads.

Folklorico dancers at the Mesilla Festival, held in historic Old Mesilla, just west of Las Cruces. Las Cruces CVB

*Below
Pete Domenici, U.S. Senator representing New Mexico since 1972, is shown here proudly wearing a watch displaying the "Zia," a modern version of an ancient symbol of the sun. The four points radiating from the circle reflect the philosophy of the Zia Pueblo who believed the number four to be sacred—representing the earth's four directions, four seasons of the year and four time periods of life (childhood, youth, adulthood and old age). Courtesy, the office of Senator Domenici*

Las Cruces is the most widely known chile-producing region in the United States. The whimsical nature of New Mexicans is evidenced by it being the only state with an official question—"red or green?" This references the frequently-asked question about what kind of chile one prefers with their food. Pecans, onions and various other crops are also produced in the area.

In the late 1980s an amateur paleontologist discovered a site in the Las Cruces area that the Smithsonian Institution considers the finest fossilized footprints from an era that existed about 600 million years ago.

Albuquerque the largest city in the state, with one of the most ethnically diverse populations in the country has a metropolitan area expected to reach 700,000 in 2000. The city is making a concerted effort to maintain its quality of life and control urban sprawl and at the same time revitalize its down-town. Present Mayor Jim Baca is concerned about uncontrolled growth impacting the region's limited natural resources. Although there have been repeated attempts to revive downtown in the past, the expectation is that this time it will be successful because it's controlled by builders who previously avoided the area.

While Santa Fe has been famous for the Santa Fe Trail, Albuquerque has long been known for Route 66, a waystation for travelers, immortalized in John Steinbeck's *Grapes of Wrath*. Albuquerque has dedicated its Summerfest in July 2001 to celebrating the Route's 75th anniversary with many events including "Flicks on 66" featuring films associated with the famous highway.

Visitors are attracted to the growing community of Alamogordo by the White Sands National Monument and the Mescalero-Apache Indian Reservation. Contributing to its growth are the nearby Holloman Air Force Base and the White Sands Missle Range. Alamogordo, displaying New Mexico's sense of humor brags that thusfar it hasn't had any earthquakes, riots, tornadoes, hurricanes, tidal waves, floods, mudslides or smog.

New Mexico's institutions of higher education continue to thrive and are led by the University of New Mexico and New Mexico State University.

The University of New Mexico, founded in 1892 began on a 20-acre campus with 25 students two miles east of Albuquerque. Today the campus sits on 600 acres along old Route 66 in the heart of Albuquerque, and is the state's largest university, with more than 30,000 students on five campuses. UNM offers nationally ranked academics, exceptional research, recognized athletics and an architecturally unique Spanish Pueblo Revival campus with a nationally recognized Campus Arboretum. UNM is a Carnegie I Research university, one of 88 in the country and one of two that is also designated a Hispanic-serving institution.

UNM faculty members include a Nobel Laureate, a MacArthur Fellow, several are members of national academies and many have been published in professional journals. The University has campuses in Gallup, Los Alamos and Valencia County as well as an education center in Taos.

The New Mexico Museum of Natural History in Albuquerque uses high-tech tools such as holograms and fiber optics to help tell its story. Stand inside a live volcano, experience the Dynamax theatre, or take the "Evo-later" back to the age of dinosaurs. Photo by Dick Kent. ACVB

Right
Chile ristras at the Farmers Market. Las Cruces CVB

Below
Visitor's can explore the subterranean fantasyland of stalagmites, stalactites and helictites known as Carlsbad Calverns, often referred to as "The 8th wonder of the world." At 750 feet below ground, the caverns are a constant 56 degrees, comfortable for touring yea round! Pictured here is "Green Lake Room." Photo by Russ Finley. Courtesy, Carlsbad Caverns National Park

UNM has seven libraries and houses federal and state documents.

Among the University's outstanding research units are the High Performance Computing Center, Cancer Research and Treatment Center, Center for High Technology Materials, and the Center for Micro-Engineered Ceramics. It offers programs from certificates to doctorates including: rural medicine program, photography, clinical law, and family medicine. The School of Medicine and the School of Engineering ranks as among the top nationwide. UNM's anthropology, biology, Latin American and Western history programs have respected national reputations.

Las Cruces is the home of New Mexico State University, New Mexico's land-grant institution—the only one classified as Research I that is also designated Hispanic and minority-serving by the federal government. New Mexico was still a territory when Las Cruces College, the forerunner to New Mexico State University, opened in a two-room adobe building in the fall of 1888. Its organizers could not have imagined the NMSU of today—a major research university with a 900-acre main campus and 15,000 students.

The early history of NMSU reflects the

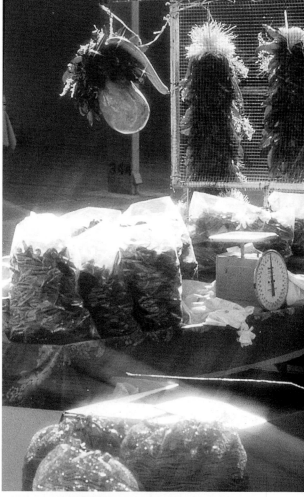

Top
Mexican folk dancers entertain the crowd in the museum's amphitheater during the annual La Fiesta de San Ysidro. Antique farm implements can be seen in the background. Courtesy, New Mexico Farm and Ranch Heritage Museum

Below
A young visitor enjoys feeding one of the dairy calves after the daily milking demonstration. Courtesy, New Mexico Farm and Ranch Heritage Museum

The New Mexico Farm and Ranch Heritage Museum sits on a 47-acre site with 25,000 square feet of exhibit space in the shadows of the Organ Mountains in Las Cruces. Its long portales gives the feel of a hacienda. Courtesy, New Mexico Farm and Ranch Heritage Museum

Right
A sculpture titled "The Quest for Knowledge" is a gathering place for students outside the Zuhl Library on the NMSU campus. NMSU

Far right
NMSU Professor Steve Stochaj works with student Ulisse Bravar on subatomic particles known as cosmic rays to understand more about the structure and evolution of the universe. NMSU

Below
The Center for the Sustainable Development of Arid Lands is the newest campus building, a state-of-the-art research facility dedicated to agricultural and natural resource studies. NMSU

New Mexico Museum of Arts and Culture in Santa Fe. © 2000 Chris Corrie

color and flavor of its Western heritage. The first commencement would have taken place in 1883 but the college's one and only senior, Sam Steel, was fatally shot, an innocent bystander in a hold-up. The first graduating class in 1884 included Fabian Garcia, a pioneer chile breeder who put the school on the map with the release of the nation's first commercial variety in 1921.

The campus itself became part of Southwestern history: famed architect Henry Trost drew up the original campus plan and designed several of the early college buildings, many still standing today around the commons area called the Horseshoe. The hallmark of the post-war years was growth—in enrollment, facilities, research and scholarship. Famed astronomer Clyde Tombaugh, discoverer of the planet Pluto, came to the college in 1955 and began a research program that today ranks among the nation's finest. And, Professor Robert Golden was the first to discover naturally occurring antimatter.

In 1960, a constitutional amendment changed the college name from the New Mexico College of Agriculture and Mechanic Arts to reflect the transition from what some had labeled a "cow college" to a comprehensive land-grant institution— New Mexico State University.

That stature was boosted in 1987 when the university was classified by the Carnegie Foundation for the Advancement of Teaching as a Research I University, another one of only 88 in the country, based on levels of federal research support and numbers of doctoral degrees awarded.

Today, research expenditures exceed $100 million a year in widely recognized areas of expertise such as arid lands and desert ecology studies; bridge inspection and safety training; bilingual special education; artificial intelligence; and optics, photonics, and microlaser development. Its degree programs are extensive.

NMSU operates one of the world's largest university-owned telescopes, at a site in the nearby Sacramento Mountains, for a consortium of universities including the University of Chicago, Princeton and others. Under a NASA contract, the Physical Science Laboratory manages the world's largest scientific balloon research program, launching probes from sites as remote as Antarctica and Greenland.

Perhaps the most important milestone, however, was the report of the team reviewing NMSU for reaccredidation in 1998.

New Mexico's state capitol, situated a few blocks south of Santa Fe's historic plaza, is known as the "Round House" because of its unusual shape. It is designed in a modified territorial architectural style. The unique design of the State Capitol in Santa Fe. ©2000 Chris Corrie

157

Members of a Zuni Hotshot Crew working "hot spots" on a hillside area during the Cerro Grande fire in 2000. Courtesy, NPS

Team members said they were impressed by the rich diversity of the student body, by the important role that students play in university decision-making, and by the fact that students described their professors as "inspirational mentors."

The state has long been proud of scientific advances at the Los Alamos National Laboratory but it was beset by difficulties as the new century began and under intense media scrutiny. On 43 square miles of mesas and canyons and 35 miles northwest of Santa Fe, the Laboratory is the largest employer in the area. Clouded by ongoing concerns of security breaches, the area was hard-hit when a "controlled burn," the Cerro Grande fire developed into a full-fledged wildfire. The fire, burning 48,000 acres, destroyed more than 200 homes and part of the Los Alamos National Laboratory, prompting concerns about safety issues at the Laboratory and also raised questions about the National Park Service officials decision to go forward with the burn. Originally set in Bandelier National Monument, on May 4, 2000, it was declared a wildfire the following day. Although structures had not been threatened for a number of days, the fire was not declared officially 100 percent contained until June 7. Bandelier Superintendent Roy Weaver, under intense criticism, retired as a result.

The stunning beauty of of New Mexico's land and the fascination of its cultures are attractive to all who have come to the state to stay. For it may be here that one finds the true, abiding wealth of New Mexico. The mesas in the evening sun are as beautiful today as in centuries past, and as long as the tricultural mix can avoid becoming too homogenized, it will continue to enrich the lives of residents and visitors alike. There is some combination here, of space and color and light, of challenge and occasional reward, that is as attractive to modern technological man as it was to the Pueblos who loved it first. It was they who first dug turquoise from the earth, a stone that is worn today by New Mexicans of every culture. Some say the stone is a piece of the New Mexican sky. If that is so, one could do worse than to wear it wherever he goes.

Barry Kennedy with the Blue Ridge Hot Shot team watches to make sure the fire doesn't cross the creek in Santa Clara Canyon. Photo by Eddie Moore, Albuquerque Journal

A spectacular view of sunflowers on the Mesa at Ruidoso. Photo by Anne Brunell. Courtesy, Ruidoso Valley Chamber of Commerce

159

Although present-day lumberjacks prefer chainsaws to double-bitted axes, timber producers continue to provide building materials that sustain the state's urban growth. From the Department of Development Collection. NMSRCA

Chronicles of Leadership

From stone age to space age, the history of business in New Mexico is a fascinating story. Long before Spanish conquistadores appeared on the Rio Grande in the sixteenth century, indigenous Indian tribes carried on an active trade in agricultural products, pottery, salt, dried meat, and turquoise. Other items unavailable locally, such as shells and exotic feathers for ceremonial purposes, were exchanged over great distances from one village to the next.

After Juan de Oñate founded New Mexico's first permanent colony in 1598, his followers depended mainly on subsistence farming for support. Lacking industry and mineral resources, the settlement produced few marketable commodities which caused a woeful balance of payments with New Spain. Besides sheep and woolen products, the colonists exported goods obtained from Indian neighbors. In return for their hides, skins, and coarse textiles, the natives received horses, metal tools, and weapons, innovations that brought profound changes to Indian cultures.

Because Spanish colonial policy mandated imprisonment for intruders, business relations with foreigners were almost nonexistent. That situation changed rapidly following Mexican independence, however. In 1821 William Becknell opened the Santa Fe Trail, the great commercial highway from Missouri to New Mexico. Besides providing local residents with a wondrous array of merchandise, the trail established contacts between New Mexicans and Anglo-Americans that prepared the way for United States conquest during the Mexican War.

When hostilities ended, the military presence in New Mexico caused a brief boom since Army payrolls and supply contracts greatly increased the amount of cash in circulation. Anglo entrepreneurs established new industries and began prospecting for precious metals despite Indian hostilities. In the towns, banks, newspapers, hotels, and other service industries sprang up.

New Mexico remained remote, however, until the railroad pushed over Raton Pass in 1878, integrating the territory into the national economy. Trains not only provided markets for livestock and minerals but also brought a throng of immigrants who introduced eastern ideas and fashions. Irrigation projects and other technological departures led to expansion in agriculture at the turn of the century. After World War I the discovery of important oil and gas reserves caused rapid development in the state's northwest and southeast corners.

World War II stimulated a new wave of economic growth. Frequently, servicemen stationed within the state decided to remain after discharge. Development of the atomic bomb at Los Alamos gave an advantage in securing peacetime nuclear energy and aerospace projects. More recently, the national migration to the Sun Belt has caused another population surge. Attracted by the climate and a pool of skilled personnel, many high-technology companies have established themselves within the state.

The organizations whose stories are detailed on the following pages have chosen to support this important literary and civic project. They illustrate the variety of ways in which individuals and their businesses have contributed to the growth and development of the state. The civic involvement of New Mexico's businesses, institutions of learning, and government, in cooperation with its citizens, has made the state an excellent place to live and work.

C H A P T E R   I X

THE ALBUQUERQUE JOURNAL

The *Albuquerque Journal* is a home-owned, independent morning newspaper, which is a rarity in today's conglomerate-run newspaper industry. Published 365 days a year, the *Albuquerque Journal* has a circulation throughout New Mexico and into Texas, Colorado and Arizona.

The *Albuquerque Journal* traces its history back to 1880. It is the successor to a newspaper called the *Golden Gate*, which was established in June of that year. In Fall 1880, the owner of the *Golden Gate* died and Journal Publishing Company was founded. The first *Albuquerque Daily Journal* was published on October 14, 1880.

The *Daily Journal* was published on a single sheet of newsprint, folded to make four pages. Those pages were divided into five columns, and the headlines were miniature compared to today's. Advertising appeared on the front page. The *Daily Journal* was published in the evening until the first Territorial Fair opened in October 1881. On October 4 of that year, a morning *Journal* was published to record the day's events at the fair. The morning *Journal* continued for six issues. The last issue was published on Sunday, October 9—making it the first Sunday newspaper ever to appear in Albuquerque.

The *Daily Journal* was first published in Old Town, a present-day

T.H. Lang, president and publisher.

tourist attraction near downtown Albuquerque. In 1882 it moved to the "new" town near the railroad tracks. The operation was housed in a single room at Second and Silver streets. That year the evening paper was discontinued and the *Albuquerque Morning Journal* appeared. The *Morning Journal* continued until 1887, when it was absorbed by the *Albuquerque Daily Democrat*, a newspaper founded in Santa Fe, which had moved to Albuquerque.

Albuquerque Journal's *downtown office in 1985.*

The paper's name changed again in 1899 to the *Albuquerque Journal-Democrat*. A change in policy necessitated the dropping of *Democrat* from the paper's name in 1903, and it appeared again as the *Albuquerque Morning Journal*. Since 1925, the paper has been known as the *Albuquerque Journal* and followed an independent editorial policy.

As New Mexico's oldest, largest and only statewide newspaper, the *Albuquerque Journal* not only keeps the state's citizens informed, but it keeps them connected. The newspaper has always been a forum for public debate and a medium for information, providing news coverage on important issues throughout the city, state and country.

The *Journal* is home to some of the state's best-known journalists, including columnist Jim Belshaw and cartoonist John Trever. The *Journal's* desks keep readers informed and involved with a wide variety of issues.

The newspaper prides itself on keeping up with the latest technology and provides a vast array of services to its readers. The *Journal's* web site hosts more than 6,000 pages of

news, features and information, as well as on-line advertising for readers. In print, the *Journal* publishes four editions a day—providing readers with up-to-date information and breaking news stories.

The Journal Publishing Co. is headed by brothers T.H. and W.P. Lang. T.H. Lang, president/publisher, has a longstanding interest in the state. An Albuquerque native who attended the University of New Mexico, T.H. Lang has been at the helm of the *Journal* since 1971. He has expanded the newspaper's presence throughout New Mexico and established *Journal* bureaus in Santa Fe, Las Cruces and Washington, D.C.

"The *Journal* has always been the

Albuquerque Journal's *current location at Journal Center.*

newspaper of record for the state, and I want our coverage and reach to live up to that," Lang said.

In addition to the *Journal's* four editions, the newspaper also publishes news and advertising sections emphasizing various regions, including the *Journal North*, covering the state Capitol of Santa Fe and northern New Mexico; the *West Side Journal*, covering Rio Rancho and the metro area's West Side; and the *Journal South*, covering Valencia County. Journal Publishing Co. also publishes the weekly *Mountain View Journal*, focusing on the East Mountains and Torrance County.

Keeping with his philosophy of being the newspaper of record and information, Lang maintains an investigative team specializing in in-depth reporting on the people and institutions that affect the lives of New Mexicans. He also has fought

against secrecy in government.

"Newspapers are empowered by the people under the First Amendment to report and record for the people in our free society. This is a duty and a privilege," Lang said.

Lang has also extended the newsroom's reach outside state borders. The newspaper has sent reporters to cover the Death Squads in El Salvador, politics in Mexico, the economic crunch in Russia and the floods in Honduras.

Community outreach is also a commitment met by the Journal Publishing Co. In an effort to give back to the community, the *Journal* has awarded nearly $500,000 in college scholarships since 1984. The *Journal* also sponsors many events, seminars, fairs and other activities aimed at benefiting charitable organizations.

"We are committed to participating in the ongoing progress and promise of New Mexico and Albuquerque," Lang says.

AMERICAN PROPERTY MANAGEMENT CORP.

Based on their mutual love of the Land of Enchantment, native New Mexicans Jim Long and Michael Gallegos formed American Property Management Corporation (APMC) in 1991. Today the corporation owns and manages 26 lodging properties encompassing 5,980 rooms throughout the United States and employs more than 4,000 people.

APMC's foundation was laid years before the partnership of Long and Gallegos began. Both men come from multiple generations of native New Mexicans. Long's family roots are from Pena Blanca, NM where his grandparents Telesfor and Guadalupe Aragon once owned and operated the town's only grocery store. Gallegos' family is from Las Vegas, NM. As an 11-year-old boy, Gallegos convinced the La Fonda Hotel in Santa Fe to give him a job parking cars. By the time he was 18, Gallegos was the assistant general manager at La Fonda.

Long is a 1978 graduate of Valley High School and Gallegos graduated from St. Michael's High School in 1977. Both men attended the University of New Mexico. Long graduated from UNM's school of architecture and Gallegos graduated with a double major in economics and political science. Out of a love of architecture and real estate, as well as with a keen sense of business, Long founded American Property in 1987.

These two successful businessmen joined forces in 1991 with the formation of APMC. The company purchased its first hotel in New Mexico, the Hilton Las Cruces. By 1999, the corporation was ranked 21 out of the top 100 hotel owners and developers in the United States.

Sensing a loss of the native culture and traditions that are indigenous to New Mexico, Long and Gallegos felt responsible for ensuring the preservation of New Mexico's unique culture and its traditions. In an effort to provide travelers with a complete New Mexican experience, they created New Mexico Heritage Hotels and *¡TRADITIONS! A*

The lobby of the Hilton Las Cruces embodies the Mexican culture that threads throughout the Las Cruces community. Just minutes away from Historic Old Mesilla, the hotel's Mexican colonial interiors create an ambiance reflective of the area's rich traditions.

FESTIVAL MARKETPLACE. New Mexico Heritage Hotels is an umbrella for a collection of New Mexico hotels owned by APMC. Each of these hotels embodies the New Mexican culture, spirit and tradition. Through architecture, landscaping, interior decorations, cuisine, art, music and entertainment, hotel guests receive a full New Mexican experience. The unique blend of Native American, Mexican, Spanish and Western cultural influences inspired the style of each hotel. The hotels were chosen because of their fertile history of New Mexico and their easy accessibility to some of the state's major attractions. APMC has hotels in all the major cities of New Mexico, guaranteeing that the traveler to the state can experience the state's offerings to their fullest.

Rising above the Rio Grande Valley, the Hilton Las Cruces is the only AAA 3-Diamond award-winning hotel in Southern New Mexico. The hotel's Mexican colonial interiors create an ambiance reflective of the area's long history and rich traditions. Its location is unparalleled—just minutes away from Historic Old Mesilla, which is surrounded by

haciendas filled with quaint shops and art galleries, and is rich in the area's folklore.

The Wyndham Garden Hotel in Albuquerque uses deep, rich, Southwestern colors and beautiful Native American style throughout its structure. Travelers can view the majestic Sandia Mountains from their rooms, take a ride on the world's longest tram or experience the Albuquerque Balloon Fiesta in October, when 900 hot air balloons fill the crystal clear New Mexico sky with magic.

Guests of the Albuquerque Old Town Inn, a Sheraton hotel, can experience 400 years worth of history at Albuquerque's Historic Old Town, which is adjacent to the hotel. The San Felipe de Neri Church, the world's oldest continuously-operated church in the United States is open for touring year round in Old Town. The Albuquerque Old Town Inn captures the history of Albuquerque through the usage of a traditional territorial style.

The landmark hotel defines a unique "Albuquerque style" through its multi-cultural design theme. The Grand Sala, outdoor portals, hand-crafted interiors and unique dining experiences provide hotel guests a memorable experience. The Albuquerque Old Town Inn creates a sense of nostalgia and revives the spirit of an earlier time in Albuquerque's history.

APMC's two hotels in Santa Fe encompass the appeal of "the city different." Located in the heart of Santa Fe, the Plaza Real is a picturesque boutique hotel featuring guestrooms and suites containing hand-crafted furnishings and art. Private balconies overlook a charming courtyard and offer enchanting views of Santa Fe. World-renowned shopping, dining, museums and art galleries are just steps away in the prominent Santa Fe Plaza. Featuring breathtaking views of the Jemez and Sangre de Cristo Mountains and just minutes from the Plaza is the Radisson Santa Fe. Guests can experience authentic music and dance from the area, with the Santa Fe Opera nearby and the internationally-acclaimed Benitez Cabaret flamenco dance troupe performing seasonally within the hotel.

¡TRADITIONS! A FESTIVAL MARKETPLACE provides a strategic site where New Mexico's unique heritage and diverse cultures can be experienced at a single location that personifies the natural beauty of the state and the warmth and friendliness of its people. *¡TRADITIONS! A FESTIVAL MARKETPLACE* is a vibrant festival marketplace that is visually appealing and provides a unique guest experience. The design of the marketplace combines typical New Mexican architectural design with colorful festive displays. The festival marketplace contains a unique wind garden, pedestrian plaza, cultural events building, hospitality center, native garden with Indian dance area and hornos, extensive landscaping, and brightly colored vendor pavilions.

¡TRADITIONS!-A FESTIVAL MARKETPLACE also hosts year-round events and performances including exhibits and shows, festivals, athletic events, educational demonstrations and traditional fiestas. All of these events showcase New Mexico's spiritual, cultural, social, historical and physical enchantment in a beautiful dance, music and drama format. In the wind garden, a 22-foot harp makes use of the wonderful wind elements out in the center. The Plaza Gazebo is utilized for musical and dance performances and elevates from two grand stairways adorned with beautiful iron lighting elements.

The Land of Enchantment is full of a rich history and blending

Nestled in the heart of Santa Fe, the Plaza Real is a picturesque boutique hotel featuring hand-crafted furnishings and art. From the Native American interiors to the private balconies that overlook a charming courtyard, guests can truly experience the culture and traditions of "the city different."

of cultures that make it a truly unique experience. Growing up in New Mexico, Long and Gallegos recognized the power of the beauty of the Southwest. By using their backgrounds and successful business strategy, the two businessmen have created a corporation that allows travelers through-out the world to enjoy the best traditions and culture New Mexico has to offer.

GERALD CHAMPION REGIONAL MEDICAL CENTER

Concern for the community has been at the heart of Gerald Champion since its beginnings after World War II.

What has become a regional medical center serving both civilians and military personnel began with the efforts of local residents to build a basic country hospital for Otero County. In 1946, when the Otero County Hospital Association formed, the only facility in the area was the Rousseau Hospital with six upstairs rooms, in the house of a registered nurse named Mrs. Rousseau.

The Association launched a fund raising campaign at the beginning of 1947; its goal was to raise $100,000 that would be joined with $50,000 in matching federal funds to build a federal aid hospital. This was the first of three steps including planning the facility's location and building it.

The successful effort was spearheaded by Gerald D. Champion, a businessman from Alamogordo and Tularosa, who became the Association's chairman. The drive was supported by the Association's directors: M.C. Cauthen, C.E. Moore, M.R. Prestridge, James E. Mahill, and L.A. Hendrix, all of Alamogordo; and Fr. Francis Redmon of Tularosa. Champion, however, did not live to see the hospital built. He was killed in February 1948 when a plane he was piloting from Carlsbad to Alamogordo crashed in the Sacramento

The original Gerald Champion Memorial Hospital in 1949.

Mr. Gerald Champion.

Mountains. The community voted to name the new facility in his honor.

The fund drive—which included a livestock auction to sell animals and other commodities donated by area residents, raffles, several dances and a carnival—surpassed its target but, because costs had risen, fell short of raising all the funds needed for construction. The community voted overwhelmingly for a $50,000 bond issue to complete the financing, and construction began. The site cost $2,000, and its owner O.G. Cady, donated $500 to the drive. The rooms were furnished largely by additional donations; plaques on their doors acknowledged these benefactors.

The 24-bed Gerald Champion Memorial Hospital was dedicated

with ceremonies on Sunday, July 31, 1949. Its complex included a dormitory for female staff, with three bedrooms, a small living room, and a kitchen. Later it became the maintenance building and 50 years later, it was the last of the original hospital structures standing.

Scheduled to open on Tuesday, August 2, the hospital actually served its first patient, three-year-old Peggy Lee Tefft of Monista, at 9:30 a.m. on Monday morning. She was brought in as an emergency with acute bronchial pneumonia. The first patient on Tuesday was Mrs. W.S. Hudman, who walked across the street from her home and was admitted at 3 a.m. She delivered the hospital's first baby, named Barbara, two hours later.

Initially the staff included a nurse administrator and a surgical nurse. A nurse anesthetist, the wife of one of the three doctors in town, also helped out, as did a number of registered nurses who volunteered when things got tight. A technician, paid on commission, ran the laboratory and x-ray, and a cook, not a dietitian, operated the kitchen.

In 1954, to accommodate an increasing number of births, the hospital acquired surplus barracks from Fort Bliss and converted them to an obstetrics unit. Five years later a two-story addition opened, adding another 26 beds, expanded laboratory facilities, radiology and dietary services, and outpatient and support areas.

The staff grew apace. In 1952, it added a second cook and by 1955, there was a lab assistant who often doubled as record's clerk, and several aides. In 1959, Charlene Ward joined the hospital as assistant administrator. Within a year she was named to the top job, a position she filled for the next decade. She was one of three female hospital administrators in the state; the other two were nuns at hospitals in Albuquerque and Santa Fe. She served as the first female president of the New Mexico Hospital Association and initiated the first visit to Gerald Champion by the Joint

Commission on Accreditation of Hospitals.

As the Tularosa basin's population grew and Medicare came into being, the hospital's need for space increased. More and more, patients had to be cared for in the hospital's corridors, which led to the addition in 1968 of a third floor with another 21 beds, bringing the total to 71.

By 1975, with needs for an intensive care/cardiac unit, expanded radiology facilities and a new obstetrics department pressing, and the original building no longer meeting hospital and building codes, the hospital underwent renovation. The oldest section of the building ceased being used for patient care, though it still housed support services.

As healthcare continued to change and the population to rise, demand for outpatient care grew. By the early 1980s, Champion's emergency department facilities were inadequate, and surgery suites too small. It had no private or isolation rooms, and patients were again being cared for in the halls. The Hospital Association turned to Otero County for help with another major capital project and in 1985, completed a renovation and the addition of another 20 beds.

The next decade saw many more advances in the hospital's capabilities. It reached a joint service arrangement with the Las Cruces renal dialysis facility to place a satellite unit on its campus, operated and staffed by Las Cruces and the building and equipment provided by Champion. It also met increased demand from the community and nearby military bases for obstetric services and ambulatory care, with major renovations on those units completed in 1992.

As the hospital's 50th anniversary approached, it focused on the future, recognizing the need for additional services as well as for flexibility to adapt to the ever-changing health care environment.

The result was a completely new Medical Center (opened in December 1999), confirming Gerald Champion's pivotal role in the region. With

149,000 square-feet and 95 beds on a 65-acre campus, the acute care facility undertook a partnership with Holl-oman Air Force Base. With 500 employees and a medical staff of more than 60 that includes both private and military doctors, it became one of the first shared civilian/military facilities in the United States. Federal funds helped bring state-of-the art equipment to the area more quickly than would otherwise have been possible, improving services for everyone in the community.

Gerald Champion Regional Medical Center entered the third millennium

Gerald Champion Regional Medical Center.

The original Board of Directors, left to right bottom row: Andrew Hendrix, Miss Grace Powe, Mrs. Jas F. Mahill, Miss Opal Haynes, A.L. George, Leo Aubel, Walter Lafferty, Ray Sowell, Mrs. Nona Champion, Karen Champion. Top row: Dan King, John L. Larkin, Dr. Ernest Faigle, Forrest Chambers, Rev. Jesse Watson, Rev. C.K. France, Mose C. Cauthen, and Walter Wingfield.

as an outstanding health care facility. In a difficult environment, it continues to grow, blending two communities under a single roof and improving, in the process, its ability to attract top physicians and nurses. It constantly looks to the future, assessing community and physician needs and working to meet them.

COLLEGE OF THE SOUTHWEST

College of the Southwest's story is an inspiring one. It is a story of dreams and determination. It is a story of hearts and hands working together. Most importantly, it is the story of one community's belief in its future.

The story begins in the early half of the 20th century, when a young man scaled the heights near Cloudcroft to gain a panoramic view of this Land of Enchantment. In prayerful meditation, the youth beseeched God to give him New Mexico for Christian education.

That young man was B. Clarence Evans, and he was destined to become the founder and first president of what would eventually become College of the Southwest.

After many prayers and many years, Evans' dream finally became a reality. In 1956, in facilities rented in downtown Hobbs, Hobbs Baptist College was chartered as a two-year junior college. It was changed to New Mexico Baptist College in 1958, when the school became a four-year college.

The college soon grew beyond its original design, however, and the need for a non-denominational college—as well as a larger, permanent location—became a motivating force. By 1961, the college obtained the present 162-acre site on the Lovington Highway.

In 1962, to reflect the expanded vision of the entire community that had embraced this fledgling institution as their own, College of the Southwest was founded. CSW was—and still is—centered in non-denominational Christian principles, free enterprise philosophy, independent support and governance, and debt-free operations. To this day, CSW is set apart from almost every other college or university in the nation by this mission.

Dr. Nell McLeroy, president from 1960-1964, said it best, "This marks a milestone...for this section of the Southwest."

In January 1964 groundbreaking at the new site finally began. With the support of the community and a new president, Dr. J.L. Burke (1964-1970),

Dr. J.L. Burke (president of CSW from 1964-1970) oversees construction of the multi-purpose administration building on the campus of the first institution of higher learning in Lea County. (1964)

CSW grew to include an administration building, Scarborough Memorial Library, and a science building.

Dr. Claude B. Wivel (1970-71) and Dr. Eugene Hughes (1972-74) witnessed the completion and dedication of the student center.

In 1975, Dr. Bruce Evans became president, and another bustling period of growth began. The Mabee Southwest Heritage Center, a 238-seat auditorium, was completed in 1976, and in 1978 CSW constructed Jane Adams Hall, the first on-campus student housing for higher education in Lea County.

That same year, CSW's budding Students in Free Enterprise program began garnering national recognition. CSW's SIFE team was ranked among a handful of top colleges in the nation, an achievement which SIFE members uphold to this day.

In 1980, with the completion of the Mabee Physical Fitness Center, CSW's campus was comprised of seven buildings. However, more on-campus housing was desperately needed; thus, the Bob and Adele Daniels Residence Hall was constructed in 1981.

As the only four-year college in a 100-mile radius, College of the Southwest served many students from the southwestern New Mexico and West Texas regions even before the campus looked appropriately "collegiate." (1970)

The addition of baseball and soccer fields in 1985, under president Robert Galvan (1984-86), allowed for a new dimension of college life through team sports.

William L. McDonnell served as CSW's next president on an interim basis during 1986-87, followed by Herman Barlow in 1987-89.

The presidency of Joan M. Tucker, which began in 1989 and continues to the present, ushered in a period of tremendous expansion and visibility. The Distinguished Lecture Series, begun in 1991, has brought a number of renowned speakers to this remote part of the state. Past speakers include Dr. Thomas Sowell; William F. Buckley, Jr.; Arthur Schlesinger; Edwin Newman; Dr. Sally Ride; Captain James Lovell; Linda Wertheimer; Dave Barry; and Catherine Crier, to name only a few.

The following year, CSW expanded again, this time into neighboring Eddy County where the Carlsbad campus currently serves the educational needs of approximately 150 students each semester.

In 1994, a new dormitory, the Thelma Linam Webber Hall, was dedicated in honor of the feisty Lea County pioneer and long-time advocate for CSW.

In 1994-95, a number of student organizations were also begun. Alpha Chi National Honor Society; the Southwest Association of Teachers; the Fellowship of Christian Athletes; and Sigma Tau Delta; the International English Honor Society, were added to the list of student associations.

In 1996-97, the college realized another milestone when a master's program in education was approved,

with majors in administration, counseling, and curriculum and instruction.

Besides the most obvious achievement of tripling its student enrollment over the past 10 years, CSW registered a number of other outstanding accomplishments in the '90s. CSW gained national recognition when it was named to collegiate guides by *U.S. News and World Report*, *Money* magazine, and *Time/Princeton Review*. CSW was even ranked among the top 10 Western regional liberal arts colleges for "Campus Diversity."

Thanks to a 1997 technology grant, CSW enjoys cutting edge technology with all on-campus network services. The college is also set apart by ELIN, the Estacado Library Information Network, a consortium which links CSW and four other Lea County libraries, thereby providing near-limitless research and information opportunities for the area.

A number of new programs have been added including an athletic training program; women's soccer and volleyball; the Center for Busi-

CSW's dedicated Board of Trustees witness an historic moment as the college breaks ground for a $6.2 million expansion of the campus. (1999)

Although College of the Southwest's enrollment and campus square footage have grown considerably over the years, there has always existed a certain "esprit de corps" among faculty, staff, and students. (1979)

ness Leadership, which offers professional development seminars to area businesses; and the privately-funded Center for Educational Excellence, which provides free on-site and off-site professional development training for Lea County teachers.

In September 1999, CSW underwent yet another groundbreaking upon completion of the largest community-supported capital campaign in the college's history. The $6.2 million campaign has prompted an explosion of construction and expansion that, when completed, will result in a 68 percent increase in total campus square footage.

Today, at the beginning of the new millennium, the surprising story of a little college in a rugged land continues. Founded on vision, faith, and determination, the college has evolved to embody the best of the great American experience. And now, looking to the future, new dreams, new successes, and new chapters await unfolding in the ongoing story of College of the Southwest.

CORONADO PAINT AND DECORATING CENTER

In August 1984, at the age of 37, Cervantes Roybal cashed in his retirement plan and sold his vintage 1959 Corvette to fulfill his lifelong dream of becoming a business owner. Cervantes, or "Buddy" as he is known to his friends, employees and business associates, began his career in paint and decorating with Sherwin Williams Paint Company, serving in a management position for more than 12 years in both Albuquerque and Santa Fe, New Mexico.

With his experience, Roybal opened Coronado Paint and Decorating Center in a converted warehouse space at 124 Chamisa, a tiny dead-end street in Santa Fe. With a small, 900 square-foot showroom, a bookkeeper and a paint clerk, Roybal was determined to establish a business based on the philosophy of "make customers, not sales." This philosophy proved successful and only three years later, Roybal was able to expand his business into the retail sales of tile, carpet, and window coverings, serving the needs of Santa Fe's growing housing industry.

This second location, at 3200 Cerrillos Road, on Santa Fe's "main street" quickly became known as the one-stop shopping place for the finishing products of new construction and remodeling projects. It also became known as a source for custom and imported tile and decorating accents, providing something a little different for a place known as "The City Different." Within the first five years of operation, gross sales surpassed the $1 million mark. Five years later, Roybal was able to secure a small business loan from The Bank of Santa Fe to purchase land and construct a new facility, providing nearly every option imaginable in the realm of paint, floor covering, wall covering, and window coverings.

This new store launched Coronado as northern New Mexico's largest paint and decorating center, and one of Santa Fe's most successful minority-owned businesses.

Located at 2929 Cerrillos Road in the heart of Santa Fe's business district, the store consists of a 7,000 square-foot showroom, a 14,000 square-foot warehouse space, and 25 full-time employees including his original bookkeeper and paint clerk, Claudia Ramirez and Phil Garcia, respectively. Ramirez now serves as Coronado's operations manager, and Garcia is paint sales manager.

After 17 years in business, the 54-year old Roybal attributes his success to his faith in God, his family, and his love for Santa Fe and its people. Through Coronado's tremendous growth and strides, it has maintained

In 1991, Coronado Paint and Decorating Center ribbon cutting cermony with Santa Fe Mayor Sam Pick and Chamber of Commerce Welcoming Committee.

a "home-owned and operated" atmosphere which builds customers' comfort, satisfaction and loyalty.

In addition to running his business, Roybal is heavily involved in the Santa Fe community, donating time to various volunteer activities and serving on the board of directors for several community organizations, including the Santa Fe Boys and Girls Club, Santa Fe Big Brothers Big Sisters, Santa Fe County Cham-

Outside view of Coronado Paint and Decorating Center.

ber of Commerce, and Santa Fe Partners in Education.

In 1999 Roybal's business and community leadership was recognized nationally with a "*Sam Walton Business Award*," for his service to the customer, respect for the individual, and persistence to strive for excellence. He was also named in the local newspaper, *The Santa Fe New Mexican,* as one of the "10 Individuals Who Made a Difference in Santa Fe."

Roybal believes that in his role as a businessman and community leader it is important to "remind the next genera-

At a local fund raising event, Buddy helped to raise over $46,000 for the Santa Fe Boys and Girls Club. From left to right: Santa Fe Mayor Delgado, Irene Roybal, and Buddy Roybal.

tion of leaders that they do not have to give in to the all-powerful dollar when doing business. The human elements of doing business—positive interaction, respect, and the successful fulfillment of needs—is so important and can really take you and your customer a long way."

A look into the future of Coronado Paint and Decorating shows projected revenues of over $7 million and a continued effort to meet the paint, flooring, and custom decorating needs of the community.

A look into Roybal's future shows a more focused enjoyment of the fruits of his labor by spending quality time with his wife Irene and his four children Dorinda, Valerie, Michael, and Melissa. He also hopes to spend more time traveling, especially on the roads of Northern New Mexico, driving a car from his collection of custom and vintage automobiles.

CREAMLAND DAIRIES, INC.

For nearly 50 years the name Creamland has been synonymous with fresh, delicious milk and dairy products. The growth of Creamland from humble beginnings to an instantly-recognized brand enjoyed today throughout New Mexico, is a story of astute business management, opportunity and foresight.

Creamland Dairies, Inc. was organized in 1937 by a group of dairy farmers, together with Albuquerque businessman Albert G. Simms. They purchased the Albuquerque Dairy Association, a dairy co-op for New Mexico, which had been established as a cooperative in 1920. They broke ground at 321 2nd Street NW to construct the first Creamland Plant. Here they produced milk in glass bottle containers under the management of Roy Campbell.

In time this site was destined to become the home of the Albuquerque Convention Center, as urban development changed the face of the downtown and forced the Creamland plant to relocate 18 blocks to the north, to 1911 2nd Street. This was in 1948, the same year that Mr. Campbell became general manager, and Creamland experienced considerable growth.

Creamland's home base remains at this location today, where its high quality dairy products are produced. During the 1960s New Mexico's first modern, filtered air, cottage cheese processing room was added here. Since the '90s significantly enlarging and modernization has occurred, utilizing the newest and finest equipment and processing techniques available, and establishing Creamland's reputation as one of the finest dairy processing plants in the Southwest.

But Creamland was destined to expand its product base beyond liquid milk. Ice cream production entered the picture in 1956, when Creamland merged with the Darrow Ice Cream Company, also located in Albuquerque. They used Darrow's processing facility at 500 Broadway SE.

Just a year later Creamland built a

Route driver delivers Creamland products in 1955.

second plant, in Farmington, in the northwest corner of the state. It was designed by Harold Schmalenberger, who also supervised its construction, and it was used for 11 years as Creamland's primary milk plant. Although the plant was closed in 1980, it continues to be useful as a distribution facility.

Other acquisitions were on the horizon for Creamland. In 1965 Earl Collins and his associates, together with Bell Dairy in Lubbock, Texas acquired controlling interest in Creamland Dairies; and Prices Creameries, Inc., of El Paso was taken over by Creamland in 1978. More consolidation occurred in July 1978 when Creamland, Bell, and Prices were all purchased by Dean Foods, a Chicago-based food company.

Creamland's base of products are sour cream, cottage cheese, ice cream and fluid milk which is sold as whole milk, light milk, chocolate milk, skim milk, and Milk Chugs. As the product line expanded, the containers

improved. Paper containers replaced the glass bottles in the early 1970s, and plastic containers in the gallon-size were introduced by 1978. Two years later Creamland built a bottle plant to produce its own plastic containers for milk products. But the latest innovation in containers is the cleverly-designed Milk Chug, presented in a handy size with easy-to-open-and-close flared cap.

The ingenious Milk Chug is one of the recent business successes for Creamland Dairies. While marketing studies showed that milk consumption among the region's predominantly older population was declining, it also demonstrated that younger people

Creamland Ice Cream Plant today.

would consume more milk if packaging, flavors, and versatility were enhanced. Creamland began generating this new product in low-fat chocolate, chocolate, 2% white, and strawberry flavors in pint, multi-pack, and quart sizes. An extensive awareness campaign ensued with a Chug Sweepstakes, nutrition events, wide-scale product sampling, and a strong presence at the 1999 Kodak Albuquerque International Balloon Fiesta. This brought Milk Chugs to the attention of 18-24 year olds, and garnered Creamland Dairies a National Award for Marketing Excellence from the Quality Chek'd Dairies. Quality Chek'd is an international, member-owned dairy co-op of which Creamland has been a member since 1960.

Another success started with Creamland's expansion into the ice cream business. When Creamland merged with the Darrow Ice Cream Company in 1956, the acquisition included Darrow's good reputation and 30 year history as one of the principal suppliers of ice cream in the state. By consolidating ice cream manufacturing operations to this plant, located at Broadway and Coal SE in Albuquerque, and with expansion and modernization to the facility over time, it became a major competitor in the ice cream market. Creamland is also the current supplier to all the Baskin Robbins stores in the Rocky Mountain Region, which includes New Mexico, Colorado and Wyoming. They are still the only manufacturer of ice cream in the state.

Currently Creamland employs nearly 300 people and maintains three facilities in Albuquerque with branches in Farmington, Santa Fe, and Gallup. Creamland fosters a family-like atmosphere with its workers who enjoy a reputation for hard work. Creamland is proud of the steady employment they provide and their stability as a leading business in the community. Also important to them is that Creamland receives all of the milk for its products from a New

Mexico farmers' co-op, keeping the milk in state for its own people. Sixty percent of the milk used by Creamland comes from the Rio Grande Valley region; the remaining 40 percent comes from the Roswell area.

Creamland commits itself to the community and the state each year by donating time, money and resources to those in need. Many causes are supported, from a 5K run for cancer awareness to local charity fund-raisers. An example of how Creamland's employees show their community spirit occurred during the Los Alamos fire disaster in Spring 2000. The Dairy donated two trailer loads of milk to the victims of the fire, but didn't stop there. Volunteers showed up on the weekend to help bottle gallon cartons of water for the firefighters and those displaced from their homes. The crisis impelled Creamland to simply react and help

Creamland Milk Plant today.

their consumers in their time of need, without looking for recognition or compensation.

In a dry climate such as New Mexico's, it is a tribute to the innovative thinking and strategic management that Creamland Dairies, Inc. could make the dairy industry there such a success. In this millennium year, Dean Foods celebrates Creamland's 75th anniversary.

Creamland Dairies Milk Plant (bottle washing room) in 1955.

THE FIRST NATIONAL BANK OF NEW MEXICO

The First National Bank of New Mexico was founded in 1963. It was established in Clayton, New Mexico near the Texas and Oklahoma borders and served communities in each of the three states. Initially, the bank was known as the First National Bank of Clayton and was an integral part of the communities it served. The bank came under its current ownership in March 1986 and has excelled as a part of Northeastern New Mexico commerce. Since coming under the ownership of the Reeves family of Clayton, The First National Bank of New Mexico has expanded its presence in northeastern New Mexico and currently serves five communities.

In 1998, the institution opened an office in Raton, New Mexico just across the border from Trinidad, Colorado. The Raton office has greatly enhanced the banking industry in the community and is highly-touted as the only "hometown" bank in Raton. Banking customers from both New Mexico and Colorado

The First National Bank of New Mexico is headquartered in Clayton, New Mexico and was established in 1963.

The First National Bank of New Mexico in Raton opened in 1998 and serves customers in both New Mexico and Colorado. There is also a loan process office in Miami, near Springer, New Mexico.

enjoy personalized service from The First National Bank of New Mexico in Raton. A loan processing office is also located in Miami, New Mexico, about 15 minutes west of Springer. Both offices have added to the quality of banking business in these rural areas.

In 1999, The First National Bank of New Mexico acquired Zia Bank in Tucumcari, New Mexico, and its branch in Logan. The Logan office was remodeled in 1999-2000 and celebrated its grand reopening in April 2000. The history and culture of the Logan office was preserved. The original teller cages still give an air of banking in the Old West. The Tucumcari office of The First National Bank of New Mexico

will be completely relocated in 2001. Construction has begun on a new building that will offer convenience to Tucumcari banking customers. The Tucumcari and Logan offices have both seen a significant number of increased deposits and both are well-respected institutions in their communities.

It was 1904 when Sim and Fred McFarland erected a building in Logan, New Mexico and began using the new building as the McFarland Mercantile. The McFarland Mercantile provided postal, general store, and banking needs to a rural area spanning in excess of 25,000 square miles along the banks of the Canadian River.

The McFarland brothers applied for and received its first state charter to conduct official banking business in 1923. Known then as the McFarland Brothers Bank of Logan, New Mexico, the volume of their banking business, combined with livestock trade, provided a living for themselves and their growing families.

Sim and Fred McFarland's own business welfare depended on the success of their neighbors. They actively encouraged settlement and the establishing of schools and churches. The bank was a central institution in the little town and provided many necessary services, contracts and bills of sale.

The First National Bank of New Mexico in Logan is rich in history and dates back to the turn of the 20th century.

Incorporated in the state banking system in January 1920, McFarland Brothers Bank obtained the required $25,000 of operating capital from family members and several Logan merchants. The major stockholders were relatives, thus the bank continued as a family-managed business, with members of Sim's and Fred's families working as bookkeepers, janitors and night guards as they grew up.

The records of the bank's status for those early years, all in handwritten entries, indicate how closely it was tied to the fortunes of the small community on which it depended. The small levels of yearly profit reflect all the difficult times experienced in Quay County, including hard winters, droughts, and agricultural depression.

Northeastern New Mexico saw its share of Wild West lawlessness including cattle rustling, gambling, bootlegging, and feuding that ended in gunfire. It was not until the 1920s and 1930s, however, that the bank was robbed in a holdup. In 1921, two young men rattled down the unpaved road from Harding County, intent on robbing the bank. Entering with pistols, they took $1,000 in silver and currency and shut Fred and his wife Nora in the vault. Fortunately, the vault door did not lock and Fred rushed out of the bank with a Winchester rifle just as the two thieves were rounding the corner heading north. A telephone call alerted the sheriff in NaraVisa and a posse started toward Logan. The posse actually passed the robbers, only to turn back when they met Fred galloping on horseback. The posse caught the bank robbers 20 miles north of Logan, out of gas and bogged down in a sandy creek bed. Not all the money was recovered and it is rumored locally that the thieves fed the silver dollars into the gas tank, located under the front seat of their Ford Roadster.

The bank was robbed again in 1930. The robbery was discovered when Sim returned from his lunch hour and released three victims from the vault. Two of the victims were Sim's children. The robbers' car tracks were followed, but the men had hidden and had escaped. Months later, the ex-girlfriend of one of the two men "squealed" and a jury sentenced him to the penitentiary. The $800 taken in the robbery was never recovered, nor was the other robber identified and prosecuted.

During the Great Depression the bank's importance was vital to the daily survival of many families. This is evident in loans granted for as little as $1.50. Letters from borrowers requesting loan extensions during the period reflect how anguishing it was for everyone, including the bankers.

Over the years, the bank has continued providing invaluable services to northeastern New Mexico. In 1999, the bank was purchased by The First National Bank of New Mexico. The bank was totally remodeled, preserving its historic significance and is an attraction that draws people from all over New Mexico to experience its history.

As The First National Bank of New Mexico forges into the new millenium, each office takes pride in claiming personalized service. Banking competition in the area is stout, but The First National Bank of New Mexico takes its commitment very seriously. The First National Bank of New Mexico continues to pride itself on convenience and community-mindedness and is happy to be the hometown bank of Northeastern New Mexico.

The new building for The First National Bank of New Mexico in Tucumcari is currently under construction and is expected to be completed in late 2000-early 2001.

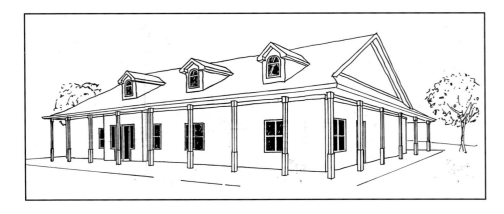

FRENCH MORTUARY INC.

The year 2000 marked the 93rd year of French Mortuary's history as the largest and oldest, continuously family-owned funeral home in the state of New Mexico.

Chester T. French was born on a family farm south of Knoxville, Tennessee. He attended Maryville College and obtained a teacher's certificate. He taught at a one-room schoolhouse and earned $35 a month.

At the turn of the century, tuberculosis was ravaging the country and several of the French family of 10 children died of the disease. Mr. French and his brother Jessie came to Albuquerque in 1904. Jessie died soon after their arrival. Mr. French later went to New York City where he graduated from Embalming College and returned to Albuquerque to start French Mortuary in 1907.

He married Elizabeth Thomas who had moved to Albuquerque from Gallipolis, Ohio. She had recently graduated from Maryville College and moved to the Territory of New Mexico to teach at Albuquerque High School. They had three daughters, Mary Elizabeth, Lillian Ruth (who died as a baby), and Lois. The family lived on the top floor of the mortuary on Central Avenue.

The business prospered, and in 1921 Chester T. French purchased a building at Fourth Street and Gold, naming it the French Building. This location would later become the Simms Building.

Chester T. French (1882 to 1966), founder of French Mortuary, Sunset Memorial Park and Mausoleum.

In 1935, a beautiful new mortuary was built at 910 East Grand Avenue (now Dr. Martin Luther King, Jr. Blvd.) across from St. Joseph Hospital.

When I-25 was built in 1959, the mortuary stood in its path. Mr. French began planning for a new place of business, his fourth location at 1111 University Blvd., N.E. This building was dedicated on February 12, 1959, Chester T. French's 77th birthday.

Mr. French's career in funeral service spanned over 60 years during which he opened branch offices in other New Mexico communities including Hot Springs, Socorro, Magdalena, Grants, Farmington, Mountainair, and San Marceal—all of which he sold.

In the late 1920s, Mr. French began a second career. He visited

Forrest Lawn Cemetery and got the idea for a modern cemetery in Albuquerque using all flat markers and having a park-like appearance. In 1930, Sunset Memorial Park was opened at Menual and Edith, N.E. It has become one of the most beautiful memorial parks in the Southwest.

In 1961, Mr. French built a beautiful mausoleum for families requesting above-ground entombment. Now Sunset Memorial Park has one of the largest, endowed perpetual care trust funds in the Southwest—over $6,000,000.

This celebrated funeral director and cemeterian, who was known for his integrity and fairness in serving families of all income levels, was also an active churchman. He taught the Lucky Band Sunday School class for teenage boys at the First Methodist Church for 40 years and rarely missed a Sunday from 1910-1950.

Mr. French's three grandsons, Rick T. Stewart, Chester French Stewart and Bob H. Stewart now operate the business.

As a Sunday school teacher, Chester French reached out to boys of all walks of life. Two more prominent class members were Charles V. Schelke who was vice-president of General Electric and Austin T. Cushman, who was chairman of the board of Sears-Roebuck.

A great joy in his life was the French Boy Choir which he founded in 1915 and reorganized in 1935. The boy choir continues today under the name The Albuquerque Boy Choir.

Chester T. French's horse-drawn ambulance in 1907, at his first mortuary at 5th Street and Central Avenue.

The fleet of cars replaced the horse-drawn carriages: hearse, passenger car and ambulance. This was the first motor hearse used in New Mexico.

At the age of 60 Chester French developed a health system in a published pamphlet titled, "One Minute A Day...Will Keep Aches and Pains Away" to help himself and others enjoy good health. At the ripe age of 82, he was quoted as saying that he was in perfect health. Thousands of people across the USA have been helped by his simple exercise routines.

Mr. French's great love for flowers, especially dahlias, was combined with his love for children. He held flower-growing contests, rewarding the young people with scholarships and prizes.

Last but not least, Chester T. French was also a successful family man who impressed the value of funeral service upon three of his grandsons—Chester French Stewart, Bob H. Stewart and Richard T. Stewart. These three grandsons have carried on the business. The story of this new generation's leadership in the mortuary and cemetery business began with Mr. French's grandson and name-sake, Chester French Stewart.

Mr. Stewart graduated from Wheaton College in 1962 and received a commission in the U.S. Army through R.O.T.C. Mr. Stewart shares the following, "After I grad-uated from college, I had a two-year commitment to serve in the Armed Forces. Three months before I got out of the service, my grandfather called and asked me to come to Albuquerque. He said he wanted me to go into the funeral business with him. At the time, I wasn't absolutely sure that that was what I wanted to do, but I had a great deal of love and respect for him and told him that I would come to Albuquerque for a year. I came to Albuquerque and after about six months I began to realize that it was a great opportunity to serve people and to minister to their needs. In September 1965, I went away to mortuary school and I completed the education needed for a funeral director's license. I returned to Albuquerque one year later. Three weeks after I returned, my grandfather ran a full-page ad in the newspaper announcing our partnership. Unfortunately, three days after that, he died very sud-denly of a heart attack. The next few months were very difficult, but we worked hard and really concentrated on the service aspect of our business. We could see that our business would grow if we would continue to provide great service with the highest integrity."

In 1986, the mortuary branched out with the completion of another chapel at 7121 Wyoming Blvd., N.E. Then, in 1996, the third mortuary location was completed at 10500 Lomas Blvd., N.E. A fourth mortuary located on the West Side at 9300 Golf Course Road, N.W. was completed in 2000.

The Heritage Plan was established to help people to pre-arrange their funerals. With a qualified staff of pre-arrangement funeral consult-ants, French Mortuary's Heritage Plan has become one of the leading pre-need programs in the country.

French Mortuary is family-owned and operated and is committed to meeting the needs of New Mexican families well into the 21st Century.

One of French Mortuary's four locations in Albuquerque.

GALLUP SAND AND GRAVEL COMPANY

Gallup Sand & Gravel Company's mission statement is "to provide quality ready mix and aggregate products to the complete satisfaction of the customer, at a reasonable price with regard to the safety of our employees, customers and the community."

Gallup in the 1940s still resembled the romantic image of the "Old West" that was seen on every billboard and sign along Route 66, "The Mother Road." It was in this setting that Gallup Sand and Gravel Company was born. George Bubany, the local lumber company owner, knew that good consistent concrete for building was scarce. The concrete being produced then was mixed on site by hand, and inconsistencies were a major problem. What was needed was a good source of concrete as an adjunct to the lumber business. This would help assure quality local sources for building the many new structures being constructed in and around Gallup and McKinley County.

A meeting with interested parties in October 1945 produced the decision to create a corporation. Mr. Bubany, along with brothers John and Tony Kozeliski formed a triad that would set the standard for other businesses in the world of ready mix concrete. There would now be a company that would batch and deliver concrete to the job site. However, due to World War II and a shortage of materials, production did not officially begin until 1947. Sand and rock had to be shipped in by rail on the main AT&SF line from Albuquerque Gravel Products and Springer Transfer in Albuquerque. Cement was shipped by rail in cloth sacks from Southwest Portland Cement in California and later from El Paso, Texas. It was also in 1947 that GS&G became one of the first members of the National Ready Mix Concrete Association.

During the first year of production there were only four employees with an average wage of 75¢ an hour! There were two truck drivers and one laborer. Orders had to be placed two to three days in advance, with a week being the norm. Tony Kozeliski was

General Motors Truck with a two-cubic yard Yeager mixer, 1947.

elected vice-president, and assumed the duties of manager, dispatcher, batcher, secretary and janitor. Tony went on to become president and principal stockholder of the company, and retained the title "Chairman of the Board" until his death in July 1999. Tony, the son of Croatian immigrants who came to Gallup to work in the local coal mines, was proud to have his sons Frank and Tom join the company. Frank and Tom serve on the company's present-day Board. Tom, with a business degree, began working with the company straight out of college in

1971, and is the operations manager and secretary-treasurer of the corporation. Frank, a registered professional civil engineer, began with the company in 1976, and oversees research and development, quality control and promotion. He is the company's current president and general manager. Frank is also in demand as an expert speaker at national and international concrete industry expos. He has also published in several industry journals.

Even before his sons were in the business, Tony, along with the community, saw many changes and exciting events. In the 1950s the first

The delivery fleet, 1955.

diesel-powered mixer trucks were purchased, natural gas lines were being installed in northwest New Mexico and northeast Arizona, and Gallup Sand and Gravel supplied concrete to pumping stations being constructed by El Paso Natural Gas and Trans Western. In 1959 Gallup Sand and Gravel became a founding member of New Mexico Ready Mix Association. Tony, Frank and Tom have all held the office of president for the state association. Frank is also a past director of the National Ready Mix Concrete Association and Tom is a past director of the National Aggregates Association. The company is also a member of American Society of Concrete Construction and the American Concrete Institute and National Stone Association.

The 1960s brought the first hydraulic powered mixers and the beginning of Interstate 40 construction through the area. Up until 1966 the company was still shipping in rock by rail from Albuquerque. Not wanting to continue relying on the often-inconsistent deliveries, the company began their own rock crushing operations in summer 1966 in order to provide the limestone needed for operations.

The 1970s set in motion the hauling of concrete for long distances, up to three or four hours from Gallup. This extended mix time was changing the ready mix industry nationwide. An increase in coal mining, construction for housing, new schools and federal projects, along with an increase in population, all led to the use of more concrete and concrete products. Gallup Sand and Gravel was there to supply the demand.

Interstate 40 through Gallup was completed in October 1980. A new electric generating station was also under construction. At that time, the cement needed to make concrete for these projects was in short supply, due to a nationwide shortage. Cement had to be shipped from as far away as Pennsylvania, Missouri and California. Also in the '80s Gallup Sand and Gravel filled

Tony Kozeliski in front of the newly-constructed rail unloading and reclaim conveyor system, 1959.

some of the old, abandoned coal mines that were running under the City of Gallup. These were the same mines that Tony's father and father-in-law—Frank's and Tom's grandfathers—mined coal when they first arrived in the area.

The original site of the first ready mix company in Gallup continues to house the main office to this day. Located adjacent to the mainline of the Santa Fe, the company's lifeblood remained with the railroad tracks

well into the 1980s. The plant on Round House Road houses dispatch, quality control labs, accounting/billing and the original batch plant. The main truck garages and mechanical and repair shops are housed at this site, as well.

Clearly visible in the central downtown area of Gallup, the high-profile silos and conveyor systems have remained landmarks for over 50 years. The main plant sits parallel to the Rio Puerco, which the locals lovingly call "The Perky." Interstate 40 runs on the north side of "The Perky" and Route 66 runs parallel to the plant site to the south. The "Perky" is usually a dry ditch, no more than 10 or 15 feet deep. However, during extremely rainy days on the mountains to the east it can become a raging torrent, and cause severe flooding in the area. The main plant and office complex has had several incidents of flooding over the years, including doing major damage in July 1973 and again in July 1990. Fire has also had its time with the old plant. Destroyed by fire in 1975, the original batch plant was refurbished and still operates today. Each time "Mother Nature" displayed her wrath, the family company worked even harder to rebuild and remodel, making new and modern changes to the original

Hasler Valley Plant, 1997.

Concrete recycles concrete crushing operation, 1999.

batch plant.

Developing a good reputation and good relations with contractors and suppliers through the years has also proven fruitful. Many new projects were awarded to the company that now encompass a service area of over 150 miles, including the states of Utah, Colorado and Arizona. Several portable batch plants were bought in order to provide concrete in these areas. Taking the business to the customer "on site" continues to be a hallmark of the company to this day.

With the advent of the 1990s, expansion and modernization were needed to deliver product in a timely and cost-efficient manner. It was also time to incorporate the newest technology. With this in mind, the "Hasler Valley Plant" was constructed in 1995. Using state-of-the-art computer hardware and software has enabled the business to realize an increase in productivity and evaluate materials in concrete mixes, thus delivering high quality ready mix concrete to all customers in both English and Metric units.

Gallup Sand and Gravel has long been involved with the welfare of the community. Generous giving has, and continues to be, an important part of the overall philosophy of the company. A total of six soccer fields were dev-

eloped for the Gallup McKinley County Schools and the City of Gallup with the help of the company's equipment and expertise. The company also began a recycling program that is widely used by area contractors and local and regional governmental agencies. Old concrete and asphalt debris is processed at the "Hasler Valley" plant with a new 400 ton-per-hour recycle crusher. In fact, some of the local roads and streets are using recycled aggregate base that was

Hasler Valley Plant with Kenworth 11 cubic yard MTM mixers, 2000.

originally produced by GS&GC in the 1940s and '50s. Gallup Sand and Gravel has also entered cyberspace by creating a web site at www.gallupsand-gravel.com, which proudly showcases innovative uses of concrete. Current employees are encouraged to develop their own decorative items, and have produced concrete snowmen, pumpkins, turtles and even little green "aliens," which are displayed in and around the city. There is also a display of concrete "sculptures" lining the entrance to the Hasler Valley Plant. Tom created these 11 sculptures in memory of his father Tony.

GSG is recognized as a leader in technical advances in the concrete industry. GSG customers expect and receive a high level of expertise, professionalism, selection of product, convenience and the personal touch. Because of the diversity of cultures in northwestern New Mexico services are offered in English, Spanish and Navajo. For over 50 years, Gallup Sand and Gravel has been the builder of "foundations" for Gallup, McKinley County, Western New Mexico and Northeastern Arizona. The company will continue its commitment to expand and evolve around community and area needs, building new foundations for new generations into the 21st century.

LA FONDA

One of the Southwest's great hotels, La Fonda stands on a corner of Santa Fe's famous plaza at the end of the Santa Fe Trail. Although La Fonda is a mere 75 years old, the site has provided lodging facilities for nearly 400 years and is a key part of the city's romantic heritage. It was not until after 1822, when the Santa Fe Trail opened, that specific references to the hotel were made in the journals and diaries of those hardy pioneers who crossed the dangerous plains. La Fonda, the only inn of Santa Fe became the trail end meeting place. Regardless of its name, many bilingual patrons called it "la fonda (the inn)."

Soon after New Mexico became a U.S. Territory in 1848, the inn became the Exchange Hotel, the name under which it operated for nearly six decades. The Exchange continued to be the rendezvous for trappers, traders, pioneers, soldiers and politicians as well as the central meeting place for town gatherings. It offered modern comfort and

Sometimes known as "the Inn at the End of the Trail," La Fonda stands at the southeast corner of Santa Fe's historic plaza.

convenience, including warm meals, a livery attendant and corral.

The Exchange fell on hard times after serving as a regional social center for several decades, but even its demise had a certain flair. As part of a Liberty Bond rally after World War I, patriotic citizens razed the building with an Army tank, crashing into the walls following each sale of a $100 bond. To nurture the budding tourist industry, city fathers solicited funds for a new hotel, La Fonda, at the same site. Unfortunately, the project foundered when capital raised from community stock subscriptions proved inadequate. After long negotiations the local promoters sold La Fonda to the Santa Fe Railroad in 1926. La Fonda was then leased to Fred Harvey, the famous managerial firm then operating tourist hotels and related enterprises throughout the Southwest. In planning the décor, Harvey personnel brought in Mary Colter, a renowned designer who gave La Fonda its distinct character.

Under Harvey's management, La Fonda became known throughout the world as the place to stay in Santa Fe. In the 1960s however, industry

leaders lost confidence in older, downtown hotels. As a result, railroad executives quickly accepted an offer to purchase La Fonda from a group of investors headed by Samuel B. Ballen, a Dallas oil man who had recently moved to Santa Fe. Although he and his associates lacked hotel experience, they had great faith in the city. By preserving La Fonda's unique charm they hoped to strengthen Santa Fe's historic downtown and prevent urban decay.

Known as Corporacion de La Fonda, the new ownership took over in 1968 and immediately began a comprehensive improvement program that has continued to the present. In addition to replacing the building's plumbing and climate-control systems, the Corporation has enlarged the bar, rearranged the lobby, and redecorated each guest room, reproducing much of the original Colter-designed furniture. Recent renovations include a three-level Carriage House topped by 14 exquisite rooms, hot tub and a native-decorated banquet room overlooking St. Francis Cathedral. La Fonda has continued to maintain and preserve itself as one of Santa Fe's most enduring landmarks.

HEEL INC.

In 1979, Biological Homeopathic Industries (BHI) began with the determination of one man, seven employees and first year sales of less than $20,000. The goal was to establish a company that would enable its founder to introduce his homeopathic medicines to American doctors.

Since then, BHI, now known as Heel Inc., has proven itself as a leader in the field of homeopathy and has grown into one of the largest companies in the industry. Still in its original building in southeast Albuquerque, the company continues to adhere to the principles that ensure its success—to produce quality homeopathic remedies while continually educating healthcare practitioners interested in the field.

Homeopathy (from the Greek "homeo" meaning similar and "pathos" meaning suffering) is a scientifically-proven system of medicine that uses minute doses of plant, animal and mineral substances. These specially-prepared substances, or 'remedies' as they are called, are administered to patients in diluted doses. Homeopathic remedies produce, in a healthy person, symptoms similar to those of the condition being treated. In this way, the body's defense system is stimulated to overcome the symptoms produced by the medication. Although homeopathy has existed for hundreds of years and is documented in the writings of Hippocrates, the founder of Heel/BHI, Dr. Hans-Heinrich Reckeweg, expanded the theory with a more modern approach.

Dr. Reckeweg was born in Germany in 1905. His interest in homeopathy began while in medical school when his father became seriously ill and was cured by a homeopath. This event influenced a young Dr. Reckeweg to study homeopathy and after receiving his medical degree in 1929, he established a homeopathic practice in Berlin. He soon realized that although homeopathy offered exciting healing possibilities, it was too

Dr. Hans-Heinrich Reckeweg, founder.

cumbersome for many physicians. Classical homeopathy requires not only a detailed recording of a patient's symptoms, but also an intimate knowledge of the homeopathic pharmacy. Unfortunately, in order to do this well and effectively, a physician needs many years of clinical experience.

In an effort to simplify the modality, Dr. Reckeweg combined the practice of homeopathy with modern, conventional medicine. Homotoxicology—the connecting link between allopathic medicine and homeopathy—was formulated in 1952. Dr. Reckeweg then began combining single ingredients into unique formulas and his patients responded so well to his combination remedies that other doctors began asking to buy them. Demand became so great, that in 1936 he created a company named Heel, to mass-produce his medications. Heel is an acronym for Herba est ex luce, meaning "plants are from light," in Latin.

Some 40 years later, Dr. Reckeweg sold Heel, moved to Albuquerque,

and developed new preparations that he would sell through BHI. His primary objective was to introduce his remedies to physicians in the United States and on October 1, 1979, Biological Homeopathic Industries opened for business. As BHI was a relatively unknown company at the time, employees were able to indulge in non-work related pursuits such as stickball in the parking lot and basketball out behind the building. While Dr. Reckeweg spent hours in the lab developing his formulas, the few employees of BHI were filling many shoes. These unhurried times didn't last for long, however. Through the years, as the staff and sales grew, the building was renovated and expanded to accommodate these welcome changes. Just as it had happened in Germany 43 years earlier, American doctors were noticing the importance of Dr. Reckeweg's remedies. Demand for the products increased and slowly but surely, and the company continued to grow.

Dr. Reckeweg continued living in Albuquerque until less than a year before his death. A dedicated man who was intent on seeing his new

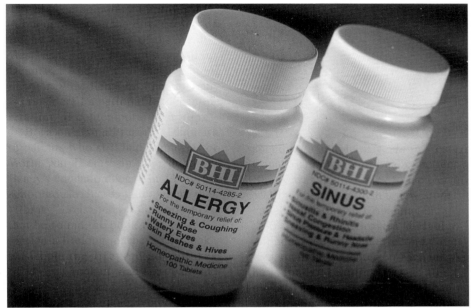

BHI Allergy and BHI Sinus are among the over-the-counter products available in health food stores around the country.

company prosper, he came to the office everyday for at least one hour, and mixed the tinctures for the formulas himself. Upon his death in 1985, 50 percent of BHI was purchased by Dr. Reckeweg's original company, and became the American distributor of Heel products. The other 50 percent remained with Dr. Reckeweg's family—his daughter Monika and her husband, Dr. Friedrich Doerper; and his grandson Stefan Doerper, who served as BHI's general manager in the early 1990s. In 1998, BHI officially changed its name to Heel Inc. and today is one of the largest homeopathic companies in the United States.

Through the years, Heel Inc. has gone through many names and even more milestones. In addition to corporate success, the years have marked some exciting innovations in the homeopathic industry.

In 1983, the first *Biomedical Therapy Journal* was published. *Biomedical Therapy* is a quarterly scientific journal for healthcare practitioners interested in exploring the fields of complementary medicine including homeopathic therapy. Published in the journal are editorials, clinical reviews and original research. After 60 issues, the original journal was discontinued in April 2000. It will be redesigned into an abridged,

newsletter version and reintroduced in Fall 2000.

In 1997, Traumeel® ointment became the first homeopathic medication to be published in the Physician's Desk Reference. It is also on the formulary of Cedar Sinai Hospital and is the leading topical homeopathic in the United States.

In 1998, Heel Inc. had another breakthrough when a scientific study

on Vertigoheel®, its remedy for vertigo, was published in the American Medical Association's peer-review journal *Archives of Otolaryngology*. It was the first time an AMA publication had acknowledged the efficacy of a homeopathic remedy.

Heel Inc. also maintains a very active role in the homeopathic community. As a member of the American Association of Homeopathic Pharmacists (AAHP), Heel has worked to improve relations with the FDA and helped address regulatory matters facing the industry.

Heel Inc.'s prescription for success has been slow and steady growth. In 1999, it celebrated 20 years in Albuquerque. Heel currently manufactures and distributes 170 formulas nationwide, with 55 over-the-counter products that are available to consumers and 115 other formulas sold to physicians, chiropractors, acupuncturists and other healthcare providers throughout the country. The company, now with nearly 50 employees and yearly sales in the millions, still believes in its beginnings—the dream of one man.

Traumeel® is Heel Inc.'s top-selling product and comes in five dosage forms.

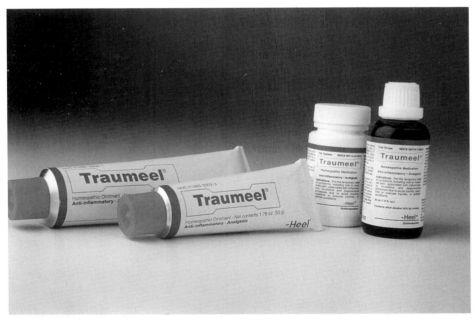

HOTEL SANTA FE

Hotel Santa Fe's history dates back some 2,000 years, to the ancestral home of its majority owners, the people of Picuris Pueblo. It was there, centuries ago, that a standard of hospitality was established which continues today at Hotel Santa Fe, the nation's only off-reservation Native American-owned full-service hotel. That hospitality is reflected in words carved above the hotel's entrance: "Mah-waan, Mah-waan," meaning "welcome" in the Tiwa language of the Picuris people. And welcome is evident everywhere—from the serenity of the exquisitely landscaped private gardens to the warmth of a roaring fire in the lobby's traditional kiva fireplace.

Hotel Santa Fe began in 1988 as the project of a group of Santa Fe-based business people who dreamed of building a luxurious new hotel in Santa Fe. The original group included hotel and real-estate developer Joseph Schepps; Santa Fe and New York real-estate developers William and Nancy Zeckendorf; Richard Yates, architect and developer; attorney Earl Potter and his wife Deborah, both leaders in the community; and hotelier Paul Margetson, now general manager of Hotel Santa Fe. Subsequently, Santa Fe businessman and former Deputy U.S. Secre-

Hotel Santa Fe.

Picuris Pueblo Governor Eagle Rael and Richard Mermejo, Lt. Governor and President of the White Buffalo, Inc.

tary of Commerce Luther Hodges joined the group. When financing for the project proved difficult, it was suggested that the investors consider partnership with a Native American tribe in order to qualify for a federal loan guarantee. The group was told about a poor Pueblo north of Santa Fe—Picuris Pueblo—that might be interested in such a project. Negotiations began, though not without concern from the Picuris elders, who feared an erosion of their tribal traditions. They were especially wary of any establishment that would serve alcohol, a banned substance at the Pueblo. Advisors from the Bureau of Indian Affairs recommended that the investment group practice the Native American tradition of patience, and strive to develop a better understanding of Native American culture. After lengthy and delicate negotiations, a partnership was finally formed, with Picuris Pueblo retaining 51 percent ownership of the hotel. The partners' dream would soon become a reality.

Groundbreaking ceremonies at the Paseo de Peralta site took place in February 1990.

Many Picuris tribal members signed up for the construction crew while others trained for staff positions at nearby hotels. On March 27, 1991, Hotel Santa Fe opened, marking a new era of economic development for the people of Picuris Pueblo and providing a culturally-unique luxury hotel for the City of Santa Fe. Today, the original staff of 60 has grown to 100 and continues to grow, with the payroll approximately 20 percent Native American. Picuris Pueblo receives certain considerations as well: tribal members receive advance notice of job openings; the Arts and Crafts Shop is exclusively-owned by the Picuris and has done much to revitalize the Pueblo's artistic traditions.

Close to the hubbub of the City Different, Hotel Santa Fe embodies the tranquility that typifies Native American life. The moment one enters the hotel's private, walled grounds there is a sense of serenity. A curving driveway traverses flowering gardens shaded by towering trees. Placed throughout the gardens are impressive sculptures by some of Native America's most renowned artists: Allan Houser, the patriarch of Native American sculpture, Doug Coffin and Doug Hyde. The hotel, designed in the Pueblo Revival style of earth-hued adobe, appears to have risen from the land itself. Allan

Houser's beautiful sculpture, "The Offering," welcomes arriving guests with an appropriate peace pipe offering.

Beyond the entrance portal lies a warmly-welcoming lobby, decorated in the lodge style, with comfortable New Mexico furnishings arranged around a traditional kiva fireplace. On chilly high-desert evenings, a roaring piñon fire blazes while a background of Native American flute music sets the mood. Dominated by Allan Houser's powerful bronze, "Buffalo Dancer," the room is graced by the work of Native American artists' pottery, paintings and weavings. Even the hotel's decorative design, from doors and mirrors to accoutrements, reflects the traditional symbolism and pure artistry of Native America. "Nothing is more central to Native American culture than its art," says Paul Margetson, general manager and partner, "and we are dedicated to creating a collection of pieces that reflects the sense and sensibilities of that culture." To that end, Hotel Santa Fe invests a large sum each year in works by Picuris artisans, including the fabled micaceous pottery, and continues to amass a world-class collection of Native American art.

The 128 guest rooms and suites of Hotel Santa Fe are furnished in authentic New Mexico style, with locally-crafted furniture and Native American art. Balconies overlook the Sangre de Cristo mountains to the east, the Jemez mountains and spectacular Santa Fe sunsets to the west. The details of each room are planned with guests' comfort in mind, from the duvets to the amenities. A concierge stands at the ready to fulfill every request; a private shuttle bus transports guests to favorite Santa Fe sites—such as world-class museums and the art galleries of Canyon Road. In the gardens, shielded from view by the privacy walls, a swimming pool and hot tub offer a perfect place to relax under the vivid New Mexico skies.

Located within the lobby is the world-renowned Corn Dance Cafe, the only Native American restaurant in Santa Fe. Here, guests dine on delicacies such as Tlingit Salmon with Rosehip Puree, Buffalo Chili and Little Big Pies, a Native American version of pizza. On summer Sunday mornings at dawn, Pueblo women bustle about the patio, firing the horno, the traditional beehive oven, and preparing hot, fragrant loaves in time for breakfast on the terrace or in the newly-installed tepee. "While the tepee is from the Plains–not Pueblo–culture," explains Paul Margetson, "we believe we have a responsibility to expose our guests to *all* Native American culture and traditions, not just Picuris." The Picuris partners agree.

It is this unique sense of place that attracts visitors to Hotel Santa Fe and keeps them returning year after year. "I've found that our guests have an insatiable curiosity about all things Native American," says Paul Margetson, "and they're eager to learn everything they can about the culture." Hotel Santa Fe strives to provide the tools for that learning process. Visitors may sign up for twice-weekly lectures by well-known Santa Fe historian Alan Osborne, who also leads the hotel's guided tours to Picuris and other neighboring pueblos. On Friday evenings in summer, dancers from Picuris Pueblo entertain with traditional drums and dancing, and on Saturday evenings an Eastern Cherokee/Chippewa hoop dancer performs his astonishing feats. The Sunday morning bread baking on the patio has become a weekly ritual for both guests and local residents. Everywhere throughout the hotel there is that unique blend of old traditions and new beginnings that makes up the essence, the very heart and soul of Native America. Capturing that special sense of place, and offering it to visitors, is both the philosophy of Hotel Santa Fe and the secret of its success.

Paul Margetson attributes that success as well to "listening to our people," whether partners, employees or guests. "It's the diversity of our cultural backgrounds and our ability to use that diversity to create a fascinating environment, that has made Hotel Santa Fe so successful," says Margetson. As for the future, Hotel Santa Fe is constructing an $8.0 million addition of 35 rooms and suites, scheduled to open in Summer 2001. When it does, it will bring ever-growing success for the hotel, the Picuris, the City of Santa Fe and a nation which, only now, is beginning to experience, understand and revere its Native American heritage.

Santa Fe Suite, Hotel Santa Fe.

KELLER'S FARM STORES

Keller's Farm Stores, a local favorite, flourishes as Albuquerque's premier supplier of the finest quality beef, pork, lamb, exotic meats, fancy poultry, fresh seafood, handmade cold cuts, sausages, and gourmet foods. The Keller's have grown their market niche by doing things differently. "Our farm fresh meats and poultry are grown for flavor, tenderness and nutritional quality," says Margie Keller Perko, one of four Keller siblings who own and operate the company. "The number one reason customers come into our shops is because they know we have the finest meats and gourmet food items available."

Keller's Farm Stores locations include a shop on Eubank at Candelaria, and a shop on Coors Road at Montano. Customers can choose from a staggering variety of fresh meat, poultry, and seafood cuts artfully displayed in full service cases, as opposed to the vacuum packaged meats offered in the self serve cases of most supermarkets. The walk-in-cooler is typically filled with grain fed sides of beef aging to perfection. "Our older customers tell us this is the way meat tasted to them when they were children— good, old-fashioned flavor and tenderness," explains Margie. Delicious deli items are prepared daily, including hot barbecued ribs and chicken, fresh salads, sandwiches and party trays.

Keller's stocks a huge selection of domestic and imported cheeses as

Nancy Keller Jackson, Michael Keller and Margie Keller Perko are responsible for production and retail operatioins at Keller's Farm Stores.

Lawrence and Helen Keller in 1946.

well as gourmet and natural groceries from around the world. Fresh pastries, baked goods and organic produce are enticingly displayed. A full time nutritional staff offers the most current health information and assists customers with natural vitamins, herbs and cosmetics.

The Keller's story begins in, of all places, a bakery, where Lawrence, working with his father, met his soon-to-be wife Helen. The Keller's, dreaming of fresh air and sunshine in the great outdoors, decided to buy a farm and strike out on their own. In 1946 Lawrence and his family began farming. Before long a line of cars was a consistent sight at the Keller's farm. People would drive out to the farm to buy fresh meats. The first retail shops were opened in the '60s. The Keller's retail shops and meat processing plant served as the test kitchens as Lawrence worked, making new and previously unimaginable products for upscale restaurants and retail sales. Lawrence became a legend in the turkey industry, famous as a leader and innovator. He received numerous awards for his products. The four Keller siblings have always worked side by side in the business with their parents, grandparents, aunts and uncles. They became the heart and soul of the business when their parents passed away, Lawrence in 1980 and

Helen in 2000. Chances are you'll end up dealing with a Keller family member when you're shopping. All eight grandchildren have been active in the family business, with their parents. Customer service is as much their concern today as it was to their parents in 1946.

Variety is the spice of shopping at Keller's. The seasoned and marinated meats offered at Keller's can go straight to the grill or stove. "Our goal is to make meal preparation easier and faster," relates Nancy Keller Jackson, who has a masters degree in Poultry Science. Hard to find meat items are a "cinch" at Keller's. For those not satisfied with the abundant selection of exotic meats, including buffalo, quail, pheasant, and emu, Keller's will seek out everything from rattlesnake and alligator to bear.

During the holiday season, a hungry crowd lines up before the store is even open. The huge smokehouse, loaded with delicious meats, runs around the clock. The store smells like hickory heaven. In the three days before Thanksgiving this family will sell 10,000 turkeys. During Christmas week more than 10 tons of prime rib roasts are cut to order. Hundreds of lambs are cut to fill Passover and Easter orders. Complete dinners are made by the hundreds, featuring smoked or roasted turkey or ham and side dishes including such family favorites as sweet potato casserole and fresh strawberry-cranberry salad. Keller's staff prepare beautifully decorated gift baskets featuring Keller's smoked meats, imported teas, exotic nuts, jams, crackers and cheese. Hundreds of local business people order gift certificates or gift wrapped boxes of choice, tender, aged steaks for their employees, clients and business associates.

In an era of mega-supermarkets and blockbuster packing houses mass producing chemically-pumped meats, Keller's has done the opposite. "We never add chemicals, MSG, colorings, preservatives or any other additives

Helen Keller with her children and grandchildren in 1998.

to any of our meats, cold cuts, sausages or bacon," explains Nancy. The entire line of deli meats are naturally low in sodium. The Keller family makes all of their cold cuts and sausage by hand in their shop. "Our sausage and cold cuts are great, really different," says Michael Keller, who heads the company's production. "There simply isn't anything comparable. We start by using our own choice beef, prime turkey and pork." Keller's hams, bacon, cold cuts and sausages are Old World recipes. Only spices and herbs are used for flavorings. The meat is hand-stuffed into natural casings and slowly smoked over a hickory fire. "It isn't necessary to disguise poor flavor with a lot of chemical additives when you start with really good ingredients," explains Nancy. Kellers' customers have repeatedly voted the Best of Albuquerque Bologna Award and Best of Albuquerque Meat Market Award to the Keller's shops. The bottom line is a wholesome, natural product a cut above the competition. The taste is phenomenal and the product is pure. "It's the food you really feel good about feeding to your family," says Nancy.

Modern agriculture is a cost-driven industry, and food prices are set with little consideration to quality. There is universal pressure on ranchers and farmers to cut production costs. The Keller family's approach goes against the grain. They do not sacrifice quality to lower production costs.

"The meats we market come from animals that are fed a carefully-balanced, very high quality diet of corn, alfalfa and other grains," explains Michael. "We do this for two reasons. First, the flavor of the meat you eat is determined by the animal's diet. Cattle that are fed rich grain, corn and alfalfa turn out meat with exceptional flavor and tenderness you just don't find in the supermarket. Our decision has been to stay with the same quality feed formula day in and day out. Our feed costs are higher, but the result is meat with consistently great taste. Secondly, the meat from animals fed a higher quality, nutritious, well-balanced diet supplies our own bodies with greater nutrition."

Keller's animals are raised in a humane manner, with plenty of fresh air and exercise. No dehorning or castration is performed. The Kellers feature USDA choice and prime grades of beef. "Choice and prime grades of beef are the most tender and flavorful," relates Paul Keller, who operates the Keller's farm and transporting. "The industry standard is USDA Select. The extra time and expense invested in feeding our meats to prime and choice results in exceptional flavor and tenderness." Keller's animals are processed in clean, USDA-inspected plants. There is an inspector on duty at all times.

The Keller family's secret ingredient for success is customer service. "Your family deserves the best" is the slogan that permeates the company. It's their customers who matter most. The Keller family is mindful of the fact that customers want a fresher, higher quality, more nutritious product than they can get in any other store, and they want valuable customer service and interaction. Providing customer-oriented service is largely a matter of being mindful of the customer in performing every task. "Our customers are wonderful, really nice people," relates Margie. "We treat our customers as guests. We help them make their selections. If they are in a hurry, we take their order by phone and have it waiting when they come in. At Christmas we smoke and gift wrap our natural hams or turkeys for everyone on their shopping list. We prepare complete dinners with all the trimmings and cater special occasions. Our goal is to make shopping fun with a friendly, helpful staff."

The Keller's selection of fresh products gives new meaning to the "farm to table" production chain, making it second to none in quality assurance. The family has developed a respected reputation for their commitment to providing outstanding customer service and the best in specialty meats and gourmet foods. The Kellers plan to stick to their slogan, "Your family deserves the best!"

Paul Keller is responsible for the family farming and transporting.

KTECH CORPORATION

As nuclear testing went underground in the 1970s, entrepreneurs with scientific backgrounds saw opportunities aboveground. One of these enterprising physicists, Dr. Donald Keller, felt the time was ripe to strike out on his own. On December 14, 1971, Keller established Ktech Corporation, a professional and technical services company that specialized in shock physics and weapons effects. Three employees supported the company's contract with the Defense Nuclear Agency (now the Defense Threat Reduction Agency) during that first year. Nearly 30 years later, Ktech Corporation employs nearly 350 people and enjoys an established reputation with government and industry for sound scientific and engineering work, outstanding technical support services, and proven management expertise.

Keller, now chairman of the board, initially established Ktech in Santa Barbara, California, but the heart of the company moved to Albuquerque within two years. His staff of three had grown to 15 in support of a contract with the Air Force to perform scientific research and operate the Material Response Impact Facility in New Mexico. New Mexico has figured prominently in the field of nuclear physics since its selection in 1942 as the site for developing the first atomic bomb. The facilities initially established for that project are now known as Los Alamos National Laboratory and Sandia National Laboratories, located in Los Alamos and Albuquerque, New Mexico, respectively.

The Material Response Impact Facility enabled scientists to study how materials reacted during nuclear fission experiments. In the 1970s, a major focus of the nuclear weapons field was to better understand and model nuclear weapons effects so that aboveground testing with pulsed power simulators could eventually replace nuclear tests at the Nevada Test Site. Early on, Ktech became a leader in designing techniques to reliably measure and model dynamic

In 1979, Ktech won a contract to operate, maintain, and design experiments for Sandia National Laboratories' Pulsed Power Research Center. One of the center's world-class high-current accelerator facilities is shown here during discharge.

material properties—measurements of effects that last less than a microsecond—and also in fabricating the sensors. This expertise, combined with the company's growing reputation, led to additional opportunities with Sandia.

Steady growth characterized the 1970s as the number of both contracts and employees continued to increase, including the hiring of former Sandian Larry Lee, Ktech's president since April 1999. However, Ktech's office needs remained relatively modest because many of its staff members supported projects onsite at Sandia and at the Air Force Weapons Laboratory (now the Air Force Research Laboratory). Thus, the administrative offices at 901 Pennsylvania Ave., NE that Ktech rented in 1973, and later bought, have continued to house Ktech staff. Ktech did expand its facilities in the 1970s, however, when it added a machine shop to enable production of its own gauges and sensors, along with machining prototypes for its engineering projects.

Staff numbers grew significantly in 1979 when Ktech won a contract to operate, maintain, and design experiments for Sandia's Pulsed Power Research Center, staffed by world-class plasma physics personnel and containing state-of-the-art accelerators. The new contract added nearly 20 employees to its payroll. In its support of the Pulsed Power Research Center, Ktech strengthened its capabilities in data acquisition, software engineering, and systems development and integration. Ktech staff made major contributions to the Center and later supported other pulsed power projects, including systems for the United Kingdom, Germany, and France.

To Keller, it has been important not only to have established a company with a solid reputation for science and service, but to have created an enjoyable, yet challenging, work environment for its employees. In fact, Keller attributes the success of Ktech over the years to the high caliber of staff that it has attracted and retained. One-third of its current employees has more than 10 years of service with Ktech—a retention rate three times the national average. Also, Ktech's dedicated and professional staff have nearly all been drawn from the New Mexico job market.

In 1988, Ktech reinforced its commitment to its employees by becoming an employee-owned company.

By the early 1990s, as the Cold War ended and the federal government's emphasis shifted from weapons development to stockpile stewardship, Ktech was also geared for a shift in focus. Many of the technologies that Ktech helped to develop in the 1970s and '80s could now benefit industry. For example, Ktech's piezoelectric sensors, originally developed to support the simulation and underground test programs, have found varied commercial applications, such as integration into loudspeaker design and as medical components.

One region of expansion has been Ktech's work with thermal sprays, which began in 1995. At that time, Ktech was called upon to operate and maintain a thermal spray research laboratory at Sandia, including the design, installation, and maintenance of thermal spray equipment and control instrumentation. Thermal sprays are a relatively new technology

Ktech's work with thermal sprays began in 1995.

Tech Reps, Ktech's technical documentation division, knows firsthand of the dramatic changes in report preparation since the 1970s.

that provide wear-resistant, lightweight, and cost-efficient coatings for a variety of engineered parts, such as automobile engine cylinders. Ktech's early involvement in their design and installation has positioned it as a significant player in this field. Ktech and Sandia have recently begun to commercialize a newer, more efficient, cold spray technique.

Other growth areas in the last five years include software engineering for satellite data systems; development and fabrication of automation systems

for manufacturing facilities; creation of engineered solutions for firefighters, such as a new heat flux sensor to measure burn damage potential and evaluation of fire-protective clothing; knowledge management software and services; and professional staffing services by Ktech's subsidiary, Albuquerque Staff Augmentation Providers (ASAP).

To round out its capabilities, Ktech decided in May 1998 to pair its expertise in scientific research with outstanding technical reporting by merging with Tech Reps, Inc., a local technical communications firm. Like Ktech's Keller, two of Tech Reps' founders, Robert C. Holmes and Donald E. Tiano, were also entrepreneur-scientists involved with the underground test program in the 1970s.

Since its inception on May 6, 1974, Tech Reps has provided engineering and scientific support when needed, but its primary focus has been technical documentation. When Tech Reps received its first contract with the Defense Nuclear Agency in October 1974, Tech Reps' staff numbered four and its office equipment basically comprised two lawn chairs and an IBM selectric. Reports were painstakingly corrected by then state-of-the-art methods: replacement of whole lines or paragraphs on paper copies by means of a razor blade and scotch tape.

Today, Tech Reps' facilities are staffed by scientists, writers, illustra-

tors, and production personnel, and its equipment includes networking and web capabilities, high-volume electronic storage capacity, multimedia capabilities, printers/scanners, large format printing, and high-production copiers. Tech Reps continues to document scientific and engineering projects, but the black-and-white typed reports have evolved into high-quality communication products such as full-color reports, brochures, exhibits, presentation materials, and web pages.

To accommodate its changing corporate structure, Ktech moved its administrative offices in 1998 (for the first time since 1973) to 2201 Buena Vista, SE in Albuquerque. (Its subsidiary, ASAP, continues to occupy the building on Pennsylvania Ave. NE.) Current facilities also include an optical laboratory, an instrumentation laboratory, an automation and fabrication facility, and a machine shop, all located in Albuquerque.

Even as Ktech enlarged its customer base, however, it has continuously supported its clients from the early 1970s—the Defense Nuclear Agency, the Air Force, and Sandia. Ktech remains dedicated to solving the most difficult and complex technical problems for both government and industry through custom engineering, accurate documentation, and a variety of professional skills.

LAGUNA INDUSTRIES, INC.

Federally-chartered Laguna Industries, Inc. (LII) was founded to provide economic development for the people of Laguna Pueblo, a Native American tribe located in west central New Mexico.

It is a high tech manufacturing and technical-services company operating in New Mexico, Maryland and Colorado producing quality products at competitive costs for very satisfied customers. From its facilities in Mesita, located about 45 miles west of Albuquerque on the 533,000-acre Laguna Indian Reservation, it serves customer locations worldwide.

LII boasts proven performance, an experienced and diverse staff, innovative team-oriented management, and strong relationships with nationally recognized organizations such as Sandia National Laboratories and the U.S. Army Research Laboratories. The U.S. military is among LII's principal customers. LII works with the Air Force's Electronics Systems Center in Massachusetts, and Ogden Air Logistics Center in Utah, the Army's Communications and Electronics Command (CECOM) in New Jersey and Research Labs in Maryland.

Other clients with whom LLI has had contracts or subcontracts include the U.S. Postal Service, Raytheon Aerospace Company, Motorola System and Satellite Technology Group, Alliant Tech Systems, GTE Government Systems Corporation, Tri-Ex

LII field engineer instructing 93rd Signal Brigade on the operation of tactical communication assemblages at Ft. Gordon, GA.

AN/TSM-210 Maintenance Shelters.

Tower Corporation, and Marion Composites.

Classified as a small disadvantaged business (SBD) in an historically underutilized business zone (HUBzone), LII is working toward measured growth—identifying and capitalizing on specific niches in the defense and federal markets—while expanding its presence in commercial and cross-over markets.

The Pueblo of Laguna (Spanish for "village of the lake") is federally-recognized, the second largest of 19 Pueblo tribes located in the state. It has more than 7,000 registered members, half of whom reside on the reservation.

It comprises six major villages: Mesita, Laguna, Paguate, Encinal, Seama, and Paraje. It lies along the San Jose River, but the lake that provided its name has disappeared.

In its own language, the tribe is known as "Ka-waikah," meaning "lake people." Its Keresan dialect is one of four spoken among the pueblos and is used by seven of them.

Laguna and the other pueblos came under Spanish rule in the 1590s, when the conquistadors laid claim to the area. These rulers provided names

for the native people. Spanish domination lasted until August 10, 1680, when a medicine man named Popé led his long-repressed people in the Great Pueblo Revolt. Their independence was, however, short lived.

The Mexican government moved into the area around 1690, taking control by 1692. The pueblos remained under Mexico until 1848. Then, in the Treaty of Guadalupe Hidalgo at the end of the two-year Mexican War, Mexico ceded to the United States 522,568 square miles which would become the states of California and Utah, most of New Mexico and Arizona, and parts of Wyoming, Nevada and Colorado. The pueblos came under U.S. jurisdiction, but it was not until 1926 that Native Americans became U.S. citizens and 1948 that the Pueblo people received the right to vote.

In the middle of the 20th century, the members of Laguna Pueblo began to develop their economic potential beyond traditional farming and raising of livestock. Initially, this took the form of exploiting the reservation's mineral resources,

Sunrise outside Laguna Industries, Inc. facility.

which included one of the world's richest uranium fields. Laguna began to mine the radioactive ore in 1952. This was the Pueblo's economic mainstay until competition from other parts of the world made operating the mines too costly. They closed in 1982.

In the 1970s, tribal members reestablished their traditional crafts of pottery, jewelry making, and painting, meeting a growing commercial interest in native handicrafts. Members of the tribe also applied skills learned from mining in employment outside the Pueblo.

In 1982, the Pueblo formed the Laguna Construction Company to reclaim the Jackpile pit, once the world's largest open-pit uranium mine. Using former miners who were excellent heavy equipment operators, Laguna Construction completed the project in six years, four years ahead of schedule.

In 1980, the Pueblo, looking to expand its economic base, did a job-skills inventory of its members. It concluded that they had the capabili-

ties to function in a repair and overhaul facility or a manufacturing operation.

The planners initially organized a tribally-chartered corporation with the name Laguna Industrial Development Enterprise (LIDE). They saw the Department of Defense (DoD) as a potentially significant market, but initial approaches directly to the Pentagon met with little success.

In 1984, LIDE made its first marketing presentation to CECOM. When it became apparent that Laguna had a chance to be accepted as a CECOM supplier, and facing the possible loss of federal grants that supported its economic development efforts, the Tribal Council decided to incorporate LIDE under state law. It became Laguna Industries, Inc. on July 26, 1984.

That October, the Army division set aside its Digital Group Multiplexer Assembly (DGMA) program for LII in anticipation of the company becoming certified by the Small Business Administration (SBA) under Section 8(a) of the Small Business Act. The 8(a) program is for small firms owned by socially and economically disadvantaged persons. Certain

federal contracts are designated specifically for its participants, which also qualify for management and technical assistance.

At the same time, LII entered into a management support, training and technical assistance contract with Raytheon Service Company. This relationship became the model for DoD's Mentor/Protégé program under which large companies help small and disadvantaged firms assess training needs and follow development of key employees in disciplines that will generate the most effective growth. In the mid-'90s, LII participated in a similar contract with Motorola.

In November 1984, LII received a federal charter. It was also certified by the SBA.

Less than a year later, it received the request for proposal for the DGMA program. It responded through the SBA, and on August 29, 1985, CECOM issued a contract. The relationship between LII and CECOM continues, with its projects a mainstay of LII's business. Their needs moved LII into engineering design and helped it develop significant expertise in Integrated Logistics Support, including publications, field engineering and new equipment training. LII has employees working at the MIL-STD-2000/A levels.

LII employee working inside AN/TSM-210 Maintenance Shelter.

Laguna Pueblo built an electronics plant to make components for appliances. Later, and still, the plant manufactured communication shelters for the U.S. military. These equipment-filled mobile stations were used for Desert Storm and in Kosovo, among other places. LII representatives travel overseas to instruct military personnel in use of the equipment.

In 1991, the Pueblo, with financial help from the Economic Development Administration, added some 50,000 square feet to LII's facilities, bringing its total size to 130,800 square feet. LII occupied the new space at the beginning of 1992.

In 1994, LII graduated from the 8(a) program. It maintains SBA designations as a small disadvantaged business and as a minority business enterprise, which provide preferred access to some designated government business.

In 1994-95, the NASA/McDonnell Douglas Space Systems Kennedy Space Center in Florida named LII its Small Business of the Year.

LII left the 8(a) program at a time when defense spending was decreasing. This government belt tightening, coupled with losing access to contracts under 8(a), caused its revenues to drop from a high of $40 million a year to $18 million near the end of the decade.

LII field engineers training the 93rd Signal Brigade on the DGM Assembly Multiplexer Program (DAMP) antenna at Ft. Gordon, GA.

Employment fell from a high of 486 to 150.

LII reevaluated its direction. While maintaining its federal business, it diversified to the private sector and toward new skills and products. In 2000, revenue was back to the $30 million a year level and the number of employees increased toward 200. Because of improved technology and productivity, this was expected to support current business and some additional growth.

Key to LII's plans is burgeoning opportunities in information technology. Fiber optic lines put in along Interstate 40 have given the Pueblo of Laguna new opportunities, with the promise of huge bandwidth generating a wide range of possibilities. The prospect of cutting-edge development is attracting the interest of younger members of the tribe, and holds a promising future for the Pueblo. LII is entertaining a variety of approaches to accelerating such expansion, including acquisitions, teaming arrangements and joint ventures.

At the same time, LII continues to offer its growing customer base a variety of high tech manufacturing and technical services, including electronic and electrical cable fabrication; electronic assembly; mechanical fabrication; system and sub-system assembly; electrical and mechanical design and engineering services; integrated logistics support; and technical publications. These are built on a technical sound infrastructure of quality assurance, networked information systems, cost accounting, training and development, human resources, and program management.

Its manufacturing plant incorporates modern machines and methods to produce high-quality products in

AN/TSM-210 Maintenance Shelter against red rocks of Laguna Pueblo.

an environment geared for just-in-time needs. Its product variety ranges from the shelters for narrow band digital communications equipment for military applications to electronic switchboards and line filters for use in commercial computer equipment.

Quality support includes calibration and configuration of advanced testing and measuring equipment, as well as document control systems. LII embraces statistical process control and total quality management and is well on the way to being ISO 9001 compliant before the end of 2000.

As worldwide logistics support LII provides training, field upgrades, maintenance and service, system installation, and operational testing and evaluation. It publishes user-friendly technical documentation and support data, both military and commercial.

LII is wholly-owned by the Laguna Pueblo and is operated by its people. It is built on the strength of individual diversity and the dreams of its community. These have enabled its well-planned, strategic growth into a competitive, far-sighted organization poised for the economic demands of a fast-paced, technology-based future.

NATIONAL CENTER FOR GENOME RESOURCES

The National Center for Genome Resources (NCGR) is an independent, nonprofit life sciences research institute based in Santa Fe. The Center was founded in 1994 at the urging of U.S. Senator Pete Domenici, and grew from human genome research occurring at nearby Los Alamos National Laboratory. Today, it is engaged in one of the most exciting scientific endeavors ever known to humankind.

NCGR works at the interface of biology, computer science and mathematics (bioinformatics). The massive amounts of data being generated by genomic research can only be understood by combining these disciplines; the essence of bioinformatics is to comprehend relationships between genetic code and the life processes inscribed in it.

More than 250 people attended NCGR's building dedication in April. Festivities included a sculpture exhibition by College of Santa Fe students who incorporated themes of science, technology and art.

Why? Such research can help ease the suffering of hunger that plagues our world, develop revolutionary medicines to fight diseases like cancer, and leave the planet a better place for our children. By conducting and facilitating bioinformatics research, NCGR contributes to these goals.

The Center's research focus is developing analytical software tools, frameworks and databases that allow scientists all over the world accessing a website (www.ncgr.org) to seek meaning in data. Among NCGR's most significant accomplishments to date are:

• The Arabidopsis Information Resource (TAIR), a collaboration with the Carnegie Institution that is funded by the National Science

President and CEO Stephen C. Joseph, M.D., visits with guests at the NCGR building dedication in April.

Foundation. *Arabidopsis thaliana* is a mustard that is closely related to many food plants and used broadly by scientists as a "model" organism for research. TAIR is employed by researchers to bolster understanding of all plants and to improve important crops such as corn, soybeans and rice.

• The Genome Sequence DataBase (GSDB), the project that started the Center. GSDB is one of four comprehensive public sequence databases worldwide that provide access to DNA sequence data and analysis tools. Researchers use the tools to identify new genes and compare organisms' genetic makeup.

• The ongoing development of an integrated biological knowledge system, called ISYS. This unique resource will allow users to comprehend and analyze a broad range of data types, including gene sequence, genome maps, gene expression and biochemical pathways, from a variety of organisms. System components will work together and suit the needs of researchers in divergent specialties.

Six years ago, NCGR began operations with one full-time employee and a volunteer. The start-up Center boasted 500 square feet of office space, a word processor, rented furniture and a couple of two-line telephones.

In 2000, the staff of 60 biologists, technologists and administrators

achieved a dream—a move into a 32,000-square-foot, custom-built headquarters that is a landmark building in Santa Fe. The new research facility houses some of the most significant computer infrastructure in the state and greatly enchances NCGR's effectiveness. The building enables the staff to better work together on collaborations and project teams and allows more flexibility in hosting visiting researchers.

The building's completion signals NCGR's commitment to New Mexico. NCGR is fortunate to be situated in this state, which has a rich scientific and cultural heritage, and looks forward to a long and productive stay.

Systems technician Mark Guillen works with the Center's lifeblood: network cable. Connectivity is crucial to bioinformatics research; NCGR is US West's largest Internet customer in New Mexico.

LEA COUNTY STATE BANK

There were no oil wells in Lovington, New Mexico in 1928, but there were over 70,000 sheep within the boundaries of Lea County. At least 700,000 pounds of wool valued at more than $200,000 was sheared.

Sheep rancher J.S. Eaves and a small group of visionary citizens including the local Ford dealer, W.M. Snyder, formed the Lea County State Bank of Lovington in 1928. At that time, Lea County had been without a bank for five years.

Lea County State Bank of Lovington was chartered November 2,1928 with capital and surplus of $31,250. The first depositor was J.E. Simmons of the Elliott Waldron Abstract Company, who made a deposit of $1,000.

Snyder was the president of the new bank. As a pioneer in trucking in Lea County, he used Model-T trucks to haul gasoline and freight. Daniel C. Berry was the cashier.

The bank was located in Lovington at the corner of Main and Central on the second floor of a building which also housed the Sweet Shop, a popular gathering place for the local residents. It had previously been an apartment for the shop owner Otto Dean.

In September 1991, First Interstate Bank of Lea County was purchased through a management buyout led by Samuel S. Spencer, Jr., left, and Robert C. Dunn, Jr., right. The bank was renamed Lea County State Bank.

The original Lea County State Bank building in Lovington, 1928. The bank was located on the second floor of the facility.

Since there was no electricity available in Lovington, due to an earlier fire at the power plant, Dean rigged up a plant to furnish power to the facility.

The State Bank of Hobbs merged with Lea County State Bank of Lovington on July 8, 1931. Two years later, in 1933, a branch of the Lovington bank was opened in Hobbs at Shipp and Broadway.

New local owners including James Murray, Sr. and Guy L. Rogers, acquired the bank in 1937. On April 5, 1938, the main office was moved to Hobbs and the name shortened to Lea County State Bank.

James Murray, Sr. was the president of the bank from 1938 to 1942. He was elected lieutenant governor of New Mexico in 1939, and he served in that position until 1942.

Murray's business partner, Guy L. Rogers, was vice president of the bank. He was one of the most widely-known figures in state banking circles. He began his career in 1901 when he started as an office boy for First National Bank in Albuquerque, at the age of 16.

Rogers was very active in Hobbs, serving as mayor for two terms. When Murray resigned from active participation in the bank, Rogers was named president in 1942, and later became chairman of the board in 1955. He held that position until his death in 1976.

Lea County State Bank's headquarters in Hobbs, pictured here, was expanded with the construction of a 6,000 square foot building.

The bank continued to facilitate the growth and development of the communities it served. On April 16, 1946 the service area expanded to include branches in Eunice and Jal. In 1951, land was purchased at Broadway and Linam in Hobbs to build the main office of Lea County State Bank.

Controlling interest in the bank was sold in 1956 to Transamerica Corporation of California. In July 1959, the bank changed its name to New Mexico Bank and Trust Company.

In the 1970s the balance of the locally-owned minority interest in the bank was acquired by Transamerica Corporation's successor, Western Bancorporation. In June 1981, the bank's parent company changed its name to First Interstate Bancorporation, and New Mexico Bank and Trust Company became First Interstate Bank of Lea County.

That same year, the bank pur-

chased and renovated the building that had housed the Safeway Super Market at 1017 North Turner in Hobbs. That location was known as the Broadmoor Branch.

In September 1991, First Interstate Bank of Lea County was purchased through a management buyout led by Samuel S. Spencer, Jr. and Robert C. Dunn, Jr. Other investors included Robert J. Kerby, Clifford G. Kerby, Keith W. Pearson, and W. Trent Stradley, James A. Clark and Samuel S. Spencer.

The name of the bank was changed back to Lea County State Bank, and the main office was moved to 1017 North Turner.

Throughout its long history, the bank has not only continued to meet customers' needs, but its directors, officers and employees have been committed community leaders. "The board of directors and management have always taken the responsibility of being a good corporate citizen very seriously," said Samuel S. Spencer, Jr., president and chief executive officer. "In our ongoing effort, the bank and

its employees will continue to consistently support and participate in local organizations, working to improve the overall quality of life in Lea County."

Lea County State Bank is proud of the past and is building for the future. The latest development in the bank's history is the construction of a 6,000-square-foot building housing the real estate department and Bank Direct Mortgage Corporation. Contruction on the building, located adjacent to the main office of the bank at 1001 North Turner, began in January 2000.

Lea County State Bank is a name that personifies perseverance, strength, and stability. It is also the name of a unique bank. Since 1991, Lea County State Bank has been the only locally-owned bank in the county, and the bank operating with the oldest charter in Lea County.

Superior customer service combined with the latest technology, local ownership, and exemplary civic involvement are traits that will continue to distinguish Lea County State Bank into the 21st century.

LUNA VOCATIONAL TECHNICAL INSTITUTE —A COMMUNITY COLLEGE

The factors that led to the creation of Luna Vocational Technical Institute-*A Community College* (LVTI-CC) have long and revered traditions in American society. From the beginning, America recognized the essential need for an enlightened citizenry, capable of constructive participation in the political, economic, social, and aesthetic dimensions of democracy. Public education for all youth was entrusted with a major role in the preparation of incipient members of society. The purposes of public education were dual—to prepare the young with knowledge and skills necessary for creative participation in society. The second was to imbue them with understanding and appreciation of the basic culture of society—the values, morals, and ethical commitments which constitute citizens' allegiance.

LVTI-CC was founded by the New Mexico Area Vocational School Act in 1969 with the express purpose of ameliorating the technical, vocational, and occupational potential of its service area residents, which is long and rich in traditional culture and history, but short on education and occupational opportunities. The northeastern quadrant of the State, where the College is located, is sparsely populated with long, rural distances between communities where poverty, lack of education, and meager exposure to the majority economic and occupational systems abound. The population has a high proportion of direct descendents of the Spanish Colonials who still maintain the pre-industrial culture of 16th century Spain, a language which is closer to Cervantes than to contemporary usages, and a general lack of educational, social, and medical services.

The main campus for the College is located on high ground at the Gallinas Gateway to the majestic Sangre de Cristo Mountains, overlooking the community of Las Vegas. This historic settlement on the old Santa Fe Trail served as the main artery for commerce and exchange

Maximilliano Luna.

between the American Midwest and the Mexican territory of New Mexico. With the annexation of New Mexico into the United States, Las Vegas gained a great deal of influence in territorial politics as well as education, rivaling the growth, stature, and influence of Albuquerque and Santa Fe. By 1890 San Miguel County was regarded as the "Imperial County." In education it took the lead, establishing the first public school system in the State in 1871, as well as a Jesuit College later moved to Denver and today known as Regis College.

Today, the community of Las Vegas has three post-secondary institutions—two that serve the public and the schools, and a third being the Armand Hammer United World College.

New Mexico Highlands University was established in 1893 as a "normal school" to prepare teachers for the public schools, and later expanded to a full university.

LVTI-CC offered its first classes in 1970 in such areas as automotive mechanics, building, carpentry and cabinet making trades, welding, culinary arts, business and secretarial skills. Later it added programs in electronics, computer-assisted drafting, nursing, medical technology, and general studies. Since 1989, it has expanded to community college status with a wide range of offerings in technical and vocational fields as well as a comprehensive two-year curriculum leading to associate degrees in various areas. Under the jurisdiction of the State Commission of Higher Education, it is fully accredited by the North Central Accreditation Association, sharing compatible credit transfer with colleges and universities.

The College has dynamic programs in various areas of institutional development. These include professional development for faculty and

Technology students.

Aerial view of LVTI-CC campus.

student support services personnel; student assessment, evaluation and diagnosis; teacher-learning effectiveness research and improvement; continuous curricular review, revision and development; distance education, community outreach, course and service delivery systems; student dropout research, follow-up surveys, remediation, and intervention systems; and curricular coordination with public schools and institutions of post-secondary education with special attention to curriculum gaps and subject matter articulation.

Two satellite centers operated by the College are located in Springer, New Mexico, 60 miles north of Las Vegas; and Santa Rosa, 60 miles south of Las Vegas. In addition, many outreach courses are sponsored throughout northeastern New Mexico.

The College also has systematic linkages with industrial and scientific installations for student placement

and faculty in-service exposure. Coordination with Los Alamos National Laboratories, INTEL, state agencies, and other employment sites provide industrial, scientific, and occupational exposure for students and faculty.

The College derives its name from Maximilliano Luna, who served as speaker of the House of Representatives for the Territory of New Mexico in 1899. Luna distinguished himself as a captain with the Rough Riders who fought under Teddy Roosevelt in the Spanish American War and with the 34th U.S. Voluntary Cavalry, dying while on duty in the Philippines.

The name and the history of the location of the College have special significance because of the need to include a strong sense of history, tradition, and cultural significance in the development and recognition of the students. LVTI-CC emphasizes the importance of cultural and historical continuity, engendering growth, identification and individual strength

on the part of minority people who have been historically excluded from major sociocultural recognition in this part of the country.

Nursing students.

MCBRIDE AND ASSOCIATES, INC.

Teresa N. McBride is the founder and CEO of McBride and Associates, Inc., the largest woman-owned business in New Mexico. Its annual revenues exceeded $200 million in 1999 and it has sustained a growth of between 30 and 40 percent annually. McBride and Associates has stood the test of time and is a leader in the information systems and technology industry. There are two intertwined aspects to this well-planned outcome. The first is Teresa McBride's strong family legacy of business ownership, of treating people with respect and of working hard; and second, is her personal quest to build a company of consequence.

The McBride Family story starts with four McBride brothers who left Belfast, Ireland, in 1772. Samuel, the eldest McBride, settled in Philadelphia and started a family. Samuel's eldest son Hugh, was born in 1852. As a young man, Hugh worked for the railroad. Hugh found himself traveling to New Mexico at the same time the Grant brothers established a railroad camp there in 1882. Hugh met his bride near Grants and they started a family and a cattle ranch.

Hugh's first grandson Luís McBride, a natural businessman, opened a garage to repair Ford's new Model Ts. His garage was across from the railroad station on the main street, which later became Route 66. Next door to the garage Luís opened a cantina and a dance hall. Because he loved helping people, he became the informal community banker to family and friends. He was respected in the community and was referred to as *Don* Luís. When he died, the family found IOU's in his safe dating back 40 years.

As one story goes, when the cantina needed to be painted, *Don* Luís hired an itinerant worker who painted the walls and ceiling navy blue and covered them with aluminum polka dots. Although surprised by the results, *Don* Luís was a man ahead of his time and approved the painter's work.

Luís married Clara Serna Saavadra, a strong and resourceful Spanish

Teresa McBride, founder and CEO of McBride and Associates.

woman with long black hair, which she wore braided and coiled into a bun. Most people remembered her ever-present apron and generous spirit. *Don* Luís and Clarita proved to be a tremendous business force in Grants and the downtown business area grew up around their home.

Clarita opened the Sun Shine Café during the early years of the marriage. She served sopaipillas, green chili, sodas and ice cream to the locals and the railroad passengers. After she retired in 1948, she continued to cook her famous green chili at home on her wood burning stove. She served it to the hobos who traveled the railroad and crossed the street from the depot to her house, where they always received a hot cup of green chili from Clarita.

Luís and Clarita's eldest son, Eduardo "Eddie" Salomón McBride,

was only 17 in 1932 when he visited a cousin in California and joined the Merchant Marines. He traveled the world before retiring, coming back with wonderful stories of all the places, peoples and cultures he had encountered. When he returned to New Mexico, he met and married Dora Lee Bustamante González, whose parents had both fled the Mexican Revolution after witnessing the execution of their fathers.

Eddie and Dora took over the McBride family business. Since the business alone could not sustain their extended and growing family, Eddie took a day job as an electrician at the uranium mine, the third largest in the United States, in 1951. Grants' economic stability helped the McBrides build a regular clientele. The business grew by catering family events such as birthday parties, anniversaries, weddings and baptisms.

As soon as it was financially feasible, Eddie quit his job in the mine and concentrated on expanding the business. He set a barbecue grill outside the cantina and displayed steaks under a glass counter. Customers were invited to pick out the steaks of their choice and cook them on the grill. This enterprise eventually became a steak house. Eddie's new business needed a name; but his budget was limited, so he scoured a neon sign graveyard and found a sign that had "dancing lights that reminded everyone of Las Vegas." The newly named restaurant, Eddie's Roaring Twenties, became the social center of Grants. Eddie's run in the family business lasted only a short time, however. His stint in the uranium mine left its mark on his health and Eddie passed away in 1977 of cancer.

Teresa McBride, the youngest of Eduardo and Dora Lee's three children, grew up in the middle of the family businesses. She spent her first six years with her widowed grandmother, Clarita. Family folklore from Ireland, Spain and Mexico colored her forma-

The McBride facility in Northern Virginia.

tive years. Stories from her father's experiences in the merchant marine opened the rest of the world to her. Her family's stories had common themes of business, challenge, opportunity and responsibility and of respect and compassion for those less fortunate. Teresa absorbed all of this.

Eddie's death had dealt the family a very hard emotional and financial blow. Teresa recalls paying the last of his medical bills 10 years after he died. The family sold the restaurant and bar and carried the mortgage for the two establishments. The new owners, however, could not maintain the businesses and stopped making payments a few years later. By then Grants' economy had become depressed. The mines were shutting down and jobs were scarce. People were either selling or deserting their property, "simply closing the doors behind them as they walked away from the town," notes McBride.

In 1983, Teresa assumed full responsibility of reopening the business. Teresa remembers, "I had to muscle it through to make it work." The bar opening was delayed until after Teresa's 21st birthday so she could reactivate the liquor license in

Don Luís and Eddie McBride in the 1930s.

her name. Slowly her hard work paid off and the businesses began supporting Teresa's extended family of five, which now included her young son.

In 1985, in order to spend more time with her son, Teresa bought a computer. She planned to automate her accounting and payroll. This was a tremendous challenge since technical support came in the form of bulky and poorly written manuals. She hired one of her brother's friends, Ray García, a recent college graduate, to help with the computer hardware and accounting software. Characteristically, Teresa spotted the opportunity here. Soon she was helping local business owners and city government officials with their own systems.

McBride and Associates, Inc. rose from this previously-unmet need for business support systems. Teresa started the business in a small room in the office building her father had built on their property. He had constructed the building and rented office space to the motor vehicle department, an insurance company, a hair stylist, a lawyer and a CPA before he died. Coincidentally, the occupancy permit

Eduardo "Eddie" McBride in 1930s.

was delivered to the family on the day of his funeral.

As soon as the bar and restaurant were doing well enough to be attractive to buyers, Teresa sold them. A few months later, in February 1986, McBride and Associates, Inc. became fully operational. Three months later Teresa transferred the offices to a small living room space in Albuquerque, to be closer to her growing customer base and to eliminate the daily one and a half hour each way commute. The space could accommodate only "four little, bitty desks."

McBride and Associates, Inc. is a business-to-business operation. "Our customers have a wide array of computing needs. We sell them computer hardware, software and highly specialized professional technical service," says Teresa.

McBride and Associates is a good example of an entrepreneurial business described by Dr. Don Sexton, a prominent author of entrepreneurial studies. When asked if successful

entrepreneurs are just lucky, his response was, "Luck is where preparedness meets opportunity." McBride was prepared to take advantage of the information technology boom. "We were working with the Internet long before it was a system for common use, because some of our larger, initial projects were with the military. When the Internet became commercially available, we were experienced and well-trained to meet the demand."

While McBride and Associates is a high technology business-to-business company, it is internally a person-to-person organization. "McBride has a great, upstanding group of individuals. They are very dedicated, loyal and enthusiastic. We have a very helpful environment. Because we help customers we

Clara Serna de McBride in the early 1900s.

tend to help each other."

Interestingly, the McBride philosophy is to hire the absolutely best people for the job. The natural outcome of this policy is a highly diverse workforce. It must be working, because McBride was ranked number one in customer service on a 1999 national survey that rated the top high tech companies in the market.

McBride and Associates, Inc. is headquartered in New Mexico, Teresa's home state, although 90 percent of its business is outside the state. Companies like McBride and Associates provide a solid tax base, high-end jobs and a national presence in the high tech arena for their home states. Entrepreneurship and high growth companies have become strategic options for cities looking for community and economic development. Many companies take social responsibility beyond providing jobs and supporting a solid tax base.

Likewise, McBride, through its foundation, gives back to the communities in which it does business. Its flagship educational program, College Bound, seeks to establish reciprocal mentoring partnerships between classrooms in high-risk schools and college students as a way of encouraging college attendance and sustained educational performance. In this innovative program the children monitor the grades and overall performance of their college mentors. In turn, the college students provide information and a field trip of the campus as a way of opening the childrens' eyes to educational opportunities.

When receiving the Entrepreneur of the Year Award from Business Women's Network, the National Foundation for Women Legislators, Inc. and the Small Business Administration on April 7, 2000, Teresa McBride said, "I have the good fortune of working with an outstanding group of individuals at McBride." Perhaps luck and *good fortune* happen when preparedness meets opportunity. For more information see their web site at www.mcbridefoundation.org.

NEWTEC

White Sands Missile Range, New Mexico was the birthplace of New Mexico Technology Group (NewTec), but the roots of this joint venture company run wide and deep. Four major aerospace companies formed NewTec in March 1997 with one goal: to provide superior quality, state-of-the-art engineering and data collection support for the testing of military equipment on the Range. One member of the NewTec team, DynCorp, shares its history with the 3,200-square mile test range located in the Tularosa Basin in southcentral New Mexico. Originally established as a bombing range during WWII and later used as a test range to analyze German V-2 rockets, the Range expanded its mission to include testing of numerous missile and rocket systems. Soon, an enterprising retired Air Force colonel saw potential in operating and maintaining Range instrumentation used to record data for these tests. He formed Land-Air, Inc., which evolved into the first and most enduring contract for the corporation now known as DynCorp. By merging its Land-Air Division into the NewTec team, DynCorp contributed experience that began in 1949 and has continually advanced to meet the stringent technical standards of the Range.

A second member of the team, Lockheed-Martin is one of the oldest names in the aerospace business, with a 90-year history in aviation. The company's story began when Glenn L. Martin launched a silk and bamboo plane in 1909 and subsequently incorporated under his name in 1912, just as Allan and Malcolm Loughead formed the Alco Hydro-Aeroplane Company (later changed to Lockheed). These two companies united in 1995 to become Lockheed-Martin.

Lockheed has been on the Range since beginning its 1965 contract to provide engineering design and development, modeling, and simulation support. These efforts have continued to date through the incorporation of Lockheed's WSMR-based

personnel and expertise into the NewTec joint venture.

Cortez III, a third member of the team, began in 1979 as a small, disadvantaged business working under contract on the Range. While Cortez III now successfully performs government contracts nationwide, they are headquartered in Albuquerque, NM, and have supported the Range with operations, maintenance, and construction services continually

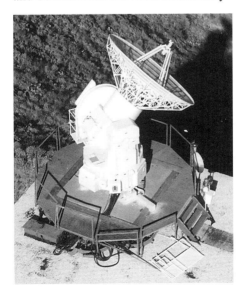

since the company's inception.

The aerospace business portion of TRW, the remaining member of the NewTec team, began in the 1950s with the birth of America's research on long-range ballistic missiles and space operations. TRW was the first company to build a spacecraft (Pioneer I) in 1958. Today it is a worldwide company providing advanced technology products and services in many industries.

In a few short years NewTec has taken its place as a force for growth and stability in the high-desert community where it was formed. Like the local community, which thrives on a blend of white settler, Hispanic, and Native American cultures, the NewTec team members work together in harmony to meet their customers' objectives. The combination of unique technical capabilities of each team member has assisted the Range in streamlining functions while continuing high-quality, cost-effective services to the various armed forces and other agencies utilizing the nation's largest military installation.

NEW MEXICO MILITARY INSTITUTE

President Benjamin Harrison was just in his third year in office (1891) when Robert S. Goss, instigated by local merchant/land owner Joseph C. Lea and his wife Mabel, established a military school—Goss Military Institute. Preceding the railroad by three years, Goss suffered from Roswell, New Mexico's frontier isolation, and his venture soon folded.

The Leas, however, were persistent souls. With the support of local merchants, ranchers and newspapermen they gained minor recognition for the fledgling school through their political representatives in the Territorial Legislature. The grant of a significant piece of real estate on the northern edge of town by industrialist and local developer J.J. Hagerman, gave the newly-renamed New Mexico Military Institute a viable future. With authorization to borrow granted by the legislature, school officials

Lea Hall in 1907.

proudly opened the doors of the Institute to the excited community of Roswell in 1898.

This lone structure provided the setting for the special educational experience still operating at New Mexico Military Institute for over a century. James W. Willson, fellow Virginia Military Institute alumnus D.C. Pearson, and early New Mexico Military Institute graduate Harwood P. Saunders, Jr. were largely responsible for building and shaping the school's character. In the roles of superintendent and commandant, this trio introduced a New Cadet/Old Cadet leadership system which they modified to meet the particular needs of high school and junior college youngsters, then largely from the rural Southwest.

In the first half of the 20th century, New Mexico Military Institute sent an extraordinarily high number of men to serve gallantly in this nation's wars. Nearly 3,000 served in World

Cadet honor guards, 1928.

War II; one received the Medal of Honor, 16 received Distinguished Service Crosses, 86 were granted Silver Stars, and 170 lost their lives in this service to their country. But, achievements were not limited to military involvement. New Mexico Military Institute proudly boasts of national championships in marksmanship and polo. Numerous former cadets, including Conrad Hilton, would earn distinction in the business world, while others chose different professions. Three would in time be honored with Pulitzer Prizes, including noted author and historian Paul Horgan, who actually won two for his work.

Social and cultural changes in the second half of the century presented new challenges for the school to overcome. After the effort to establish a four-year college proved futile, New Mexico Military Institute met the demands of racial and gender integration. Nathaniel Colbert, the first African-American student, joined the Corps of Cadets in 1967. Contrary to some military schools, New Mexico Military Institute chose to follow the lead of national service academies, and in 1977, several young women were admitted to this

Coed in 1977, cadet Lieutenant Colonel Heather Christensen, first female Regimental Commander, 1998.

Toles Learning Center, state-of-the-art on-line research library.

same student body. Females have held important positions in the Corps of Cadets ever since, and in 1998 Cadet Heather Christensen assumed the highest rank of Regimental Commander. The aggressive effort to diversify the Corps to include international students and to provide a quality education for young people regardless of race, ethnicity, or gender characterized the school as the 21st century approached.

As New Mexico Military Institute negotiates the swift currents of its second century, different components take on special significance. Sensitivity to ethical behavior as directed through the Cadet Honor Board and a designated Honor and Ethics Officer reinforces the school's commitment to character development. The ROTC Early Commissioning Program (sometimes called the ROTC Contract Program) provides critical support for the junior college and commissions as many U.S. Army second-lieutenants as any school, with the exception of West Point. Increasing focus on academic excellence, with its strong liberal arts curriculum functioning within a computer-based teaching environment, strengthens NMMI's prep school role. As a result, NMMI

sends between 50 to 60 students to the West Point, Annapolis and the Air Force academies annually. Over 90 percent of its graduates subsequently attend senior colleges and universities while that same number earn at least a bachelors degree or higher.

Various intercollegiate and inter-scholastic sports use the numerous facilities upon the beautiful, military gothic campus both to compete as well as to complement the academic demands. Heisman Trophy winner and National Football League Hall of Fame member Roger Staubach honed his rather formidable athletic skills on the playing fields of this school before attending the Naval Academy.

As the country's only state-supported college-preparatory high school and university-parallel junior college operating in a military environment, NMMI has been able to keep it costs very much in line. Truly, New Mexico Military Institute, still steeped in the traditions of decades past while rapidly adjusting to the technological demands of the future, offers a very special educational experience.

PIC QUIK STORES, INC.

Pic Quik Stores, Inc. was founded April 1958, in Las Cruces, New Mexico by G. Franklin McKinney. Franklin grew up in the grocery business originated by his parents. He came back from the U.S. Air Force after World War II and managed his parents' store in Mesilla Park, NM. He asked a friend and mentor in El Paso to predict the next trend in the grocery business, and his immediate reply was convenience store business. Franklin continued to manage the store in Mesilla Park for his parents and opened his first convenience store on Idaho street in Las Cruces, NM in April 1958, followed by number two on West Picacho Street.

The trend was to put convenience stores in small strip centers without gasoline. Franklin saw the opportunity to lease a location for number three on North Main Street, in an ideal strip center. Next, he bought the Mesilla Park store from his parents. That was number four and he was off and running.

His business continued to grow, adding numbers five, six and seven, and then expanding his territory to Deming, NM with number eight. In 1975 he added a liquor license and it is to this day the only store without gasoline. Then numbers nine and 10 were purchased in Las Cruces. Number 11 on Elks Drive was the first newly-designed Pic Quik. Number 12 opened in Old Mesilla followed by number 14 in Mesilla Park, where Franklin bought the property. It was the first store to stand alone. He expanded again and built number 15 in Hatch on property he purchased. Franklin then wisely realized the need for gasoline, and during the '70s added fuel pumps to all stores that stood alone. Typically, the islands were two pumps with a single pole canopy. The community loved the gasoline convenience.

Number 16 located on Solano was built and leased from the Las Cruces mayoral family. Then Franklin purchased number 17 from

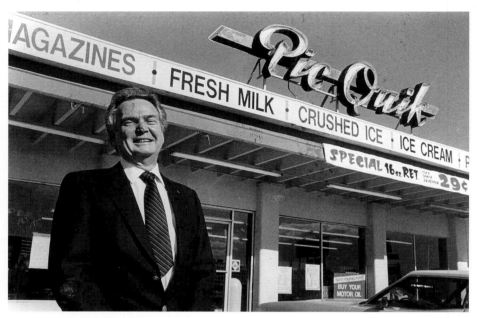

Franklin McKinney standing in front of the first Pic Quik store on Idaho Street.

his parents, in an effort to spare his mother long hours of standing on her feet, so that she could retire. Number 18 on Walnut was next in line. Number 19 on Telshor Blvd., a main thoroughfare, needed special zoning, which presented another challenge. Number 20 sprouted up in Dona Ana in the North Valley followed by number 21 on Valley Drive, number 22 in Fairacres and number 23 on Valley Drive. Number 24, an hour north on I-10 in Truth or Conse-

quences, complete with a deli, finalized the development of the McKinney enterprises.

In the '80s the office was computerized. The first computer was the size of a small desk. Pic Quik continues to upgrade its computers as technology changes. Long hours and hard work combined to make Pic Quik a success. Franklin often said, "I'm not in the grocery business, I'm in the people business." The customers would, and still do, talk about "their" store, and will positively

New gasoline pumps with Oregon mountains in the background in 1998.

Franklin and Frances McKinney in front of new store #14 Mesilla Park in 1998.

and served until United Bank sold to Norwest in 1994.

Times changed in the '80s and customer needs changed; they wanted to purchase gasoline. Most of the stores in strip centers had to be closed, because gasoline could not be added.

In 1992 Franklin became ill with two aortic aneurysms, and was sent immediately to Houston for surgery. After extensive surgery he slowed down a bit, and in January 1994 his wife Frances McKinney came to work at Pic Quik. Frances became president, and Franklin CEO.

With 15 stores left, Frances decided to close down numbers 10 in Las Cruses and 24 in Truth or Consequences. Everything changed— managers and supervisors quit and clerks did not show up to work. It seemed as though Pic Quik was starting over, with only one person in the office remaining.

Frances checked the stores daily in an attempt to learn the business. She rode with the maintenance man to see exactly what his job was, hauled ice, mopped floors, stocked merchandise, and observed constantly.

In June 1994 Franklin suffered a minor stroke. Frances knew she had to do something. She called all the people she had ever met in the business and asked for recommendations. She needed a name. A businessman in El Paso advised her to call a young man by the name of Oscar Andrade, who had worked for 7-11 stores for 13 years. He was the only applicant to interview, and after some negotiating decided to come on board as general manager. That summer was hot and the challenges multiplied. One store was even set on fire.

Things began to turn around; changes were in the wind. Remodeling and sprucing up the stores began in 1996. New gasoline equipment and canopies, new paving, lighting, and flooring were added to several stores. Sales began to climb again with the new image.

demand whatever another store has that "their" store does not.

In the '60s, Franklin helped start the New Mexico Food Dealers Association, headquartered in Albuquerque, and has served on that board continuously. He made numerous trips to legislative sessions in Santa Fe to monitor pertinent legislation related to his business. Franklin was one of the founding members of Tri-State Wholesale Grocers of El Paso, TX. He was the only member nominated from the floor and elected to serve on the Tri-State board, where he served as president and member for many years.

Although Franklin was active in the Las Cruces Chamber of Commerce and the Aggie Booster club, his hobby was work; his passion was Pic Quik.

In 1984, he became one of the founding board members for United New Mexico Bank of Las Cruces. He loved his bank board challenges

Franklin McKinney at an El Paso Tri-State board meeting in 1983.

In 1997 Franklin and Frances decided to tear down the old number 14 in Mesilla Park and build a new store on the same location. New state-of-the-art gasoline equipment, card readers, and a local fast food outlet, Santa Fe Express, along with new color and design were incorporated into number 14. Then their flagship store, number 19 on Telshor was torn down and a new store, car wash with more pumps, and three rental spaces were built in 1998. A new store on a new site on Highway 70 opened April 1999. The next project was a complete renovation of store seven on Missouri Street, including a new Santa Fe Grill kitchen, and the addition of new corporate offices.

Two stores were closed in March 2000, bringing the total number of locations to 12, with two more on the drawing board.

There are 70 store employees at present, two supervisors, two maintenance men, a general manager-vice president, office staff of four and an inventory auditor. Pic Quik is striving to bring the best service, convenience and image to Las Cruces, keeping customers and employees happy in "their" stores.

When traveling the state of New Mexico, the McKinney's noted many instances of meeting people from all walks of life who had put themselves through New Mexico State University by working at Pic Quik. There are now three generations of customers shopping at Pic Quik.

Franklin McKinney went in for quintuple heart bypass surgery November 1999. He had a massive stroke and never recovered. He died November 29, 1999.

Franklin McKinney was a quiet man, and a deep thinker with a keen sense of humor who silently helped many. Franklin was a pioneer in his business, a leading citizen, good

McKinney Plaza with old #19 before it was torn down and the new store Pic Quik #19 was built.

friend and father, and wonderful husband. Everyone misses him, for he was "Mr. Pic Quik."

It seems as though Pic Quik has come full circle. Each store still has a full line of groceries, and the rebuilt store on Telshor is in a new modern strip center with state-of-the- art equipment inside and out. In Las Cruces, Pic Quik is the leader in its industry, in all regards.

McKinney Plaza new strip center with gasoline pumps at #19 on Telshor.

TALBOT AGENCY, INC.

Insurance is an important element in any state's infrastructure. Businesses need insurance to start and to grow. Homebuilders cannot create communities without the right bonds and policies. Schools must manage their considerable risks. And families need insurance to achieve security and prosperity.

When Lyle Talbot founded his insurance agency in 1957, Albuquerque was a fairly small city and New Mexico a very small state. The city, the state, and the agency have grown tremendously, each fueled in part by the other. Talbot has grown locally from one man in 1957 to 170 employees in New Mexico and over 500 others in states from California to Illinois. Today, it is the second largest insurance agency headquarted in the Western U.S. And just as it has grown, Talbot has contributed in a meaningful way to the state's growth.

By helping employers devise and offer attractive employee benefit plans, Talbot makes it easier for them to attract new talent to the labor pool.

By providing the businesses of New Mexico with world-class insurance services, Talbot makes the Land of Enchantment an easier place to thrive and grow. By helping non-profit agencies and governmental entities find affordable, quality insurance, Talbot helps them serve their constituencies more efficiently.

In three eras of leadership Talbot's history has included changes in office location, major expansions in services, acquisitions and new offices. Lyle was succeeded by his son Randy Talbot in 1988, and Randy passed the reins to David Weymouth in 1998. However, in the most important ways, Talbot's history is one of non-change: no change in values, no change in commitment to New Mexico, and no change in its high standards of service and professional conduct.

As this book about New Mexico's history was being prepared, the Cerro Grande wildfire was making history in the Los Alamos area. An insurance agency must mobilize in the face of a disaster just like fire-

fighters or the Red Cross. During the crisis, Talbot set aside normal routine to find every possible way to help its customers who suffered losses. They got out-of-state claims adjusting teams set up, oriented, and working. They created a central claims directory phone line for all victims, and got the media to publicize it. They helped clear up misinformation about flood insurance. And its employees and offices contributed generously to relief funds. Overall, the situation was approached by every Talbot employee as an unprecedented call for extraordinary professional efforts. The Cerro Grande fires tested the resilience of Los Alamos' residents, the courage of the fire eaters, and the hearts of many New Mexicans. For Talbot, the test was one of their ability to respond when clients needed them the most, and it proved Talbot's mettle.

Talbot has offices in Albuquerque, Santa Fe, Las Cruces, and Rio Rancho.

PORTALES NATIONAL BANK

Portales National Bank is the oldest family-owned bank in New Mexico.

James Polk Stone came to eastern New Mexico in 1885, as a cowboy, with his father Micajah, and younger brother Andrew. Jim worked at the DZ Ranch for the privilege of branding and owning the calves that followed his father's cows. The DZ Ranch's cowboys gathered cattle as far south as Carlsbad and drove them to Fort Sumner, NM; Dodge City, KS; and later, Amarillo, Texas.

In 1896 he moved to the Running Water Draw nine miles north of the present site of Clovis. In 1889 he married Lula Beasley and moved her to his home 40 miles from the nearest woman, who lived at the DZ Ranch

James and Lula Stone on their 12th anniversary.

near Arch. Forty miles was a long day's ride by horse and wagon. Every several months, the husbands would get the two women together so they could talk and talk and talk.

In approximately 1900 the railroad came to Portales, bringing many people, including women. Mr. & Mrs. J.P. Stone then moved to Portales, where Mrs. Stone distinguished herself as a leader in Portales and its various organizations. She was actively involved in the Women's Club, the First Methodist Church, United Daughters of the Confederacy and was the first woman in the state

James P. Stone (center), president of the Bank of Portales, 1902

of New Mexico to serve on a school board. Mrs. Stone was on the local school board before women had been granted the right to vote.

James (Jim) P. Stone founded the Bank of Portales in 1902, which was the first bank in Roosevelt County. He later changed the name to Citizens Bank and then merged it into the First National Bank of Portales. Jim founded the Portales Bank and Trust located at the present site of the Tower Theater. He founded the First National Bank at Elida on August 30, 1906, which later became the Portales National Bank. He also founded the First National Banks located at Ft. Sumner, Texico, and in Hereford, Texas.

Jim died in 1913 at the age of 46, owning an 87,000-acre ranch in Bailey County, Texas, 5,000 head of cattle and five banks. Not bad for a man with a fifth grade education who came to New Mexico owning the shirt on his back and the horse between his legs.

Around 1900, when free land could be filed upon, many home-steaders came to eastern New Mexico and Roosevelt County to file claims on open territory. Because transportation and communication were limited, communities were generally established along the railroad. Each community had to be self-reliant because of the great difficulty in reaching neighboring towns. Each had its own school, stores, doctors, lawyers, banks and

James (Jim) Polk Stone, rancher and president of five banks.

whatever was necessary to make the community self-sufficient.

Around 1910, there were six banks in Roosevelt County: three in Portales, two in Elida, and one in Kenna. At no time prior to 1930 did the total resources of all the banks in Roosevelt County exceed $500,000.

The entire economy of Roosevelt County was based upon agriculture, and the prosperity of the county depended on adequate rainfall, cattle and farm prices. Numerous hardships were encountered and many families

The total number of cars in Roosevelt County, July 4th, 1911. Jim Stone's Cadillac is front right. Doug Stone is the baby in his mother's lap on the back seat.

were forced to give up their homesteads and return to their former homes in other states. For the most part, the people who had the fortitude and ingenuity to stay, prospered and became strong citizens. These early homesteaders who remained, passed their heritage on to their children and grandchildren, many of whom live in Roosevelt County to this day.

In 1906, there were 967 registered voters in Portales, with 136 telephones. Elida had 338 registered voters and only 42 telephones. In 1912, the First State Bank of Elida, owned by W.O. Oldham, was merged with the First National Bank of Elida, and in 1941, the Kenna Bank and Trust Company of Kenna, owned by Charles Sims, was similarly merged.

On October 12, 1935, the First National Bank of Elida was moved to Portales and became the Portales National Bank. In its 94 years, the Portales National has had only five presidents: James. P. Stone, 1906-1913; A.A. Beeman, 1913-1929; J.S. Click, 1929-1959; Douglas B. Stone, 1959-1981 and David L. Stone, 1981-present.

The bank had the dubious distinction in 1928 of being the only bank ever held up by armed bandits in Roosevelt County. The bandits ran out of gas near Arch. The stranded bandits managed to hitchhike to Amarillo and rent a hotel room. As they were counting the stolen money, they were apprehended after being turned in by a maid.

Roma, Douglas and Gladys Stone, 1934.

Twenty years later one of the bandits came by the Portales National Bank, walked up to the president, Mr. Justin Click, and said, "Do you remember me?" Mr. Click looked at the stranger with a puzzled expression. The ex-con smiled and said, "I'm one of the guys that robbed your bank 20 years ago. I just got out of prison and thought I would see how you're doing."

As a young man, Jim's son Douglas B. Stone, learned to operate a car while driving his mother to Elida to attend the monthly board of directors meeting of the First National Bank. In 1935, Douglas (Doug) worked for the Security Pacific National Bank in Los Angeles, California, when he met Dona Locke, his future wife who was attending the University of Southern California. Doug was a tall, thin, nice looking young man who wore white linen suits and drove a new Ford Roadster convertible. His future wife Dona, planned on living in Southern California and being a "California girl" the rest of her life.

Doug took his new wife to Portales, NM to see where he had grown up and to meet his family's friends. After a nice visit in town, he and Dona drove to Elida. Doug

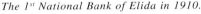

The 1st National Bank of Elida in 1910.

The board of directors in 1970. Left to right: Eldridge Mears, Frantelle Bryant Hatch, Gayle Ferguson, Douglas B. Stone, Gordon Hatch and Dona Stone.

and his sisters Gladys and Roma owned a large share of the First National Bank of Elida. Doug wanted to visit with Mr. Click, the bank's president, and see how the bank was doing.

Elida looked like the end of the world to Dona, as she sat impatiently in the car while Doug went into the bank.

Mr. Click was especially glad to see the young banker and shareholder. The night before John Beeman, the bank's cashier, had been playing poker with some out of town cardsharks and had lost heavily. The winners forced John to open the bank and its vault after midnight to pay his gambling losses. Mr. Click was furious when he discovered his cashier's indiscretion and fired John Beeman on the spot.

Mr. Click quickly found himself in a dilemma. The bank no longer had a cashier, and John Beeman's mother owned 48 percent of the stock in the First National Bank of Elida. If Mrs. Beeman did not support Mr. Click's decision to fire her son, he would no doubt be looking for a new job.

Mr. Click could hardly believe his luck when Douglas B. Stone walked in his door. Doug and his sisters also owned 48 percent of the bank stock. Mr. Click's small ownership plus the

Stone's would exceed 51 percent. His job could be secure.

Mr. Click listened intently as Doug spoke of his banking experience at the Security Pacific National Bank in Los Angeles, California. Mr. Click suddenly said, "How would you like to be the cashier of the First National Bank of Elida?" He then explained what John Beeman had done the night before.

"That is exactly what I would like to do. I'll take the job!" Doug replied breathlessly.

Outside in the hot sun, Dona waited. "Guess what?" Doug said, as he ran up to the car.

"What, darling?" Dona replied, trying to hide her impatience.

"I am the new cashier at the First

National Bank of Elida, We are moving from California to Elida! We're home!"

Dona sat dumbfounded, unable to reply. She began thinking about her recent marriage vows in which she promised to "love, honor and obey till death do us part!"

"I thought we would be living in California," she stammered, trying to keep from crying.

"I did too, but now I have this wonderful job offer and this is exactly what I wished would happen," Doug said, almost unable to keep from jumping up and down with joy.

Doug took his new wife back into the bank to meet Mr. Click and to see their new business.

Dona was quiet all the way to California. "Love, Honor and Obey," she kept repeating.

After living in prosperous California, Doug could see that Elida had passed its boom and that the growth potential in neighboring Portales was much greater. He talked the other directors, Justin S. Click, president; Thomas E. Mears, a prominent lawyer in Portales; and Graham Bryant, the New Mexico state senator into moving the bank to Portales and changing its name to the Portales National Bank. At the time of the move the total assets of the Portales National Bank were $250,000 and its competitor, the First National

Graham Bryant and Justin Glick.

Bank of Portales was 10 times its size with total assets of $2,500,000.

Both T.E. Mears and Graham Bryant were helpful in attracting new business to the bank. Senator Graham delivered the new college, Eastern New Mexico Junior College, to Portales almost single-handedly.

The most important boost to the Portales economy was the opening of the junior college that later became Eastern New Mexico University. In 1912 the New Mexico Constitution called for "a normal school which shall be established by the legislature and located in one the counties of Union, Quay, Curry, Roosevelt, Chavez or Eddy." A normal school was described as being a teachers' training institution.

During the 1927 session, the state legislature was in the process of deciding the location of this institu-

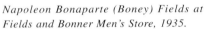

Napoleon Bonaparte (Boney) Fields at Fields and Bonner Men's Store, 1935.

an answer. Senator Bryant, in a compromise, agreed to support Tucumcari's request for road money in exchange for Tucumcari's support

tion of higher learning. All the towns in eastern New Mexico were competing for the opportunity.

Clovis was the largest town in the area and was favored to win. Tucumcari was competing hard. Roswell was home to the New Mexico Military Institute, so they made no serious attempt. Carlsbad, however was a serious contender.

The senator from Roosevelt County was Graham Bryant, a tenacious bulldog who would not take "no" for

Eastern New Mexico Junior College before it opened in 1935.

for locating the new school in Portales. This deal was to be good only on the first vote. This was one obstacle down and still a few to go.

Senator Bryant then negotiated with the Clovis city fathers. Clovis leaders Cash Ramey, A.W. Scarta, John Barry and Senator Sterling A. Jones agreed to support Portales for the college on the first ballot, but

only if Clovis would receive Senator Bryant's support for a new National Guard Armory. Wrestling was popular in those days, and Clovis needed a big facility in which to hold wrestling matches. It was good for business in Clovis. The Clovis leaders knew that state money was already approved for an armory; and college money was still questionable. They were certain that Portales could not get the votes to obtain the new normal college on the first ballot. Clovis, they thought, would end up with the armory *and* the college. Little did the leaders of Clovis realize that "Bulldog Bryant" was wrestling the college away from them.

Senator Bryant, Coe Howard, Sam Seay, Ezra Watts and Earl McCollum drove to Encino, the home of Governor R.C. Dillon, to obtain his support for the location of the college in Portales. Governor Dillon's support

Eastern New Mexico University, 2000.

was critical. A big snowstorm immobilized Bryant's car and the Portales crusaders had to make the return trip by train. However, their trip was worth all the trouble and inconvenience; the governor supported Portales on the first ballot!!

On the day before the big ballot, Senator Bryant lacked the support of only one senator. He was close in his quest to locate the college in Portales on the first vote. It was now or never. All his support would dissolve if he lost on the first ballot. He was desperate. He had run all his traps and he was still one vote short. He knew this was Portales' only chance to get the college!

Mrs. Louise Coe, the senator from Hondo, was unescorted while in Santa Fe. Her husband, a paraplegic, stayed in Hondo and managed their ranch while she was at the legislature. She was the only senator undecided on the college location issue.

Senator Bryant was a gruff, serious minded lawyer. It is hard to imagine passionate or seductive thoughts ever crossing his mind. However, when the future of Portales was at stake, Senator Bryant would persevere. He quickly began to analyze the problem at hand. Who could persuade Senator Coe to vote for Portales? She would undoubtedly need an escort to a Santa Fe celebration on the eve of the big vote. Who could escort her and sell Portales in the process? Bryant's chances for succeeding increased as he carefully selected Senator Coe's escort.

Barry, David, Dona and Doug Stone in 1981.

Napoleon Bonaparte Fields, known as "Boney," was a handsome, debonair, smooth talking men's clothing store-owner in Portales. He was an impeccable dresser and drove a new Buick Roadster convertible. More importantly, Boney was the most eligible bachelor in Portales.

Senator Bryant appeared to be a rock of power who never asked for help. On that day, however, he knew he needed help from a man with different talents than he possessed. What Senator Bryant needed was a lady's man—one that could deliver that final vote.

Soon after Senator Bryant explained the situation to Boney, Boney washed his car, packed his best suit and was on his way to Santa Fe. Boney Fields carried the hopes of Portales with him.

History does not show how "Boney" Fields entertained Senator Coe, or even *if* he did indeed entertain her. It

does show, however, that on the first ballot, Senator Coe voted to locate the new Eastern New Mexico Junior College in Portales.

After the college was officially located, the grateful citizens of Portales presented Governor Dillon with a white horse and silver mounted saddle as a token of their appreciation. Portales saddlemaker J. Harv Baker, made the trophy saddle.

Senator Graham Bryant was, and still is, recognized as the man who delivered ENMJC to Portales. This institution grew to become Eastern New Mexico University, the third largest university in New Mexico. Senator Bryant served as chairman of the board of regents and directed its future with wisdom and tenacity. He is rightfully called "the Father of Eastern New Mexico University."

A tragic event occurred on Thursday March 5th, 1981, when Doug Stone died of a heart attack, leaving a grieving family and community.

The family gathered in Portales for the funeral, all shocked by the unexpected suddenness of his death. David Stone, current president of the bank, sat alone in the funeral parlor the night before his father's service and said all the things to him that he wished he'd said when he was alive. Most importantly, he promised to listen to the advice he had given him throughout his life that he'd heard in spite of having fingers in his ears.

David had been in banking since 1964. In March 1981 he was the executive vice president of the First National Bank in Richardson, Texas.

The board of directors in 1980. Left to right: Frantelle Hatch, Barry Stone, Dona Stone, Douglas Stone, Ruby Mears, Gordon Hatch and Gayle Ferguson.

His brother Barry had been a bank attorney in Amarillo since 1964, and both were ready to take their places in bank management. Barry was elected chairman of the board and David was elected president at an emergency meeting of the Board of Directors.

Doug Stone and T.E. Mears at the ground breaking of the new bank in 1964.

The third Stone generation was now in charge.

After the meeting, David went into his dad's old office and sat in his chair for the first time ever. He could hear his father's voice, suddenly making clear the things he had told him. Since March 7th, 1981, David has "shared my office with my dad, or at

least his guiding spirit. We have made a good team."

The Board of Directors were D. Barry Stone, chairman; David L. Stone, vice-chairman, Dona L. Stone, Gordon Hatch and Frantelle Hatch; the son-in-law and daughter of Graham "Bull Dog" Bryant, Gayle Ferguson, and Ruby Mears the daughter-in-law of T.E. Mears.

Douglas Barry Stone, Jr. (Doug) came to work after graduating from Texas Tech in 1987. He was elected

The board of directors in 2000. Left to right: Richard D. Hood, Gordon M Hatch, Deanna Stone Waddell, Douglas B. Stone, Jr., D. Barry Stone, David L. Stone, Robin Stone Willingham, Deborah Stone Ingraham, and Charles Good. The picture of Jim Stone, the founder, looks over everyone's shoulders.

Derek Stone, David L. Stone and Madison Willingham, 1999

Portales National Bank's executive vice president in 2000.

Robin Stone Willingham came to work in 1993 and graduated from Eastern New Mexico University in 1998. She was elected Portales National Bank's senior vice president in 2000.

Doug's sister Deanna Waddell and Robin's sister Deborah Ingraham both serve as advising directors to Portales National Bank.

The fourth generation is preparing to receive the baton and run with it when the time comes for their leadership.

By the end of 2000 James David Ingraham, age 11; Madison Sanders Willingham, age 4; Derek Taylor Stone, age 4; Lauren Michelle Stone, age 1; and Joseph Locke Willingham, age 4 months make up the 5th generation. It is never too early to prepare for continuation of the family legacy.

The board of directors as of April 1, 2000 are D. Barry Stone, chairman; David Locke Stone, vice chairman; Douglas Barry Stone, Jr.; Robin Stone Willingham; Gordon M. Hatch; Charles Good; Richard H. Hood, Sr.; and Preston Pratt. James G. Hatch, Carol Mears Staggs, Deborah Stone Ingraham and Deanna Stone Waddell serve as advising directors for Portales National Bank.

ROSES SOUTHWEST PAPERS

Just as the Empire State Building was built in the midst of the Great Depression, Roses Southwest Papers was born in what founder Roberto Espat remembers as a time of severe economic downturn for New Mexico. Still, it was a more stable economic and political environment than in Central America, which surrounds Espat's native Belize, where he and Guatemalan wife Rose Marie had built a similar paper production operation.

"Central America was about to boil over," Espat recalls. "We wanted to immigrate to somewhere in the United States where we could find peace and quiet. We did not want to live in any rat race city."

The Espats immediately fell in love with Albuquerque's blue sky and friendly people. "We wanted to find a nice, small business to buy, but there were none available. So we decided to go with a business in which we had some experience," and in January 1986 Roses Southwest Papers opened its doors for business.

With just 20,000 square feet and a dozen staff members, the company earned less than $500,000 in

Rose Marie Espat, owner.

Roberto Espat, owner.

revenues that first year. "The biggest challenge," remembers Espat, "was getting through that first year. It was difficult starting out totally unknown in a strange community." The consumer market proved difficult to penetrate; therefore focus was shifted to the institutional market. But after 18 months, doors were opening, the numbers were looking up, and by the second year, Roses

was "in the black." The Espats have steadfastly refused to look anywhere but straight ahead since.

Diligently promoting themselves and affiliating with organizations such as the Greater Albuquerque Chamber of Commerce and Hispanic Chamber of Commerce, the Espats proved their business was viable and gradually gained customers' confidence. Milestones were reached as the company received recognition both locally and nationally from organizations such as the Small Business Administration and the United States Hispanic Chamber of Commerce. The company really took off in 1989 when it began producing paper bags for the McDonald's chain, which became Roses Southwest Papers' biggest customer. Since then they've added Burger King and several other fast food chains. Revenues grew to $8 million, then to $20 million. Today, with 240,000 square feet and more than 150 employees, Espat expects revenue to exceed $36 million dollars in 2000, up from $31.6 million in 1999.

What's particularly special about this paper production company is that all of its products are made from 100 percent recycled materials, proving that success can be environmentally-friendly.

Napkin converting equipment and process.

Finished goods tissue inventory.

"It's called converting," Espat explains. The raw materials are jumbo rolls of paper that measure five feet in diameter and stand nine feet tall. The plant operates 24 hours a day, seven days a week in order to produce the hundreds of millions of paper bags and rolls of tissue each year. Though presently the Espats purchase the raw material and packaging materials, plans are in the works to change those parts of the business within the next couple of years. A recycling and de-inking plant, together with a paper mill, will not only allow the totally-integrated company to produce their own raw materials, but will keep $18 million in purchases in the state, and create another 150 jobs. Espat estimates, "Within seven years, we should be approaching 500 employees."

It's an ambitious plan, but Roses Southwest Papers has been on a fast track of growth for years. The momentum has carried the company straight into its second year listing in the prestigious *Inc.* Magazine's Inner City 100, which ranks the fastest growing inner city companies in the United States. The Inner City Initiative, as it's called, is what Espat describes as a joint venture between *Inc.* Magazine and Harvard University to encourage businesses to locate inside city areas to revitalize downtown areas.

"When we came here," Espat explains, "there were lots of big businesses downtown. In many cities today, the downtowns are being abandoned. We want to try to revitalize these areas."

Through Roses Southwest Papers, Roberto and Rose Marie Espat have certainly contributed to a healthy economic life in Albuquerque and the state of New Mexico, and are reaping the rewards for their contribution. It's a tightly knit family operation. While Roberto Espat, Jr. is in charge of sales and publicity for the company, his wife, nephew, and son-in-law are also closely involved in running the company. Rose Marie, chief operations officer, handles the day-to-day operations, employee relations, pro-duction, inventory and quality control. "Everything it takes to make the plant run smoothly," she summarizes. "We have stringent quality standards. Our success, we believe, is principally due to our quality of product, performance, service and our personnel. Without these qualities in place we could not boast the major customers we have today." Running the company not as a large corporation but as a family-oriented team as close-knit as the two generations of Espats themselves, the doors are always open to all employees. "We're a family-owned company and we treat our employees as family and team players. If you don't lead with integrity, you can't expect to have good followers or customers. Our customers are the cream of the crop, and so is our staff."

It's only one way Roberto Espat seeks to contribute to the economic health of the area. "We are deeply involved in quality of life issues," says Espat, who serves or has served on boards or is a member of many various community and civic organizations. He has donated his time and services to United Way; Better Business Bureau; Albuquerque Economic Development; Association of Commerce and Industry; Greater Albuquerque Chamber of Commerce; Hispano Chamber of Commerce; ACCION New Mexico; Del Norte Rotary Club of Albuquerque; Albuquerque Convention and Visitors Bureau; Rio Grande Minority Purchasing Council and US Hispanic Chamber of Commerce.

While Espat maintains his family really hasn't done anything more than just work hard and with determination, his philosophies of persistence, consistency and risk are very important. "The world is made up of leaders and followers, but I do not believe there is anything you can't accomplish if you decide to. You just have to be prepared to put everything on the line. In the beginning, you live and dream the business. You work 24 hours a day. You go to sleep thinking, 'what will I do tomorrow? How can I make this better? How will I meet our bank commitments?' If you have little or nothing to lose, your chances of success are lessened."

Today the Espats' dream is a reality embodied in Roses Southwest Papers, and New Mexico is reaping the rewards of their willingness to risk and their determination to make this community the best possible.

ROWLAND NURSERY, INC.

"Work hard, treat your customers right, invest wisely, pay your bills, and develop a business that provides an honest living for family and trust-worthy employees—Because Life Should Be Beautiful."

That was the motto of M.P. (Pat) and Reba Rowland, founders of Rowland Nursery, Inc. Following this formula, the Rowlands have developed the largest family-owned nursery in New Mexico.

In the year 2000, Rowland Nursery, Inc. operates six retail stores—five in Albuquerque and one in Las Cruces. Rowland's also has two growing locations, one four-acre and another 14-acre site. But when M.P. (Pat) Rowland and Reba Sanders were married in October 1935, running a nursery was not in the picture. Instead, Pat Rowland, who loved traveling, drove a bus with Continental Trail-ways. On vacations, the young couple headed west from their Kansas City home. Reba remembers passing through New Mexico and hoping she never had to live in "that barren country."

However, Pat was transferred to New Mexico in 1938, and they both grew to love the area. Over a two-year period, they lived in Taos, Socorro and Albuquerque, where Reba had her first experience trying to make things grow in her new surroundings. She planted a small patch of grass in her yard and mowed it with a pair of scissors!

They moved again with Pat's transfer to California in 1940. Pearl Harbor was bombed in 1941, and Pat immediately joined the Army Air Corps, serving as a flight instructor until the War was over in 1945. Continental Trailways was happy to have him back driving again— "California." In November 1946, the young couple adopted a baby girl, Sharon, and *life was beautiful.*

New Mexico was on Pat's mind, so he requested a transfer. An opening in Albuquerque came in 1949, and Pat and Reba returned. A different kind of opportunity came in disguise in 1952, with a bus strike. During

Newlyweds M.P. (Pat) and Reba Rowland, 1935.

the strike, Pat's plans to install a sprinkler system at their home changed when a neighbor asked to have sprinklers installed at *his* home. Pat took the pipes purchased for his own system and installed them in the neighbor's, making enough money to purchase more. Seeing this as a "golden opportunity," he and another bus driver, Al Landon, began installing sprinkler systems on their days off from driving, after the strike was over. They formed a partnership, called ROW-LAND, taken from both their last names, and in July 1953, the first retail store opened for business.

The little store, complete with a swing set in front for customers'

children, was located at 7402 Menaul, NE—then a two-lane dirt road. "When it rained, the water came in the front door and ran out the back door," recalls Reba Rowland. She laughs and continues, "Here we were with a nursery, and Pat didn't know one plant from another." Over time, the Rowlands educated themselves— becoming experts on plants and grasses appropriate for the environment.

In those early days, Pat Rowland wanted nothing to do with credit cards—only cash, checks and personal charge accounts. Records of 1953 personal accounts show customers identified as "Mrs. Metzger" or

The Rowlands: Sharie, Michael, Reba, and Pat, 1965.

"Mr. Stevens" on a simple ledger sheet; the Rowlands *knew* their customers personally, many of whom (or their children) are still customers today.

Two major events occurred in 1953: son Michael was adopted in July, and the original partnership was dissolved with the Rowland's buying out Mr. Landon. The company was incorporated shortly thereafter, becoming Rowland Landscaping and Sprinkler Co. It was amended to Rowland Nursery, Inc. in 1986 to reflect a broader scope of business.

Sharon (Sharie to all who know her) and Michael helped their parents. Sharie's first job was dusting the pottery and garden ornamentals. Sharie recalls that her parents often didn't cash their paychecks for weeks—ensuring that their employees and vendors were paid first. In late December 1956, the bank balance was $6.56. The company employed 15 to 25 people the first few years, when the average wage was $1.25 an hour.

Michael began his nursery career when he was about four, pulling his little red wagon around their neighborhood selling the latest plants to friends and neighbors. As Sharie and Michael grew older, they were more involved with the Nursery. Under the DECA program, in the 9th grade Sharie gained credits by helping with bookkeeping in the office. She continued working in the family's business through school, then married and had one son, Tom. Sharie went to teacher's college, and taught for three years at Christ the King Lutheran School, a little one-room school in Los Lunas, New Mexico, before returning to the Nursery in 1983.

Michael learned the business literally from the ground up—working with plants and customers, running the cash register, and years of digging ditches. He attended

Kenzie (front) and Erica (the 3rd generation) with Dad Michael—Summer 2000.

Ft. Lewis College in Durango, Colorado, graduating with a degree in horticulture and business. He returned in 1977 to assume more responsibility with the growing Company. The following year, Michael and Lisa were married.

Michael and Lisa have two daughters, Erica, in college, and Kenzie, in high school. The *third* generation of Rowlands in the company, they're following their father's footsteps—learning from the ground up during the summers. Sharie's son, involved with nature in a different way, opened his own exotic bird store, "For the Birds," in 1994, in Albuquerque.

Pat Rowland had a keen eye for real estate. During the early 1960s the family acquired additional property near Menaul, expanding to include warehouses, a greenhouse of 2,700 square feet, a 32,000 square feet lath house and 4,700 more square feet of sales area. Reba and the kids frequently drove a truck to California in late summer. They brought the nursery stock into Albuquerque and let it acclimate to the high desert climate over the winter, to be ready for sale in early spring.

Carefully planning the company's expansion, the Rowlands bought more land for two future operations. The second location, smallest of the retail stores in the chain, was developed

and opened in 1968 in the 'Old Town" section of the city— popular with visitors as well as residents.

Near disaster struck in Winter 1971-72! January temperatures remained below zero for over three days, and the nursery stock stored for spring was severely damaged, costing the company close to $75,000. The Rowlands learned from this experience (this kind of cold is rare in New Mexico) to always have financial protection for losses. They also decided to grow their own plants.

In 1974 they began building greenhouses and the third retail store on land used for growing. The San Mateo store opened in early 1976. Michael became manager in 1977. With over four acres of selling space, it is the largest store. Success required remodeling in 1997 to include an atrium connecting the greenhouse with the main store, and interior redesign to provide better customer service. Rowland Nursery Farms at San Mateo grows approximately 135 varieties of perennials (100,000 per season), vegetables and annuals, and also produces over 17,000 of Rowland's own Poinsettias.

From 1980-1985, expansion continued. Additional land, trailers for hauling stock, forklifts, and other equipment were purchased. In February 1985, the fourth retail store opened, at 4344 Irving—to serve customers on the West Side. Until then, Pat Rowland had resisted credit cards, but the customer demand was so strong at the Irving store that the transition was made company-wide. Rowland's also switched to computerized cash registers and office equipment.

The next five years brought many changes. Pat Rowland passed away in March 1987 from complications associated with diabetes. Reba Rowland became the chief executive officer, Michael assumed the role of president, and Sharie became treasurer and chief financial officer. With strong leaders, Rowland

Nursery continued to flourish. Carrying through M.P. Rowland's plan for southern New Mexico, the company opened the fifth store, in Las Cruces in March 1989.

Early in 1990, the family acquired property from a nursery that had gone out of business at Montgomery and Tramway at the base of the Sandia Mountains. The building required extensive refurbishing from the inside out, but with the skilled help of S&J Construction, everyone working almost night and day, the sixth retail store held its Grand Opening in April 1990. Customers could hardly believe the accomplishments attained in just over 60 days— fresh nursery stock, the large bedding plant area, and the gifts and hardware so attractively displayed. Upgrading continued on the property and in 1992 the City of Albuquerque awarded a Certificate of Beautification to the Montgomery store.

Plant World, a wholesale division, was created during this time to serve small and large landscapers alike. Operating from three leased acres just outside the city limits, Plant World soon outgrew the space, so the Rowlands purchased nine nearby acres in 1991. By 1999, even more growing area was needed, and an adjacent parcel of seven acres was added. Plant World currently supplies 75 plus varieties of trees as well as shrubs, perennials, and sod to New Mexico and southern Colo-

San Mateo, the largest store, after remodeling,1998.

The Menaul store, circa 1956.

rado landscapers and Rowland stores.

The Rowland Nurseries and Plant World differ dramatically from many garden centers by producing a large percentage of their own plant life. The best varieties, specially suited for the New Mexico climate are grown. These plants outperform those produced out of state and shipped into an arid climate, where water conservation is on everyone's minds. Rowland's has been flexible in developing a water xeric plant life selection, tools, attitude and garden tips to help people understand that they can have a great quality of life *and* conserve water.

After the fall season, sections of the stores begin the transformation into a "Christmas Wonderland." After years of providing trees for customers, the company ventured into decorations on a trial basis. The "trial" was so successful that the *Christmas Crew* now work year round out of a large warehouse to provide the best of the newest and most unique in

Michael, Reba (puppy Noel) and Sharie Rowland—June 2000.

Christmas products. Buying, inventorying and preparation consume nine months of the year. It takes an entire week to outfit each store, but by mid-November all stores are breathtaking showcases of Christmas spirit. Customers look forward to the Open House, coming year after year to add to a collection, or start a new theme for their own home.

The Rowland family is extremely proud of their community, their employees, and the quality of the product and services they provide. They believe in giving back to their communities. For many years, the company has worked hand-in-hand with schools and clubs to provide education, seeds and plants. During 1989, Rowland Nursery began a continuing partnership with the City of Albuquerque in a Christmas Tree Recycling program, turning the trees into mulch.

The company supports many civic and cultural events, including sponsoring two plays at the Albuquerque Little Theater. It has provided both expertise and product for landscaping projects including at Civic Plaza in downtown Albuquerque and the Biological Park.

Both Pat Rowland and Michael Rowland were active in the New Mexico Association of Nurseries' Industry. Quentin Doherty, the company's vice president is currently the president of the group. Sharie has served two terms as chairman of the American Diabetes Association of New Mexico, and in 1999, Rowland Nursery was one of the sponsors for the Mayor's Ball, which benefited several non-profit agencies.

Rowland Nursery, Inc. still follows the basic formula established by M.P. Rowland, and has added practices and technology to secure the future for this company with its roots in New Mexico. Providing Legendary Products *and* Service is taught in the company's training programs. "Ours is a very personal business," says Michael. "Our customers and employees interact with *living, growing* things. We don't just sell the product; we guarantee it, and we're here to help our customers be successful gardeners. We're very proud of the 50-plus, specially-trained certified nursery professionals among our staff."

Significantly, Michael makes sure he stays current with his own certification. *This* president doesn't just sit behind a desk. Most any day will find him at the stores and Plant World, talking with staff and seeing to customers' needs—whether it be a problem with their roses or a question about the best type of grass seed to use in their yards.

Indeed, in the 1990s the Rowland team focused on fine-tuning the basics and upgrading services. A landscape designer was brought on board to advise customers. Additionally, the company hired an educator from the New Mexico State University to provide training on plant life and chemicals to employees as well as educational seminars for the public all over the state. Garden Talk, a Saturday morning live program on 770 KOB radio, is immensely popular. It features Michael or another Rowland team garden expert in a question-and-answer format. Pertinent questions asked at the stores are often addressed on Garden Talk; following each show, the information is printed and distributed through the stores, further serving customer needs.

Upgraded training for sales staff and cashiers was instituted with the addition of a corporate trainer. In recent years, hiring earlier for the Spring season, coupled with the Rowland Mentor Program, has resulted in a more stable staff of educated and satisfied employees.

Keeping pace with changing technologies, the company has invested heavily in a company-wide point-of-sale system that not only speeds up the checkout process at the registers, but also allows for up-to-date inventory keeping.

As for employees—many a young person has received their first paycheck as a result of the seasonal employment offered by Rowland's or Plant World. The company is equally proud of its team members with 10, 15, and 20—in fact, 40 plus years of working side by side with the owners. Joe Griegos was one of the first employees at Menaul, retiring in the late 1980s. Carrying on the "family" tradition today is Joe's grandson Mike, just beginning his Rowland career. The company maintains an Employee Profit Sharing Plan and a formal program recognizing and rewarding the dedication and service of the staff.

At this writing, Reba Rowland, who turned 86 in March 2000, is still an avid gardener and still comes to the office. Michael plans to continue managing the operations side of the business, with Sharie overseeing the accounting/financial area. A fourth generation of Rowlands is now growing up— Averee and Emilee, the young son and daughter of Tom Rowland and great grandchildren of Reba. Learning from past experience, and with a mature, trained staff in place, the Rowland family and nursery management are confident in the company's potential. *Life Should Be Beautiful* in the 21st century.

CITY OF SANTA FE

Santa Fe, New Mexico—it has become synonymous with southwestern culture, Georgia O'Keeffe, fine art, the Old Santa Fe Trail, world-renowned opera and incredible natural beauty. For hundreds of years visitors and newcomers to Santa Fe have come to the same misunderstanding—they arrive here thinking "desert" but within time they come to cherish the spectacular beauty of its physical landscape, its allure, and the uniqueness of its multi-cultural heritage—past and present.

Santa Fe's history, cultures and traditions go back centuries. The existence of Native American cultures is evident throughout the region. The Anasazi or "Ancient Ones," ancestors of today's Pueblo Indians, originally inhabited Santa Fe and its surrounding area about AD1050. For New Mexico's Native Americans, the centuries from 1539, when Europeans first set foot in the state, to modern times, have been filled with major trials and minor triumphs. The unrelenting attempt at acculturation impacted the Indians in tragic ways and forced into secrecy performances of tribal ceremonies—a practice that continues today.

Uprisings during colonization bolstered the natives' sense of identity.

Santa Fe's Saint Francis Cathedral was the first Roman Catholic cathedral to be constructed between Durango, Mexico and Saint Louis, Missouri. The 1869 cornerstone was stolen a few days after it was laid and never recovered. This photograph of the cathedral was taken in the 1950s.

During a Pueblo revolt in 1680, 400 of 2,500 European settlers were killed. The remainder fled to El Paso, ceding the natives their land for 12 years. In 1692, the Spanish colonists achieved a successful reconquest.

Today a Pueblo Indian stands on the same cliff as his ancestor centuries before. A major advantage for New Mexico's indigenous people today is remaining on their ancestral lands, resulting in strength of identity and empowerment. The 20th century has been a time of major transition for the state's indigenous people. They successfully integrate their cultural beliefs with those of the greater society and incorporate strong links to the past with an ever-clearer sense of the future. They educate their youth in traditional wisdom, yet send them off to be educated so they impart newly acquired wisdom to the tribe.

Composing 19 pueblos, two Apache reservations and a large portion of the Navajo reservation, New Mexico's Indians stand as leaders in the national Native American community, poised to successfully confront the challenges of the new millennium with the same strength and endurance they have demonstrated for the past thousand years.

The founding of the City of Santa Fe predates the English settlement of Jamestown. In 1607 a group of Spanish settlers established a small

This photo of San Francisco Street looking east along Santa Fe's plaza was taken around 1880. In the background are the two towers of the Saint Francis Cathedral which was under construction. Construction of the cathedral, which dominates Santa Fe's downtown, was initiated by Santa Fe's Archbishop, Jean Baptiste Lamy of France.

community in Santa Fe and in 1609 Spanish soldiers and colonists began to construct the capital of New Mexico in Santa Fe. Today, the Palace of the Governors, built in 1610, is the oldest public building in the United States. It has been

A Native American from Santa Clara Pueblo, north of Santa Fe, poses in traditional dress. The photo was taken in the 1950s.

the seat of government for nearly three centuries and witness to colorful histories including Spanish, Pueblo, Mexican and American. That statement brings into perspective the age, significance and diversity of this country's oldest capital.

Like their earliest ancestors, the Hispanic people of Santa Fe are varied, resourceful and sophisticated. Past history often has portrayed the first settlers as naïve peasants struggling to survive on the fringes of the New World. But their survival is due to a worldly combination of tradition, innovation and faith. Here on the isolated frontier that was once the northernmost point of New Spain, Hispanics have drawn on the intellectual, aesthetic and religious influ-

ences of their forebears to create the rich culture that is at the heart of the city today.

Few Americans had seen New Mexico in the early 1800s. It was the northernmost point on a prosperous trade route to Mexico City and its Spanish rulers guarded it closely. Foreigners were not welcome. But

In 1976 a wagon train from St. Louis, Missouri entered the Santa Fe Plaza, which marks the end of the Old Santa Fe Trail in celebration of America's 200th birthday.

in 1821 Mexico won its independence from Spain and a torrent of American adventurers, explorers and traders poured in seeking opportunity. The first of these was a Missouri explorer who returned home to tell of abundant profit that others quickly followed in his footsteps. The Santa Fe Trail was born.

Fur trappers, lumbermen and farmers followed the Trail; the number of Americans in Santa Fe grew steadily. In 1846 the United States went to war with Mexico, consumed with the notion that the U.S. should extend to the Pacific Ocean. General Stephen Kearney and his "Army of the West" rode into Santa Fe and claimed New Mexico as an American possession. New Mexico became a U.S. territory in 1850 and a state in 1912. An important Civil War battle at Glorieta, near Santa Fe, was a victory for the Union. As the military presence in northern New Mexico increased, so did the need for food. Vast ranches sprang up and soon cattle drives and cattle barons were a common sight.

The safety of Territorial status attracted even more pioneers, including young German Jewish immigrants, many of them brothers or cousins.

The Ninth Cavalry Band, a group of black soldier-musicians (Buffalo Soldiers) under the direction of Professor Charles Spiegel, entertained Santa Feans on the Plaza in the last quarter of the nineteenth century. In this photo by Ben Wittick, the band posed in front of the plaza's gazebo in 1880.

Taos Pueblo is located two hours north of Santa Fe. The pueblo Indians of Taos have lived there for over 1000 years. It is the oldest continuously inhabited multi-level adobe building in North America.

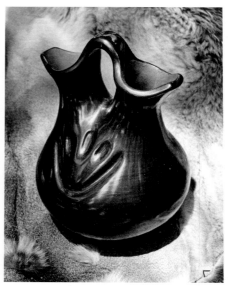

World renowned Santa Clara Pueblo potter, Maria Martinez, made famous her "black-on-black" pottery designs. Pictured is a traditional "wedding vase" given to newly-weds on their wedding day.

They established important commercial links to the East Coast, to Europe and to the Indian reservations. They eventually brought their families to Santa Fe, built mercantile businesses and opened the first banks.

The whistle of train engines in 1879 announced that the modern world had arrived on Santa Fe's doorstep. The railroad brought manufactured goods and the first tourists. The area became famous for open, untamed spaces and personal freedom. Artists, writers, eccentrics and those who were fed up with East Coast society flocked to Santa Fe.

Around the turn of the century, another industry had a major impact on the development of the city. Tuberculosis was the public health scourge of the day. Doctors believed high altitude, dry air and plenty of sunshine could cure the disease. Those who came to Santa Fe sanatori-

Built in 1610, the Palace of the Governors is the oldest public building in the United States and now a unit of the Museum of New Mexico. It was the seat of nearly three centuries of government and witness to colorful histories including Spanish, Pueblo, Mexican and American.

ums and stayed included prominent physicians, lawyers and business people. Their skills brought a new level of sophistication to the frontier town.

Santa Fe has long been known as a literary haven for such acclaimed writers as Richard Bradford (*Red Sky at Morning*), Willa Cather (*Death Comes for the Archbishop*) and Lew Wallace (*Ben Hur*).

Only recently has the rest of the United States begun to recognize and appreciate the significance of New Mexico's rich history and its important place in American heritage. There are very few places in this country where people's ancestry goes

back so many generations to the same place where they still live today. Santa Fe truly is a triumph in multiculuralism. Modern Santa Fe is a unique blend of the ideas and influences of many cultures and countries. It has long been a center of civilization. It is a city with the power to adapt to the new and cherish the old. It is in its history and through its people that Santa Feans are able to maintain their cultural awareness. Those who arrive become as fiercely protective of its special qualities as those who count their local roots in centuries. Santa Fe is a city with a soul.

TEMA CONTEMPORARY FURNITURE

TEMA Contemporary Furniture in Albuquerque was the direct result of Benny Kjaer's dreams of the Wild West, as a young boy growing up in Denmark. And now, at the beginning of the new Millennium, the company is considered a national leader in the retailing of contemporary furniture.

Born on a small farm in Denmark to parents who still had memories of World War II fresh in their minds, Benny's education began in a one-room schoolhouse. It was here, where the "library" consisted of one bookshelf, that he found the book that started him on a lifelong journey. The book was about the life and adventures of Davy Crockett, and six-year old Benny was hooked.

After high school, Benny became an apprentice/student and graduated with a degree in furniture marketing from the University of Copenhagen. However, he still dreamt of someday getting to the American West.

The opportunity presented itself in 1976 when he was offered one of the few slots to spend a year in Denver, Colorado, as a trainee in a Danish furniture store. Benny Kjaer had finally found his home. After

Benny Kjaer, president; Soren Thomsen, senior vice president merchandising, and Graham McInnis, senior vice president marketing and Internet.

Tema Contemporary Furniture, Albuquerque.

spending a couple of years in Western Canada gaining additional experience, Benny was invited back to Denver in 1980 to help establish a new store called Christian of Copenhagen.

In 1982 Benny drove a U-Haul to Albuquerque to open a second outlet in a small strip center on Menaul. As he is fond of retelling, "I was all alone. There were days when I had no customers, and not even the mailman would open the door. There was no money, and I would make deliveries at night and on weekends." It was during these years that the company's ingrained philosophy of customer service and "The TEMA Way" developed.

After five years Benny was able to buy out his partners, and in 1988 his new company, TEMA Copenhagen, moved to its present location on Montgomery in Albuquerque's North East Heights. The move proved very successful, and within two years the company took over the entire building

and created MILAN International, a store with value-priced furniture from around the world. A few years later the stores were combined, and today the company is known as TEMA Contemporary Furniture.

Over the years the company has been fortunate to attract managers with exceptional leadership skills and entrepreneurial drive. The company now imports furniture and accessories from around the world, and sells nationally through its website.

"We've been in business for 18 years, but it feels like we've just started," remarks Benny Kjaer. "There are so many opportunities in this great country, and with the organization and leadership team we have today, the possibilities are limitless. Right now we are aiming to become a top furniture retailer on the Internet, establishing several specialty stores in the region, building a large centralized distribution system and founding the TEMA University for our employees. And, the list goes on and on."

In 1994 Benny married Sylvia Linder, who among her ancestors counts Comanches; Benny's dream has come full circle. He has become somewhat of a history buff and he and Sylvia travel extensively.

Through his involvement with Rotary and charity organizations Benny has become involved in the community in numerous ways. He takes the most pride in his ability to sponsor other young Danes as trainees, and in his involvement with Accion New Mexico, a micro-lending organization that helps budding entrepreneurs throughout the state.

THE SANTA FE NEW MEXICAN

To the average person, anything from over 50 years ago is antique. Anything more than 100 years old creaks with the dust of eld.

Something older than that? Except by the rare antiquary, eminently forgettable.

The Santa Fe New Mexican proudly gives the lie to that view. At 151 years, it is the oldest newspaper in the American West—and anything but out of date.

Since its 1999 150th anniversary year, the newspaper has added microzoned editions for nearby communities and launched a direct mail product for non-subscribers in the region. With its oft-visited website, www.sfnewmexican.com, it is prepared to continue being the number one information provider for northern New Mexico.

The New Mexican's weekly arts and entertainment magazine, *Pasatiempo*, won the coveted Missouri Lifestyle Journalism Award for best regularly scheduled feature supplement in 1999. The paper publishes a monthly *Real Estate Guide*, endorsed by the Santa Fe Board of Realtors.

Another publication is the official Indian Market program for the nearly 100,000 visitors to that acclaimed

Robert M. McKinney, owner since 1949.

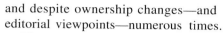

The New Mexican *in 1937. Photo T. Harmon Parkhurst, courtesy Museum of New Mexico, Neg. No. 10725*

annual Santa Fe event. *The New Mexican* also sponsors the Pancakes on the Plaza program that attracts 12,000 people to the heart of town each July 4th.

Since its first issue of November 24, 1849—a four-page tabloid with two pages in English and two in Spanish—everything has come under the journal's purview. And this whether as a weekly or daily, in English or in Spanish, through temporary setbacks

and despite ownership changes—and editorial viewpoints—numerous times.

The paper enjoys the rare distinction of ownership by one man for a third of its lifetime. Robert M. McKinney, of a family active in the West since Civil War days, acquired the paper in 1949.

His grandfather came to the region in 1857 in an ox-drawn wagon along the Santa Fe Trail. McKinney's father, a circuit-riding preacher, first brought him to Santa Fe in 1920. McKinney's daughter, Robin McKinney Martin, will succeed her father as publisher and is the owner of *The New Mexican's* sister publication, *The Taos News*.

Despite its senior status, *The New Mexican* is younger than the city it serves. Santa Fe was founded between 1605 and 1607, during the great adventures of Spanish explorer Don

The New Mexican's *composing room, 1899. Photo courtesy Museum of New Mexico, Neg. No. 10560*

Juan de Oñate. Construction of its impressive Palace of the Governors—whose occupants have included Lew Wallace, author of *Ben Hur*—began in 1609.

A printing press first reached Santa Fe in 1834. Oral history says that Don Santiago Abreu, local delegate to the 1833 Mexican assembly, bought the machinery in Chihuahua and shipped it over the Camino Real to Santa Fe.

But Yankee trader Josia Gregg, active in Santa Fe between 1833 and 1840, said in his memoirs that the press reached the city in 1834 from the United States, via the Santa Fe Trail. No matter where it came from, the press was one of the first in the West.

The New Mexican *in 1911. Photo courtesy Museum of New Mexico, Neg. No. 28798*

The first paper published in the area was *El Crepusculo de la Libertad (The Dawn of Liberty)* in Taos, N.M. Four issues came out in August and September 1834, printed by Padre C. Antonio José Martínez on the Abreu press.

E.T. Davies and W.E. Jones were the first publishers of *The New Mexican*, in 1849, one year after the end of the Mexican-American war made New Mexico a territory of the United States.

Nothing is known about the founders today, but the first issue included a glowing prospectus of their intentions to serve the community. It also included a list of locals who had received mail that week; a description of Queen Victoria's recent state visit to Ireland; a legal insertion dealing with a Santa Fe County Circuit Court filing; and an advertisement for the American Theater's offerings for November 28th.

All this can still be read on a copper printing plate of that first issue, in *The New Mexican's* offices.

The next extant *New Mexican* dates from 1850. Ceran St. Vrain— Kit Carson associate, politico and mountain man—was publisher. To keep matters in historical perspective, Nathaniel Hawthorne published *The Scarlet Letter* that year; two years later Harriet Beecher Stowe's *Uncle Tom's Cabin* took the world by storm.

In 1863, William J. Manderfield bought the paper from Charles P. Clever, who had purchased it from Dr. Charles Lieb, who probably acquired it from St. Vrain. In 1864, ownership passed to William H.

Manderfield and Thomas S. Tucker. At that time, the Spanish-page masthead was changed to *El Nuevo-Mejicano.*

On July 8, 1868 the paper became a daily morning publication. An advertisement in that issue announced that U.S. mail delivery time from Santa Fe to Denver "has been reduced to three and a half days by four-horse Concord coaches."

After some 10 years of regular appearance, *The New Mexican* suspended publication on December 31, 1879. It was revived on February 27, 1880, under a stock company controlled by the Atchison, Topeka and Santa Fe Railroad. At that time, the Spanish-language section of the paper became a separate weekly issue with its own advertising.

E.B. Purcell of Manhattan, Kansas bought the paper effective December 31, 1881. On May 27, 1883, Purcell suspended publication and offered press and equipment for sale. *The New Mexican* was reorganized that July 27th as a joint stock company

President Roosevelt and Bronson Cutting, U.S. Senator (R-N.M.) and New Mexican *owner, in 1932. Photo courtesy Museum of New Mexico, Neg. No. 138126*

The exterior of The New Mexican. *Photo by Clyde Mueller.*

and became an evening publication.

On the evening of July 20, 1888, a fire completely destroyed the paper's building at the northeast corner of the Plaza, including the press, subscription lists and back-issue files. With the $4,500 insurance proceeds, Colonel Max Frost secured a press from Topeka, Kansas and paper from San Francisco. Publication resumed one month later on August 20, 1888.

In April 1911, a site at the corner of Palace Avenue and Sheridan Street was purchased from the school board and a new two-story brick building, designed by the famous architect I.H. Rapp was erected, complete with an Otis elevator and new equipment. Publication continued there from December 31, 1911 until June 1942.

New Mexico was still sensitive about its persona in those early days. In his 1949 memoirs, long-time editor Paul A.F. Walter recalled a *New Mexican* reporter who tattled to an Eastern paper that Santa Fe women smoked in public. "No sooner had a copy of the paper reached Santa Fe when the reporter was informed he had better leave town `poco pronto,'" Walter recalled. The young man fled

via the old Denver and Rio Grande Railroad to Denver, where he became publisher of a successful farming weekly.

In 1912, New Yorker Bronson M. Cutting, who had come to New Mexico in search of health, acquired controlling interest in *The New*

The New Mexican's *news room. Photo by Clyde Mueller.*

Mexican. Cutting was appointed U.S. Senator in 1927 to succeed the late A.A. Jones, and held that position until his death in an airplane crash in 1935.

On Cutting's death, his close friend Jesús Baca took control of *The New Mexican*. He sold it in June 1937 to the Kansas-based Oscar Stauffer company. Rolla Clymer, a former staffer with William Allen White's *Emporia Gazette*, took over editorship.

Frank C. Rand purchased the paper as of June 1, 1940. *The New Mexican* built its current quarters on Marcy Street, in the heart of Santa Fe, in June 1942. That was a few months after Pearl Harbor, when the government took over the old building for the Manhattan Project.

January 17, 1949 marked the start of a new era for *The New Mexican*. George M. Reynolds, president of Southwestern Newspapers, and Robert M. McKinney took over *The New Mexican*. Within a few months, McKinney became sole owner.

In 1972, *The New Mexican* installed a new offset press and switched to cold type. In February 1976, McKinney merged *The New Mexican* with the Gannett Company, Inc.

Gannett later breached the contract,

The New Mexican's *press room. Photo by Clyde Mueller.*

firing McKinney's general manager Stephen E. Watkins, who is today president of the company and praised by McKinney as "my most important business associate for 50 years." McKinney, who was in Europe when he heard his "number one man" had been fired, took Gannett to court. The case went to trial in 1980. It took 13 weeks, the longest civil case ever in a New Mexico Federal court.

U.S. District Judge Santiago Campos noted of the Gannett men who appeared to testify in court during the trial that, "some of them acting together struck for themselves and the corporation they represented a deliberate course of conduct which willfully and wrongfully dishonored Gannett's obligations and, bit-by-bit, day-by-day shamelessly destroyed the rights bargained to McKinney."

Judgment was given in favor of McKinney, but Goliath was determined to win over David. Gannett appealed on various grounds over the next seven years, including two appearances before the 10th Circuit Court of Appeals.

When all appeals were exhausted, McKinney was authorized on September 1, 1987 to resume management of the newspaper under his contract. Gannett agreed to sell the

paper back to McKinney in November 1989. On December 17, a full-page house ad announced the paper's return to family control.

McKinney is still active and closely involved in the paper in his ninth decade. A Democrat, he served as ambassador to the United States Atomic Energy Commission in Vienna in the 1950s and as United States ambassador to Switzerland in the 1960s. He held presidential appointments under every chief executive from Truman to Nixon.

The New Mexican has long been active in the community. Working with John Gaw Meem, founder of the Santa Fe school of architecture, the paper pressed the city to adopt a building ordinance and establish a central historical district.

When what McKinney called "a circular California-style plate glass arena" was proposed for the new state capital building, *The New Mexican* worked to change the plans to something more appropriate to the area. Meem's territorial-style building, built on the initial round foundations, stands today with the fond name of "The Roundhouse."

McKinney and *The New Mexican* worked closely with U.S. Senator

The New Mexican's *web site.*

Clinton P. Anderson to support the Chama Water Project for tunneling headwaters of the Colorado River under the Rocky Mountains to the Rio Grande Valley. Water remains a paramount issue closely monitored by the newspaper.

The New Mexican is a supporter of John Crosby and his internationally-famous Santa Fe Opera. McKinney was instrumental in persuading St. John's College of Annapolis, Maryland to establish a western campus here.

During its lifetime, *The New Mexican* has enjoyed the services of scores of fine writers, including sports writer Bill Bailey, editor Will Harrison, women's editor Calla Hay and "reporter" Will McNaulty. McNaulty's funeral, McKinney recalled, included "three brass bands and free whiskey."

Oliver La Farge, acclaimed author of *Laughing Boy*, was a regular columnist for years. His 1959 *Santa Fe-The Autobiography of a Southwestern Town* told the story of *The New Mexican* up to that time. Best-selling mystery writer Tony Hillerman was once managing editor.

Today, the paper's annual Empty Stocking Fund raises more than $100,000 each year to help needy Santa Feans during the holiday season. A pilot program of *New Mexican* employees who mentor and tutor in the Santa Fe Public Schools enjoys 25-percent employee participation.

Under the day-to-day guidance of Martin and associate publisher Billie Blair, and with McKinney's oversight, *The New Mexican* remains committed to Santa Fe. With 200 employees, it enjoys a circulation of 24,500 daily and 27,000 Sunday and the respect and acclaim of its peer journals throughout the nation.

No matter what the issue, *The New Mexican* continues, as it has for a century and a half, to encourage, to warn and to seek solutions. It is the most important type of newspaper—a local institution, owned by a local family who puts the welfare of its community first.

SMPC ARCHITECTS

The architectural firm of SMPC Architects has been an Albuquerque and New Mexico institution since World War II. As such, SMPC Architects is the oldest architectural firm in the State of New Mexico.

In 1944, Gordon Ferguson went from part time practitioner and college instructor to full time architect, operating out of his house until he opened a new office at 111 Amherst Street, SE in the developing Nob Hill neighborhood of the city. A major addition to that structure was built in 1955 and the firm continues to provide services from those offices. The firm name has officially changed a few times; Gordon Ferguson, Architect changed to Ferguson Stevens and Associates in 1949, then Ferguson, Stevens, Mallory and Pearl in 1959, Stevens, Mallory, Pearl and Campbell in 1972 and SMPC Architects in 1993. The tradition of innovative quality service has remained throughout the years.

Gordon Ferguson was a true entrepreneur. He developed the

SMPC received the AIA 25 Year Firm Award for the St. Marks on the Mesa Episcopal Church in Albuquerque, designed and constructed in 1955.

firms' client base of private and public work primarily through social contact. Commissions for the Bernalillo County Indian Hospital, the Bataan Memorial Methodist Hospital and the Lovelace Clinic established the firm as the local experts in medical facility design. Donald Stevens had taught architecture at the University of Texas until he joined the firm as a partner in 1948. Don's career spanned over 35 years with the firm. Don became the medical expert and he was responsible for the continued relationships with Lovelace, Presbyterian and Anna Kaseman Hospitals.

Three very accomplished students followed Don from Texas to Albuquerque. Bob Mallory, George Pearl and Van Dorn Hooker joined the firm in the early '50s. Bob and George stayed on and became partners. Van Dorn went on to the University of New Mexico to become the University architect. Bob Mallory was an 'architect's architect,' a stickler for detail and a careful wordsmith. Bob became an excellent mentor to those in the 'drafting room' as his work ethic set the example for many in the firm to follow. George Pearl became the lead designer for the firm in the late-'50s, and his designs helped the firm gain regional and national recognition. George led the design efforts until his retirement in 1990. His unswerving efforts rewarded George with a Fellowship (for design) by the American Institute of Architects and the Western Mountain Region AIA Silver Medal for design. The firm benefitted with many awards, most notably the AIA New Mexico 25 Year Firm Award.

The Albuquerque Academy Dining Room addition was carefully detailed to blend into the campus architecture, while the interior offers patrons a commanding panorama of the Sandia Mountains.

Bob Campbell joined the firm while attending the University of New Mexico in 1955 and continued until retiring in early 2000. Bob was very influential in continuing the high level of client service during his tenure with the firm. Bob has served on many professional and local boards and is currently national treasurer of the National Council of Architectural Registration Boards.

In 1985 four members of the firm, Bob Moraga, Chris Willadsen, Glenn Fellows and Mike Dickson were made associates. They now run the firm as senior principals with the help of recent principals Allison Abraham, Dave Cook, David Hassard, Karl Schindwolf and Patricia Hancock.

SMPC Architects continues to provide architectural services to a variety of clients. The primary areas of practice are healthcare, educational, high tech and related office or commercial facilities.

Architecture, interior design, planning and landscape architecture services are offered in house. The firm is dedicated to providing clients the type of service that they need, designing facilities that are responsible to budget, function and place. SMPC has completed well over 4,000 projects in its 56 years of service to the community, and owes a great deal of thanks to its many clients, for the opportunity and the experience and especially for the friendships built.

A short list of SMPC current and past clients includes Presbyterian Healthcare Services; Lovelace Medical Center; Carrie Tingley Hospital; Cibola Medical Center; Clovis High Plains Hospital; Colfax Miners Hospital; Espanola Hospital; Sandia National Laboratories; University of New Mexico; New Mexico Tech; Eastern New Mexico University; Albuquerque National Bank (now Bank of America); Los Alamos National Bank; Albuquerque Public Schools; Moriarty Municipal Schools; Los Alamos Public Schools; Albuquerque Public Schools; Manzano Day School; Menaul School; AT&T; US West; Motorola;

SMPC Architects received the American Institute of Architects Western Mountain Regional Award of Honor for the Main Branch of the Albuquerque Public Library.

NASA; NRAO; the Hotel St. Francis and many more.

SMPC enters this new century with a renewed dedication to client service through building a better environment in which to work and live. SMPC Architects is currently involved in exciting research park projects associated with the Los Alamos National Labs and Sandia National Labs. These projects should

Construction completion is scheduled for early 2001 for the Los Alamos Research Park Phase I Building which will house office and light laboratory space promoting tech transfer.

help to shape and define the next generation of technological advances for our society. You can learn more about SMPC Architects by visiting their website at smpcarch.com/smpc.

THE TELEPHONE PIONEER MUSEUM OF NEW MEXICO

History of the old west and the role of the telephone comes alive in the Telephone Pioneer Museum of New Mexico. In 1881, the first telephone exchange established in New Mexico was developed at the end of the railroad expansion lines in the bustling little town of Las Vegas. It was here, in the northern part of the state that the legacy of the telephone people of New Mexico began.

The original "museum" was just a room set up by the Mountain States Telephone & Telegraph Company's public relations manager, Ray Gifford, in 1961. It was kept presentable by a volunteer group of then-current and retired employees of the company, called the Telephone Pioneers. It was equipped with an eclectic assortment of switchboards and telephone handsets, as well as the era's new technology. The dedication of "The Pioneer Room" as it was known, took place at 625 Silver, SW in Albuquerque and coincided with events surrounding New Mexico's 50th anniversary of statehood and the 50th anniversary of the Telephone Pioneers of America. Throughout the '70s and '80s The Pioneer Room moved to different locations around the city. With help from co-workers, the current chairperson of the Museum Board of

"Bob, the Lineman" exhibit is an up close view of the 25-foot-high telephone pole and equipment used to construct a telephone line.

Museum director, Neal Roch's, 21-foot high mural of "Electricity," a gold-plated statue which once stood 434 feet above street level on the AT&T headquarters building and is fondly referred to as "Golden Boy."

Directors, Gigi Galassini, continued adding interesting items salvaged from nearby telephone offices that were being closed or renovated. Other individuals from throughout the state also saved various telephones and equipment from being destroyed. After retiring, Gigi embarked on a mission to find a permanent, suitable home for the collection. Thus, in 1990 she began calling and writing letters which finally "landed" the building she had always dreamed would become a museum.

The perfect place for the Museum was the 1906 Mills Building (the first telephone exchange building in Albuquerque) located in the heart of Albuquerque's downtown business hub. The front section was abandoned, although still part of the AT&T office building, but it was not up to modern building codes. The architect and the building engineer brought the building up to code, while also keeping Gigi's plan for a museum in mind. The exterior of the building was even refaced to resemble the 1906 style of architecture. In December 1996, the three-story building, which had been vacant since 1983, was ready to become home to the Telephone Pioneer Museum

of New Mexico. In June 1997, after countless hours of volunteer work, the Museum welcomed its first visitors!

The history throughout the three floors of the Museum is incredible. The Museum's uniqueness is witnessed not only through the hundreds of phones, telephone equipment, historical exhibits, gift shop, murals and vintage photographs, but also through its entirely volunteer operation! Most of the volunteers are retired "telephone people" and some are community citizens who are entrenched in the State's history with interests in the city's development. Since the Museum opened in 1997, more than 4,000 visitors have visited each year including seniors from local retirement homes, university-level architectural students, elementary school children and tourists from as far away as Poland and Hong Kong.

The Museum is managed by a nine-member board of directors composed of three persons from each of the pioneer entities of AT&T, Lucent Technologies and US West. Its operation relies entirely on its 60-plus volunteers who do everything from greeting visitors and conducting tours to dusting, vacuuming, painting and carpentry. Each volunteer donates at least one day per month (10 a.m.-2 p.m.) to the Museum. In 1998, the newly-formed Museum won the Albuquerque Convention and Visitor Bureau's Hospitality Award. This annual honor is bestowed on a business or organization that helps promote and revitalize the City of Albuquerque.

Visitors enjoy the variety of switchboards that were once the "link to the world" including the actual one used in Columbus, New Mexico to warn of the attack by Pancho Villa. There are hundreds of telephones on display as well as Teletype machines used for news broadcasts. The balcony gallery features many photographs documenting the telephone era in New Mexico.

Children today are awed by a rotary telephone set and thrilled by the old can and string telephone set that was popular in yesteryear. In the Museum's Learning Center children are invited to become "really connected"! They are taught to operate a switchboard by actually connecting the caller to the called party. They can even earn their "Junior Operator Certificate." The field phones also give them a GI Jane or GI Joe experience in operating actual phones used in combat. A "Stepper Switch" connected to Designline telephones like Elvis, Mickey Mouse, Goofy, Barbie and a Harley Davidson works in full view as connections are being made. This exhibit was created when volunteers realized that in today's telephone technology children often did not know what a rotary telephone was or how to use it. Lessons of electricity and magnets, as well as those involving the oscilloscope, make it quite an adventure to learn about the telephone and other items of communication. The object of the Learning Center is not only to educate but also to inspire young inventors!

A Research Center is available to the public seeking information about the past using old phone directories or telephone magazines printed as far back as 1912. Annual Reports of the Bell System back in the early 1900s are also available to research. Collectors enjoy the varieties of insulators and cable (from coaxial to fiber optic) that are proudly displayed in the Museum.

Displays feature switchboards dating back to 1882. These early switchboards were small and used in the rural farm communities, often in someone's home. At the turn of the century, most operators in New Mexico made a salary of 10¢ an hour and were "on-call" 24-hours a day! A New Mexican "hero" was one such operator and is depicted in one of the Museum's audio-visual exhibits. She was actually a telephone operator in Folsom, New Mexico in 1908, when a devastating flood tore through the town in the early morning hours. A 21-foot wall of water, created by debris caught at a railroad trestle, broke loose and gushed toward the town as Sally Rooke, the local operator, warned the townspeople of

The Museum building as it was in 1906. It has been restored to look this way today.

the impending danger. Sally saved many lives that morning, but was washed away to her death. Operators throughout the system years later donated an hour's wage to erect a monument for Sally's grave. Their tribute resurrected her story for all to remember the bravery and courage of operators everywhere who stay at their phones to serve the public. The sound and lighting effects of this exhibit make it worth taking an additional five minutes at the Museum.

The Columbus, New Mexico exhibit is equally exciting. It displays three parts of the story of Pancho Villa's 1916 raid on the small border town of Columbus and how the local operator, with her baby clinging to her, called the cavalry to save the small town. Although she was wounded, she kept nearby towns alerted to the raid and successfully brought help to her townsmen. General John J. "Blackjack" Pershing commended her bravery and dedication after he took charge of the town. Visitors viewing this display are captured by the high drama as they listen to the story unfold.

The Museum invites guests to

become active learners as they discover the "what, when and how" of communications. Through the work of the Museum, visitors develop an appreciation for preserving history and gain new insights into the legacy of the many dedicated people who devoted their work years to the telephone industry. Thanks to early leaders like Theodore Vail, service has always been valued in the telephone industry. The tireless efforts of telephone man Angus Macdonald, are depicted in the "Spirit of Service" mural at the Museum. In the midst of the 1888 blizzard that hit between New York City and Boston, Angus and his crew grabbed their tools and snowshoes and went to restore phone service on the New York-Boston Line. In the midst of their work, they came upon a snowbound train and walked back to town to bring food to the passengers. Being assured the passengers' needs were met, the crew returned to their efforts to restore phone service.

Future plans for the Museum include exhibits featuring Alexander Graham Bell's laboratory, a Teletype simulation of the John F. Kennedy assassination news script coming over the wire, the Telstar communications satellite launch and a display illustrating the breakup of the Bell System.

THE WILSON CORPORATION

The Wilson Corporation was founded by Clarence Alfred Wilson and his wife Gertrude Wilson, in 1957. Clarence was born on a homestead in the New Mexico Territory on December 21, 1909, several years before New Mexico became a state. At the time, people still carried side arms. In fact, his father had stopped wearing his only after New Mexico received statehood. Clarence lived through the Depression, when the government bought cattle for little to nothing, shot them and buried them in mass graves due to lack of market demand.

While other ranchers saw this as a hopeless situation and were selling out, Clarence's father saw it as opportunity. He bought their land, eventually owning 2,000 acres of New Mexican land. Not bad, considering that he had started with 160 acres. He sold the land for five dollars an acre.

Clarence joined the Navy in 1941 after the bombing of Pearl Harbor, at age 32. He was discharged October 1945 at the age of 36. He started the Wilson Oil Company with his wife when he was 48, after trying his hand at a number of businesses with his brother-in-law.

He began the business with a bulk plant, used mostly for home heating.

Clarence Wilson in 1942.

Clarence Wilson in 1935.

Many a night Clarence went out in a snowstorm to fill a customer's fuel tank because they hadn't thought to order any before the cold weather arrived, and were without fuel. Later, he bought and ran several stations, and was a jobber with Frontier, El Paso, which later became Chevron. The Wilson Corporation has been a Chevron distributor for over 25 years, and now includes Total, Diamond Shamrock.

The Wilson Corporation was incorporated in 1975 with Clarence, his wife Gertrude and his three children Elaine, Gary and Kathy. When Clarence retired, Gary operated the business until his death in a car wreck in 1994, leaving the business to Elaine and Kathy. The sisters knew little about the business and their parent's attorney advised them to sell. Their father had faith in them and persuaded their mother and his attorney to let them try.

Needless to say, the employees were nervous and several of them quit and went to work for the competitors. Offers for the business came from all over; people thinking that the poor little girls couldn't possibly run it. But they have survived and conquered, assembling their own team.

Three loyal employees stayed with the business, including Sam Bernal, who has been with Wilson for 20 years, Randy Moore, who has been with Wilson for over 18 years and Randy Garcia, who has been with them for 15 years. Through fate they found one of the best financial minds in the area to work with them, when Dennis O'Connor from Maui, Hawaii, just happened to be in Raton, New Mexico (population 8,500).

"As far as I know, we are the only women-owned fuel jobbership in New Mexico. There may be others but I have not met them yet," says Kathy Atwater, corporation shareholder, president, and daughter of Clarence and Gertrude. Her sister Elaine is vice-president, secretary and treasurer, and their mother, 83 and now retired, still shows up everyday. Clarence died in 1997 at age 87.

"I guess our motto is, 'if there is a will there is a way,'" offers Kathy. "Or maybe it's Clarence's saying, 'who said life was suppose to be easy?' Or my great-uncle, better known as Uncle Sam, 'Give your customers a good deal and they will be back.' You know Uncle Sam, he was a meat packer from Troy, New York during the war of 1812. If the soldiers received meat marked U.S. they knew it was good meat."

The future of The Wilson Corporation is unclear. At the rate the major oil companies are merging and buying each other out, it's hard to say what will happen or which ones will survive. There are some who predict, when all is said and done, that there may only be five large oil companies left in the United States. The Wilson Corporation remains steadfastly dedicated to its New Mexican roots.

ACKNOWLEDGMENTS

I have incurred many debts while assembling the photographs reproduced in this volume. Although it is impossible to thank everyone who rendered assistance, I am particularly grateful to the following: Michael Miller, Christine Roybal, Louellen Martinez, and Kay Dorman of the New Mexico State Records Center and Archives; Arthur Olivas, Richard Rudisill, and Sue Critchfield of the Museum of New Mexico; Jan Barnhart of Special Collections, University of New Mexico General Library; and Fred Mang, Jr., of the Southwestern Regional Headquarters, National Park Service. All have been generous with time and welcome advice.

John O. Baxter
Santa Fe, New Mexico

The New Mexico Historical Society is the memory of New Mexico. The Society has long shown that it is dedicated not only to assembling and preserving knowledge of the heritage we share, but in making it available to all comers. I am just a storyteller, and everyone knows that a storyteller without a memory is not worth much. We all are grateful to the society; I am just the one to be saying it here.

I owe special thanks to Dr. Myra Ellen Jenkins, former director of the New Mexico State Archives, for keeping me on track. Storytellers can play only where historians have labored.

There are two other historians, not specifically connected with this manuscript but who have taught me much about New Mexico, to whom I owe much: Drs. Marc Simmons and John Kessell.

Dan Murphy
Santa Fe, New Mexico

The publisher is especially grateful to Ken Mompellier and Jeff McAdoo of Las Cruces Convention and Visitors Bureau and Gary Romero of the New Mexico Department of Tourism who were extremly helpful in providing detailed information. We would like to also offer a special thank you for the assistance of individuals at Convention and Visitors Bureaus around the state: Kristina Marzano of Alamagordo, Steve Lewis of Santa Fe, Tonya Armenta of Albuquerque, Laura Doth of Ruidoso and Renee Valliere at Carlsbad Chamber of Commerce. Mildred Evaskovich of the Tularosa Basin Historical Society and Nena Singleton of New Mexico State University at Las Cruces provided important information.

American Historical Press
Sun Valley, California

SUGGESTION FOR FURTHER READING

New Mexico is a fascinating state, and every day a scholar somewhere is digging into yet another corner of its history. Any good library has publications with the details unearthed: Marc Simmons on Spanish Colonial ironwork or early witchcraft; Al Schroeder on the history of the Apaches; France Scholes on the seventeenth century; Polly Schaafsma on rock art; Paige Christiansen on mining; Stuart Northrop on fossils; Erna Fergusson on anything; the list goes on and on and will be longer tomorrow. But there are a few books that are bedrock. Some are old, some are not, but they are good places to begin to read about this very special place. Here are a few of my favorites, with a blanket apology for the many left out.

Ross Calvin, Sky *Determines,* University of New Mexico Press, 1965. The book ties the events of the state to its climate, landforms, and natural history, and is a good antidote to histories which deal only with humans interacting with humans.

David Lavender, *The Southwest,* University of New Mexico Press, 1984. Many of us waited anxiously while this skilled researcher and writer worked on this book. (His *Bent's Old Fort* already had captivated us.) Worth the wait, the book places New Mexico in the broad context of the Southwest.

John Kessell, *Kiva, Cross, and Crown,* Government Printing Office Press, no date. The best thing the Government Printing Office ever did, the book is the story of Pecos Pueblo and the mission established there, which serves as the focus for a much broader history. Fine writing and scholarship characterize this volume, and, unexpectedly for GPO, it is well designed with wonderful illustrations. When each new character appears, so does his florid signature, copied from a document. This is my favorite book for sitting by a fire, reading slowly.

Herbert Eugene Bolton, *Coronado: Knight of Pueblos and Plains,* University of New Mexico Press, 1964. This is the "old reliable" we all had in college and an exciting rediscovery for me twenty years later. If you've, not read it lately, get it out again. Bolton is always good for demolishing the silly idea that there wasn't much here before the Anglos (including me) came.

John Nichols, *The Milagro Bean-Field War,* Random House, 1974. I debated whether to put in this hilarious novel, but it may be the best (and most enjoyable) way to understand a small New Mexican village.

I have five friends who assure me they know exactly which village he used for a model-and each insists on a different village. This means Nichols has grasped something essential.

Paul Horgan, *Lamy of Santa Fe, The Centuries of Santa Fe,* and of course his masterpiece, *Great River.* Some people have made a career of trying to find mistakes in the latter, but no mind: you can't miss with a great writer and a vast subject.

Robert and Florence Lister, *Those Who Came Before,* Southwest Parks and Monuments Association, Tucson. Well illustrated, this is the best overview of the state's archeological story. Dr. Lister was the chief archeologist of the National Park Service and director of the Chaco Project.

Bernard DeVoto, *The Year of Decision: 1846,* deals with New Mexico via the Kearny Expedition only, but is still a treasure for its writing. No objectivity here: DeVoto flaunts his opinions, but in prose so absorbing that you don't mind. You can actually do the old trick of putting your ringer anywhere and finding a superlative sentence.

New Mexico's Blue Book, Cuarto Centennial Edition (1598-1998) provided invaluable details about the state, especially its "historical dates."

INDEX

CHRONICLES OF LEADERSHIP INDEX

Albuquerque Journal, The, 162-163
American Property Management Corp., 164-165
Champion Regional Medical Center, Gerald, 166-167
College of The Southwest, 168-169
Coronado Paint and Decorating Center, 170-171
Creamland Dairies, Inc., 172-173
First National Bank of New Mexico, The 174-175
French Mortuary Inc., 176-177
Gallup Sand and Gravel Company, 178-180
Heel Inc., 182-183
Hotel Santa Fe, 184-185
Keller's Farm Stores, 186-187
Ktech Corporation, 188-189
La Fonda, 181
Laguna Industries, Inc., 190-192
Lea County State Bank, 194-195
Luna Vocational Technical Institute— A Community College, 196-197
McBride and Associates, Inc., 198-200
National Center for Genome Resources, 193
New Mexico Military Institute, 202-203
NewTec, 201
Pic Quik Stores, Inc, 204-206
Portales National Bank, 208-213
Roses Southwest Papers, Inc., 214-215
Rowland Nursery, Inc., 216-219
Santa Fe, City of, 220-222
Santa Fe New Mexican, The, 224-227
SMPC Architects, 228-229
Talbot Agency, Inc., 207
Telephone Pioneer Museum of New Mexico, The, 230-231
Tema Contemporary Furniture, 223
Wilson Corporation, The, 232

GENERAL INDEX
Italicized numbers indicate illustrations.

A
Abiquiu, 55, 145
Abó, *45*
Acoma, 31, *46*
Agriculture, 6, 20
Alamogordo, 7, 145, *146,* 153, *154*
Albuquerque, 31, *35, 108, 127, 135, 139,* 148, 152, 153, *153*
Alburquerque, Duke of, 53, *139,* 148
Albuquerque, Villa de, 6
Albuquerque Journal, The, 162-163
Alvarado, Hernando de, *6,* 30, 31, 32, *33,* 35
Alvarado Hotel, *96*
American Property Management Corp., 164-165
Anasazi Basketmakers, 6
Anasazi culture, 6, *21,* 22, 23, 27, *94*
Anderson, Clinton P., 116
Angle of Repose, by Wallace Stegner, 145
Anza, Don Juan Bautista de, 6, 55
Apache Canyon, *67, 79*
Apache Indians, 6, 7, *43,* 45, 48, 54, 80, 81, 91, *92,* 151
Apartment houses (adobe), *6*
Archaic period, 20
Arenal pueblo, 34
Arizona, Confederate Territory of, 7
Armijo, Manuel, 7, 66, 67, 69, 71, 80
"Army of the West," 71, *72*
Arroyo Hondo, *22*
Art, primitive, 27, *123*
Artists, *93,* 108, *109, 111,* 113, *133,* 145
Atchison, Topeka & Santa Fe Railroad, 87, 90
Atlantic and Pacific Shops, *98*
Atomic bomb, 7, *119*

B
Baca, Cabeza de, 6
Baca, Jim, 152
Bandelier, Adolph F., *90*
Bandelier National Monument, 26, *124,* 158
Baking, *32*
Balloons, hot air, *134*
Bandelier National Monument, 26
Basketmaker period, 20
Bataan Death March, 7, 113
Bataan Memorial Building, *115*
Battle at Acoma, 6
Battle of Arenal, 34
Battle of Valverde, 7, *77*
Battle of York, *58*
Baumann, Gustave, *133*
Beaubien, Charles, 84
Beaubien-Miranda land grant, *85*
Becknell, William, 59, 61
Benavides, Fray Alonso, 43
Bent, Charles, 7, *63,* 71, *74*
Bent's Fort, *63,* 71, *72*
Bernalillo, 31
Berninghaus, Oscar E,, *98*
"Big Ditch," 94
Bigotes, 30, 31, 32, 34, 35
"Billy the Kid," 7, 82, *83,* 145
Bison, *18,* 19, 32, *33,* 34
Black Mesa, 51, *128*
Blumenschein, Ernest, 108, *140*
Bonney, William H., 82, *83*
Bosque del Apache Natural Wildlife Refuge, *126, 127*
Bosque Redondo, 7, 81, *82, 83*
Bradford, Richard, *140,* 145
Bradley, John, *65*
Bravar, Ulisse, *156*
"Bridal Chamber," 94
Buffalo, *18,* 19, 32, *33,* 34
Butch Cassidy and the Sundance Kid (film), 145
Butterfield Overland Mail Company, *75*

C
Cabezon Peak, 16
Cachupín, Don Tomás Vélez, *54*
Cactus, cholla, *12,* 13
Camel Rock, *11,* 146
Camino Real, 39, *59, 63*
Campus Arboretum, 153
Canby, Edward R.S., *77,* 79, 80
Cancer Research and Treatment Center, 153
Capitan, 145
Capitol, New Mexico's, *127, 157*
Capulín Mountain, *15*
Cárdenas, García López de, 32, 34
Carleton, James H., 80, *81, 82*
Carlos II, King, 51
Carlsbad Caverns, *17*
Carnegie Foundation for the Advancement of Teaching as a Research University, 157
Carnegie I Research university, 153
Carrasco, José Manuel, 91
Carreta, *40*
Carrizozo, 16, *17*
Carson, Christopher "Kit," 62, 80, *81*
Casinos, 146
Cassidy, Gerald P., *30, 31, 121*
Castañada hotel, *107*
Cather, Willa, *140,* 145
Catron, "Tomcat" Thomas, 83, *85*
Cattle ranching, *98, 107, 134,* 145
Center for High Technology Materials, 153
Center for Micro-Engineered

Ceramics, 154
Center for the Sustainable Development of Arid Lands, *156*
Cerro Grande fire, 158
Chacoans, 23
Chaco Canyon, *21, 22,* 23, 27, *94*
Chaco Civilization, 6
Chacon, Soledad, 7
Chaco Villages, *21, 22,* 23, 27
Chama river, 6, 15
Champion Regional Medical Center, Gerald, 166-167
Chamuscado, Francisco Sánchez, 37
Chavez, Fray Angelico, *140*
Cháves, Manuel A., 80
Chihuahua, 63
Chile, *131,* 151, 152, *154,* 157
Chili Line, *120*
Chimayo Revolt, 7
Chivington, John M., 79, 80
Christian population, 42
Christin, Judith, *138*
Christmas lights, *116*
Church of San José de Gracia, *57*
Cimarron Cutoff, *62*
"Citizen" Legislature, 148
City of the Garden of the Crosses, 151
Civil War, *76,* 77, 79, 80, 87
Clemente, Esteban, 45
Cloudcroft trestle, *130*
Clovis, 7
Clovis Man, 19
Coal mining, 104, *105, 134*
Cochise people, 6
Cochito pueblo, *143*
College of Santa Fe, 145
College of The Southwest, 168-169
Colon, Cristobal XX, 7
Colorado, Territory of, 7
Colorado River, 6
Colorado Volunteers, 79
Columbia (space shuttle), 7
Columbus, 7
Columbus, Christopher, 7
Columbus Quicentenary, 7
Comanche Indians, 6, 54, 55, 56
Commerce of the Prairies, by Josiah Gregg, *61*
Compostela, 29
"Conquistadora, La," 49, *50, 131*
Constitution, 7, *100*
Continental-Shell refinery, *105*
Contreras, Diego José de Vargas Zapata y Luján Ponce de Leon y, *38,* 49, 51, 53, *128, 131*

Cooke, Regina Tatum, *16*
Corbeil, Claude, *138*
Corona, 7
Coronado, Francisco Vásquez de, 6, 29, *30,* 31, 32, *33,* 34, 36, 37
Coronado Paint and Decorating Center, 170-171
Cowan, R.H., *76*
Coyotes, *13*
Crafts, Indian, *108, 111*
Creamland Dairies, Inc., 172-173
Cronau, Rudolf D.L., *122*
Crosby, John O., *138*
Cross of the Martyrs, *49*
Cuarto Centennial, 7
Cumbres and Toltec Scenic Railway, *130*
Cumbres Pass, *89*

D
Dead Man's Journey, 39, 57
Death Comes for the Archbishop, by Willa Cather, 145
Denver & Rio Grande Western Railroad, 87, 98, *89, 120*
Díaz, Porfirio, 96
Dolan, James J., 82
Domenici, Pete, *152*
Domínguez, Fray Francisco Atanasio, 6, *52*
Dripping Springs, *142*
Duke City, *108*
Dunton, Herbert "Buck," *109*
Dynamax theatre, *153*

E
Eastman, Seth, *122*
Eckles, Isabel, 7
Edison, Thomas, 7, 92, 145
Education, *95,* 97, *115,* 148, 153, 157
Elephant Butte Dam, *113*
Elephant Butte Reservoir, 14
Elizabethtown, *94*
Elkins, "Smooth Steve" Stephen B., 83, *85,* 86, 97
El Morro, 6, 40, *41,* 51, *117*
El Paso, 29, 57, 148
El Paso del Norte, 6
El Pueblo del Jardin de las Cruces, 151
El Santuario de Chimayo, *128*
Enchanted Mesa, *8*
Escalante, Fray Sylvestre Vélez de, 6, *52*
Escalona, Luis de, 36
Espejo, Antonio de, 37

Estancia Basin, 19
Estancia Valley, *27*
Estevan, 6, 29
"Evo-later," *153*

F
Fall, Albert B., *96, 101*
Farmers Market, *150, 154*
farolito, *144*
Federal Reclamation Service, *113*
Film industry, 145
Fire companies, *101*
First National Bank of New Mexico, The 174-175
"Flicks on 66," 153
Fogelson, Buddy, 145
Folklorico dancers, *152*
Folsom Man, *18,*19
Fort Craig, 77
Fort Defiance, *122*
Fort Fillmore, 77
Fort Sumner, 7, *83*
Fort Union, 76, *78,* 79
47 Star Flag, 145, *146*
Franciscans, 42
Fray Cristóbal Mountains, 14
"Free Spirits at Noisy Water" (sculpture), *150*
French Mortuary Inc., 176-177
Frijoles, *26*
Fritz, Emil, 82

G
Gadsden Purchase, 7, 73
Galisteo Basin, *89, 123*
Gallegos, Hernan, 37
Gallup, 29, 153
Gallup Sand and Gravel Company, 178-180
Garcia, Fabian, 154
Garrard, Lewis H., *72*
Garrett, Pat, 7, *83 101*
Garson Theatre Center, Greer, 145
Gas industry, *105*
Genízaros, 55
Georgetown, *7*
Geronimo, 7, 153
"Gettysburg of the West," *80*
Gila Cliff Dwellings, *23*
Gila stream, 15
Gilpin, Governor, 77
Glorieta, *80*
Glorieta Pass, 7, 31, 34, 71, *79,* 88
Golden, Robert, 157
Gold prospecting, 32, *92,* 94

Gorman, R.C., *146*
Grants, 7
Gran Quivira, *43*, 46
Grapes of Wrath, by John Steinbeck, 153
Great Depression, 7, 103
Gregg, Josiah, *61*
Groves, Leslie, 113
Guías, *65*

H
Harding, Warren G., *104*
Harvey, Fred, 90, 106, *107*
Harvey Houses, 106, *107*
Hawikuh, 6, 29, *30*, 31, 34
Heel Inc., 182-183
Herrera, Velino, *132*
High Performance Computing Center, 153
Hills of Santa Fe, The, by Leon Kroll, *133*
Hilton, Conrad, *140*
Holloman Air Force Base, 7, 119, 153
Holly, Buddy, 7
Hopi Indians, 30
Horseshoe, 157
Hotel Santa Fe, 184-185
Hubbard Museum of the American West, 145, *150, 151*
Hurd, Peter, *141*

I
Indian and Pueblo Cultural Center, *127*
Indian Day School (film), 7, 145
Indian Detours, 106
Indian Market, *136, 148*
Indians: Apache 6, 7, *43*, 45, 48, 54, 80, 81, 91, *92, 126,* 151; Comanche, 6, 54, 55, 56; Hopi, 30; Mexcalero Apache, *134*; Navajo, 6, 7, 80, 81, *94*; Pecos, *48*; Piro, 39; Plains, 27, 31, 34; Pueblo, 6, *27, 36, 42,* 46, 53, *131*; Ute, 48, 54, *57*; Zuni, 29, *30, 31*
Inscription Rock, 6
Interstate Commerce Commission, *120*
Isleta, *47*

J
Jackalope pottery, *146*
Jemez mountains, 11, *12,* 14, *118*
Jemez pueblo, 31
Jemez volcano, 16
Johnson, Gary E., 148, *148*

Johnson, Lyndon B., *116*
Joint Statehood issue, 7
Jornada del Muerto, 39, 57

K
Kearny, Stephen Watts, 7, 71, *72, 73,* 74, 97
Keller's Farm Stores, 186-187
Kennedy, John F., *116*
Kirtland Air Force Base, 119
Kivas, 22, *36, 125*
"Kneeling Nun, The," *106*
Kroll, Leon, *133*
Ktech Corporation, 188-189

L
La Bajada, 58, *59*
Ladrón Mountains, *10*
La Fiesta de San Ysidro, *155*
La Fonda, 181
Laguna Industries, Inc., 190-192
La Mesilla, 7
Lamy, *150*
Lamy, Jean Baptiste, 7, *89*
Larrazolo, Octoviano A., 103
Las Cruces, *142,* 148, 151, 152, *152,* 154, *155, 159*
Las Cruces College, 154
Las Trampas, 54, *55, 57*
Lava flow, 17
Lawrence, D.H., 108, 145
Lea County State Bank, 194-195
Letrado, Fray Francisco, 43, 44
Lincoln County Courthouse, *70, 83*
Lincoln County War, 7, 82
Loma Parda, *78*
"Long Walk," 7
Los Alamos, 7, 14, 113, *118, 119,* 153
Los Alamos National Laboratory, 158
Luhan, Mabel Dodge, 108
Lujan, Manuel, Jr., *141*
luminarias, *139*
Luna Vocational Technical Institute— A Community College, 196-197

M
McBride and Associates, Inc., 198-200
McDonald, William C., 97, *101, 102*
Machbeuf, Joseph Priest, *89*
McKinley, William, *99, 100*
McSween, Alexander A., 82, *84*
Madrid, Roque, 49
Magoffin, James Wiley, 71, *72*
Manhattan Project, *119*
Marcos, Fray, 6, 30
Mariachis, *147, 155*

Martínez, Antonio José, 6, *60*
Martínez, Maria, *111, 142*
Maxwell, Lucien, 84, *85,* 86
Maxwell Land Grant, 84, *85,* 94
Medoff, Mark, *140*
Melgares, don Facundo, 58, 60
Mendoza, Viceroy Antonio de, 29
Meredith and Ailman Bank, *7*
Mesa at Ruidoso, *151*
Mesa Verde, 23, 27, *94*
Mescalero-Apache Indian Reservation, 153
Mesilla Festival, *152*
Mesilla Valley, 77
Mexican War, 7, *67*
Milagro Beanfield War, The (film), 145
Mimbres culture, 23, *25, 123*
Mining, *86,* 91, 92, 104, *105, 134,* 145
Mix, Tom, 145
Moho, 34
Mongollón culture, 6, 23
Montezuma Hotel, *91*
Morley, Sylvanus G., *140*
Morley, William R., 87, *88*
Mountain Branch, *62*
Mount Taylor, 11
Murphy, Lawrence G., *70, 82*
Museum of the Horse, 145, *150, 151*

N
Narváez, Pánfilo de, 29
NASA, 157
National Center for Genome Resources, 193
National Guard, *114*
National Park Service, *124,* 146, 158
Navajo "Codetalkers," 7
Navajo Indians, 6, 7, 80, 81, *94*
Navajo Reservation, 7
New Deal, 7
New Mexico College of Agriculture and Mechanic Arts, 157
New Mexico Farm and Ranch Heritage Museum, *155*
New Mexico Institute of Mining and Technology, 94
New Mexico Military Institute, 202-203
New Mexico Museum of Natural History, *153*
New Mexico State University, 153, 154, 157
New Spain, 151
NewTec, 201
Niza, Fray Marcos de, 29, 30

Northern Rio Grande Valley, *26*
Nueva Galicia, 29

O
Offenbach, Jacques, *138*
Ohke, 6, *28, 41*
Oil industry, 7, *105*
O'Keeffe, Georgia, 113, *140,* 141, 145
Old Mesilla, *152*
Old Mesilla Plaza (painting), *124*
"Old Santa Fe Trail," 63
Old Town Plaza, *108*
Oñate, Juan de, 6, 7, *28,* 39, 40, 41, *42,* 145
100 Best Small Art Towns in America, The, by John Villani, 145
Opera, *90, 138*
Oppenheimer, J. Robert, 113, *119*
Ordinances of 1753, 36
Organ Mountains, *142, 155, 159*
Orpheus in the Underworld (opera), *138*
Ortega, José Benito, *57*
Ortiz gold fields, 6, 92
Ortiz Mountains, 7
Oterím, Governor, 47, 51
Otero, Miguel A., *100*

P
Pacheco, Don Bernardo Miera y, *52, 55*
Padilla, Fray Juan de, 36
Palace of the Governors, 6, *44,* 47, 58, 71, *111,* 145
Paleoindians, 20
Parajito Plateau, *119*
"Paso del Norte," 39
"Pass wine," 57
Pearl Harbor, *116*
Pecos Indians, *48*
Pecos National Monument, 145
Pecos pueblo, 27, 31
Pecos River, 15
"Peggy Sue" (song), 7
Peralta, Pedro de, 6
Perea, José Leandro, 88
Pérez, Albino, 7, 64, 65, *66*
Permian Basin, 106
Pershing, John J. "Black Jack," 97, *103,* 104
Petroglyph National Monument, *35*
Petroleum industry, 104, *105*
Petty Studio, Norman, 7
Philip II, *28*
Phillips, Bert, 108

Physical Science Laboratory, 157
Pic Quik Stores, Inc, 204-206
Picurís pueblo, 27, *125*
Pigeon's Ranch, *79*
Pike, Zebulon M., 6, 57, *58,* 59, 60
Pino, Don Pedro Bautista, 58
Piñon trees, *13*
Piro Indians, 39
Pit houses, 6
Place of Governors, *140*
Plains Indians, 27, 31, 34
Plains of San Augustin, 19
Polk, James, 71, *72*
Popé, 46
Population, 7, 148, 152
Portales National Bank, 208-213
Prospecting, 92, 94
Pueblo Bonito, *21,* 22
Pueblo Indians, 6, *27, 36, 42,* 46, 53, *131*
Pueblo Mother, by Velino Herrera, *132*
Pueblo Revolt, 6, 44, 45, 46, *47, 49,* 53, 64
Pueblos, 22, *127,* 146
Punitive Expedition, *104*

Q
Quarai Mission Church, *43*
"Quest for Knowledge, The" (sculpture), *156*
Quivira, 35

R
Rafting, *149*
Railroads: Atchison, Topeka & Santa Fe, 87, 90; Chili Line, *120;* Denver & Rio Grande Western, 87, 88, *89, 120;* Santa Fe, *88, 89, 107;* Santa Fe Southern, *150*
Ralston, New Mexico, *86*
Ranchos de Taos plaza, *133*
Raton, *87*
Raton Pass, *137*
Rattlesnakes, *14*
"Red or green?" (state question), 152
Red Sky at Morning, by Richard Bradford, 145
Riley, John G., 82
Rio Grande, 6, 7, *10,* 14, 15, *28, 126, 139, 149,* 151
Rio Grande Valley, 23, 27, 31, 34
Road building, *120*
Roberts, Clarence J., *102*
Rodríguez, Augustín, 6, 37
Roosevelt, Theodore, *99, 117*

Rosario Chapel, *131*
Rosas, Luis de, 6
Roses Southwest Papers, Inc., 214-215
Roswell, 7, 113
Roughriders, *99*
"Round House," 7
Route 66, 153
Rowland Nursery, Inc., 216-219
Ruidoso, *134,* 145
Ruidoso Downs, *150*
Ruidoso Downs Race Track, *134*

S
St. Francis Cathedral, *131*
St. Vrain, Ceran, *63*
Salinas Province, 42
Salpointe, Jean Baptiste, *89*
Sandia Cave, 19
Sandia Laboratories, 119
Sandia Man, 19
Sandia Mountains, 11, 19, *139*
Sandia Peak, *135*
Sandia people, 6
Sandoval, Governor, *110*
San Agustin, *142*
San Gabriel, 6
San Gabriel Ranch, *107*
San Gerónimo Church, *126*
San Gerónimo mission, *75*
Sangre de Cristos, 9, 14, 15, 53, *125*
San Gregorio church, *45*
San Ildefonso, *128*
San Isidro Labrador, *57*
San José Church, *123*
San Juan, 42
San Juan Basin, 106
San Juan de Los Caballeros, 6
San Juan pueblo, 31
San Rafael, 55
Santa Bárbara, 37
Santa Cruz de la Cañada, 6
Santa Fe, 6, 7, 53, *93, 136, 144,* 145, *146, 147,* 148, *149, 150,* 151, 152, *157,* 158
Santa Fe, City of, 220-222
Santa Fe fiesta, *131*
Santa Fe New Mexican, The, 224-227
Santa Fe Opera, *138*
Santa Fe Railroad, *88, 89, 107*
"Santa Fe Ring," 82, 83, *85*
Santa Fe Ski Basin, *137*
Santa Fe Southern railway, *150*
Santa Fe Trail, 6, 61, *62, 63, 64,* 68, 71, *121, 139, 140,* 152
Santa María, Fray Juan de, 37
Santander, Fray Diego de, 44

Santa Rita copper mine, 91, 92, *106*
Santa Rosa Bank, *99*
Scholder, Fritz, *133*
School of Engineering, 154
School of Medicine, 154
"Seven Cities of Cíbola," 6, *30*
Shakespeare, New Mexico, *86*
Shiprock, *16*
Sibley, Henry H., *76, 77*
Silver City, *7,* 92
Simmons, Marc, 90
Ski Apache, *134*
Skiing, *137*
"Sky City," 31
Smithsonian Institution, 152
Smokey the Bear Museum, 145
SMPC Architects, 228-229
Sopete, 32, 35, 36
Sosa, Gaspar Castaño de, 37, 39
Southwestern Brewery and Ice
    Company, *95*
Spaniards, 29, 30, *31,* 34, 39, 40,
    41, 46, 54, 55
Spanish-American War, *99*
Spanish Inquisition, 6
St. Francis Cathedral, *136*
Stables, *76*
Stagecoach service, *7,* 74, *75*
State Council of Defense, 103
Steel, Sam, 154
Stegner, Wallace, *140,* 145
Steinbeck, John, 153
Stein's Pass, *75*
Stieglitz, Alfred, *141*
Stochaj, Steve, *156*
Stradling Collection, Anne C., *151*
Summerfest, 153
Sweeney, James G., *65*

T
Taft, William Howard, *96*
Talbot Agency, Inc., 207
Taos, 6, *6,* 27, 31, *33, 126,* 145, 151,
    153
Taos Rebellion, 7
Taos Society of Artists, *140*
Taxation, 64, *66*
Teapot Dome scandal, *104*
Telephone Pioneer Museum of New
    Mexico, The, 230-231
Tema Contemporary Furniture, 223
Tent Rock, *143*
Tewas, *128*
Texas-Santa Fe expedition, *68*
Tiguex, 32
Tijeras Pass, 53

Timber industry, *140*
Tombaugh, Clyde, 157
Tomé Jail, *93*
Tompiro linguistic group, *45*
Tourism, 145
Treaty of Guadelupe Hidalgo, 7, 73
Trinity Site, 7
Trost, Henry, 157
Tularosa Basin Historical Society
    Muesum, 145, *146*
Tulurosa Basin, *129*
Tunstall, John G., 82, 84

U
United World College, *91*
University of New Mexico, 153
Uranium, 7
Ute Indians, 48, 54, *57*

V
Vado, San Miguel del, *68*
Valdez, Francisco Cuervo y, 53
Valencia County, 153
Valle Grande, *16*
Vargas, Diego de, 6, *38,* 49, 51, 53,
    128, 131
Velasco, Fray Fernando de, 46, 47
Versylvania, *115*
Vial, Pedro, 59
Vigil, Frederico, *147*
Villa, Francisco "Pancho," 7, 97, *103,*
    104
Villagra, Gaspar de, 6
Villani, John, 145
VLA, National Radio Astronomy
    Observatory, *142*
Volcanism, 15

W
Weaver, Roy, 158
Wellge, Henry, *93*
Wetherill, Richard, *94*
White Oaks, *95*
White Sands Missile Range, 153
White Sands National Monument,
    129, 153, *154*
White Sands Space Harbor, 7
Willow Springs, *87*
Wilson, Woodrow, *103*
Wilson Corporation, The, 232
Windmills, *112*
Wootton, "Uncle Dick," 87, 88
World War II, 7, 113, *114*
Wyatt Earp (film), 145
Wyeth, Andrew, *141*
Wyeth, Henriette, *141*

Wyeth, N.C., *141*

Z
Zaldívar, Juan de, 40
Zaldívar, Vicente de, 40
"Zia," *152*
Zia Pueblo, *152*
Zuhl Library, *156*
Zuni Hotshot Crew, *158*
Zuni Indians, 29, 30, *31*